# Guidebook for Directors of Nonprofit Corporations

## Second Edition

Committee on Nonprofit Corporations

Editors
George W. Overton
Jeannie Carmedelle Frey

Section of Business Law
American Bar Association

Defending Liberty
Pursuing Justice

The material contained herein represents the opinions of the authors and editors and should not be construed to be the action of either the American Bar Association or the Section of Business Law unless adopted pursuant to the Bylaws of the Association.

Nothing contained in this book is to be considered as the rendering of legal advice for specific cases, and readers are responsible for obtaining such advice from their own legal counsel. This book and any forms and agreements herein are intended for educational and informational purposes only.

Library of Congress Cataloging-in-Publication Data

Guidebook for directors of nonprofit corporations / editors, George W. Overton, Jeannie Carmedelle Frey ; Nonprofit Corporations Committee.— 2nd ed.
    p. cm.
Includes bibliographical references.
  ISBN 1-59031-043-8 (pbk.)
 1. Directors of corporations—Legal status, laws, etc.—United States.
2. Nonprofit organizations—Law and legislation—United States.   I. Overton, George W.  II. Frey, Jeannie Carmedelle.   III. American Bar Association. Committee on Nonprofit Corporations.

 KF1388.7.Z9 G85 2002
 658.4'22—dc21                                                              2002003245

Discounts are available for books ordered in bulk. Special consideration is given to state and local bars, CLE programs, and other bar-related organizations. Inquire at Book Publishing, American Bar Association, 321 N. Clark Street, Chicago, Illinois 60610

06  05  04                    9

# Summary of Chapters

# Contents

## Chapter 2
**Duties and Rights of Nonprofit Corporation Directors** . . . . . . . . . . .    17

## Chapter 3
## Committees and Advisory Bodies

## Chapter 4
## Taxation

## Chapter 6
## Supervision of Internet Activities . . . . . . . . . . . . . . . . . . . . . . . . . . . .    103

# Preface

This second edition of the *Guidebook for Directors of Nonprofit Corporations* has been prepared by the Committee on Nonprofit Corporations of the Business Law Section of the American Bar Association. The purpose of the *Guidebook* is to assist the director of a nonprofit corporation in performing his or her duties. Primarily designed for the lay reader, the *Guidebook* provides a description of general legal principles as they apply to nonprofit corporations. On a more practical level, the *Guidebook* offers what we hope will be useful suggestions and procedures for both the individual director and the corporation that he or she serves.

The *Guidebook* is designed to serve as a useful reference book for directors and prospective directors of the thousands of nonprofit corporations in the United States—from the smallest corporation that operates principally at a local or even neighborhood level, to the largest nonprofit corporation having operations that extend not only across this country but internationally as well. Nonprofit corporations have always played a large role in American life; they play a bigger role today than most people realize. In the future, it is likely that even more people will look to nonprofit corporations to help address issues and solve problems.

In general, the *Guidebook* addresses general legal principles and broad areas of concern and is not intended to be a source of specific legal advice or solutions to particular problems. Rather, its goal is to provide nonprofit corporation directors with an overall understanding of their role. It is designed to help directors identify the information they need in certain areas, and to suggest methods for obtaining such information within the framework of the corporation's particular circumstances.

In this second edition of the *Guidebook*, we have tried to reflect the issues that affect directors of nonprofit corporations today. In many respects, the issues facing nonprofits now are unchanged from what they were when the first edition came out: What does a director do? What is the scope of his or her duties? Although these questions may be timeless, the answers necessarily reflect today's realities and legal developments. We have also tried to identify developing trends and legal issues that are likely to affect nonprofit corporations and their directors in the future. It has been said that those who select directors of nonprofit boards should look for the following qualities: "wealth, wisdom, and work—never settle for less than two."[1] Through this *Guidebook*, we hope to add to your wisdom, and make your work as a nonprofit director more effective; as for wealth, we can't do much for you. But if all who care for the nonprofits that they direct are wise and dedicated, there will be wealth, in many forms, for all.

The principal authors and editors of this edition are George W. Overton, of Chicago and Jeannie Carmedelle Frey, also of Chicago. Mr. Overton was the principal author of the first edition, together with William Humenuk, of Philadelphia, and other members of the Committee on Nonprofit Corporations of the ABA Business Law Section. Mr. Overton and Ms. Frey wish to acknowledge the significant contributions made by the following individuals who served as contributing editors for specific chapters and subject matter:

- Attorneys Robert Louthian and Elizabeth Mills of Washington, D.C. and Chicago, respectively (Tax Exemption, Chapter 4);
- Attorneys Catherine E. Livingston, of Washington, D.C., and Amy R. Segal, of Boston, Massachusetts (Internet Activities, Chapter 6);
- Attorney John T. Hansen, of San Francisco (Bankruptcy Section, Chapter 10); and
- Attorneys Natalie Hanlon-Leh and Jo Frances Walsh, of Denver (Volunteers and Employees, Chapters 7 and 8).

In addition, special thanks and appreciation are owed to attorneys Lisa A. Runquist of Toluca Lake, California, and Cynthia Rowland of San Francisco, for editorial assistance in several areas, and to the following young lawyers and law students who provided valuable research and editorial assistance: Thomas Asmar, Daniel Gottlieb, Anne McNicholas, and Elizabeth Savard, all of whom are now practicing in Chicago, Illinois.

GEORGE W. OVERTON
JEANNIE CARMEDELLE FREY
Co-Chairs, *Guidebook* Revision Project,
Committee on Nonprofit Corporations

# Notes

1. A common variant of this qualification standard is "time, treasure and talent." The originators of the sayings are unknown.

# Introduction

## Who Should Read This Guidebook?

This *Guidebook* was prepared to aid the director of a nonprofit corporation in performing his or her duties.[1] It is written for anyone presently serving as such a director, as well as anyone contemplating such service.

There are a wide variety of nonprofit corporations: art museums, health care providers, social clubs, trade associations, foundations and homeowner associations, just to name a few, and we write for the directors of all of them. You may ask how this *Guidebook* can address the needs of directors of all nonprofit corporations, given the vast range of nonprofit activities. Despite their variety of purposes, nonprofit corporations have many things in common. For instance, most nonprofit corporations are organized and maintained pursuant to a single state statute, and are managed by a single governing board. Although the size of the resources managed by nonprofit boards varies widely, their fundamental responsibilities are the same.

The rights and duties of directors of nonprofit corporation are in many respects similar to those imposed on directors of for-profit or business corporations. In a large number of states, the statute governing nonprofit corporations has been modeled at least to some degree on the statute governing for-profit corporations. Further, the legal analysis of many corporate governance issues in the nonprofit context often draws upon the lessons learned from the law applied to for-profit businesses. A new or prospective director of a nonprofit corporation who is familiar with the workings of for-profit boards is therefore likely to feel comfortable that he or she understands the basic requirements of this new role. However, *nonprofit directors need to be aware that, because of the unique nature of nonprofit organizations, in some circumstances state and federal law may impose additional or different duties on directors of such organizations*—especially directors of tax-exempt corporations and corporations deemed to be public charities or public benefit corporations.

A wide range of leaders in the political, philanthropic and scholarly world predicts an increasing role and responsibility for the nonprofit sector, not only in this country, but also in the international setting. We share in this prediction. The conduct of all nonprofit boards is important not only to their organizations, but also to the constituencies they serve. To help effectively direct such organizations, a director needs two things: an informed understanding of his or her role, and effective procedures for making decisions and taking action.

Directors of smaller nonprofit organizations may initially feel that many of the suggestions in this *Guidebook* are only applicable to larger entities, with bigger staffs and greater resources. While we readily acknowledge the practical limitations imposed on directors of many nonprofits, we believe that the consistency and regularity in board procedures typically found in established, well-managed corporations (whether for-profit or nonprofit) are not accidental. This *Guidebook* aims to help all directors of nonprofit corporations, big and small, to use their resources to greatest effect.

# A Few Definitions

A *nonprofit corporation* is an artificial creation of a government—usually a state—that issued the certificate of incorporation. Corporations do not exist simply by mutual agreement of members or directors but come into being only by a specific act of a state or federal government and are kept in existence only by compliance with the regular requirements of that government.

As part of the creation of the corporation, the *articles of incorporation* are filed with the government. These articles are sometimes referred to as a charter or constitution. We use the term articles of incorporation.

The detailed rules of the corporation's governance of the corporation, as adopted by the directors, are usually referred to as the *bylaws* but sometimes are labeled with other names, such as standing rules. We use the term bylaws.

Every nonprofit corporation statute provides for a *board of directors*; however, in a given corporation, the name of this body varies with the history, tradition—and whim—of the organization involved. It may be called a board of trustees, a board of overseers, a governing committee, or any one of a dozen other names.[2] We shall refer to it as the board of directors or board, and to its members as directors. Throughout this *Guidebook*, the term director is used to denote a member of the governing body of a nonprofit corporation. Any other type of director will be qualified in the text.

There is similar variety in the titles of officers. The individual who is responsible for overseeing the day-to-day operations of the corporation may be referred to as the president, CEO, executive director, or other title. In this *Guidebook*, we use the term *chief executive* to describe the principal executive officer of the corporation, and *chair* to describe the individual who presides over the board of directors.

In the nonprofit world, the word *member* may refer to an individual or entity having the power to elect one or more of the corporation's directors. On the other hand, a nonprofit corporation's members may have no voting rights—or they may have voting rights that are similar to, or even greater than, those of a stockholder of a business corporation. The term member is sometimes simply cosmetic, used by a charitable corporation to express appreciation to its donors. Numerous nonprofit corporations have different categories of members, with differing rights and powers, while many nonprofit corporations have no members at all. In some states, the term *delegate* identifies individuals, such as persons participating in conventions or other representative assemblies, who may also be members but whose rights may be limited to the context of a specific assembly or gathering.[3] In this *Guidebook*, the term member is used only to refer to a person or entity with voting or other significant rights.

In general, we shall conform our terminology to that of the ABA's Revised Model Nonprofit Corporation Act (the Model Act).[4] We shall refer in this *Guidebook* to the three classifications of nonprofit corporations set forth in the Model Act:

(1) *Public benefit corporations,* which operate for public or charitable purposes;
(2) *Mutual benefit corporations,* which operate for the benefit of their members; and
(3) *Religious corporations,* which operate to advance or maintain the religion motivating their members or directors.

This *Guidebook* deals only with nonprofit entities that are organized as corporations. Other nonprofit entities, such as unincorporated associations, charitable trusts or labor unions, are outside the scope of this book.

# Legal Requirements versus Good Corporate Practice

Throughout this *Guidebook*, we seek to answer two principal questions:

- What does the law require?
- What is good corporate practice, as shaped by the needs of the particular corporation involved and the practical limitations of the director's service?

Neither of these questions has a simple answer. Much of the law concerning a director's responsibility is derived from practices in business corporations where the accountability of a director may differ from that arising in a nonprofit context. What constitutes good corporate practice will also vary with the nature and resources of the corporation, its purposes and the nature of its exposures. The practical opportunities available to the director are further shaped by the needs and resources of each corporation involved. Nonetheless, there are significant areas of common ground that apply to all nonprofit corporation directors.

## The Law's Commands

In writing for directors we must first, as lawyers, alert our readers to the commands and prohibitions imposed by the law. All legal systems necessarily deal with minimum requirements of behavior: "You must do at least X" or "No matter what the circumstances, you must not do Y." This *Guidebook* indicates legal *requirements* by the use of imperative verbs such as *must, must not, shall, shall not, is required to,* and the like.

Our statements of the law's commands is sometimes a summary of a specific statute or regulation—such as the Internal Revenue Code and the related regulations—and sometimes a reference to the body of judge-made law concerning corporations. We shall use the Model Act as the prototype or presumptive guide to issues of statutory corporate law. However, directors should be aware that state statutes and legal precedent, applicable to specific nonprofit corporations, may differ from the Model Act in various respects.

## Good Corporate Practice

Equally important is the *Guidebook*'s advice—based on our experiences as lawyers for nonprofit corporations—outlining what a director *should, is expected to, should not,* or *may* do.

The *Guidebook*'s statements as to what a director should do reflect: (a) policies underlying legal requirements; and (b) general standards of corporate management evolved from the experience of both business and nonprofit corporations.

In writing about good corporate practice, we are describing in part what a director is generally expected to do today and in part what a director *may* be expected to do in the near future. Good corporate practice also describes the behavior we think a dedicated director will want to see from his or her fellow directors, and hence from himself or herself.

# Limitations of Time versus the Corporation's Needs

The most important practical limitation on a director's service is time. Each individual director should determine how much time she or he can devote to the corporation's affairs. The board of directors as a whole should organize its affairs on a shared assumption as to the time all directors can give. Given that most directors are chosen on the basis of their experiences and activities, director time constraints is an ever-present issue. The board needs to determine how much time directors should spend to appropriately carry out their duties, and make sure that each director is willing and able to do so.

In many of the areas examined in this *Guidebook*, we can offer no ready-made answer to the conflict of needs versus resources; it will be up to the directors to evaluate how to mediate between these conflicts, and to reassess such decisions periodically in the light of current circumstances. Directors need to be aware of changes in the legal and business climate that affect their corporation, and that may change the determination of what is "enough" time to fulfill their individual duties to the corporation and their fellow board members.

# The Organization of This Guidebook

This *Guidebook* is organized as follows:

Chapters 1 through 3 discuss matters of concern to all directors of all corporations: how a board works, the directors' rights and duties, and the functions of committees and advisory bodies.

Chapter 4, on taxation, surveys tax-exemption issues, an area of concern for most nonprofit corporations and their directors.

Chapter 5 discusses the tax-exemption issues that arise when tax-exempt nonprofit organizations create for-profit subsidiaries or contemplate joint ventures with for-profit corporations.

Chapter 6 discusses a host of potential legal issues that may be relevant to a nonprofit organization's Internet activities, including fund raising.

Chapters 7 (Volunteers) and 8 (Employees) discuss legal issues relating to use of a nonprofit corporation's human resources, and suggest standards and procedures for the effective use of volunteers and employees.

Chapter 9 notes some of the general legal issues that arise in special circumstances, including change-of-control events and bankruptcy.

Chapter 10 covers issues relating to insurance and other liability protection for nonprofit corporation directors.

Chapter 11 offers suggestions on the steps that a nonprofit's directors can take to understand the legal environment in which the organization operates, and on how to select and use legal counsel.

Chapter 12 discusses best practices for orientation of new board members, and ways to revitalize existing board members and the board as a whole.

At the end of each chapter, the reader will find questions that we suggest each individual director review concerning the issues discussed in the chapter. Following the questions in each chapter is a checklist that board members may find helpful to review in light of their organization's specific circumstances.

# Notes

1.  This *Guidebook* is the work of the Committee on Nonprofit Corporations of the Business Law Section of the American Bar Association (the ABA).

2.  The Model Act and most state laws specifically reject the trust law standard for the conduct of nonprofit directors. *See* Model Act § 8.30(e). Thus, the use of the term trustee does not connote duties different from or additional to those of a director. However, in some states and in certain circumstances, nonprofit directors may be considered trustees of charitable assets and thereby subject to duties beyond those generally applicable to nonprofit directors. See the *Guidebook* chapter "Duties and Rights of Nonprofit Corporation Directors."

3.  *See* Colorado Revised Nonprofit Corporation Act, 7-121-401(10). *See also* Indiana Nonprofit Corporation Act, §§ 23-17-2-8 and 23-17-9-1.

4.  The Model Act was published by the Business Law Section of the American Bar Association in 1987. Readers should be aware that the statute applicable to a nonprofit corporation in a particular state may differ from the Model Act. When faced with a specific problem, directors and their counsel should examine the particular statute governing the corporation in question. As of this writing, the ABA Business Law Section has begun a project to review and revise the current version of the Model Act. Some of the references herein to the Model Act's provisions may not be completely accurate with respect to the new Model Act, once it is complete.

# The Nonprofit Corporation and Its Directors: What They Do, How They Do It, and For Whom

## *Contents*

CHAPTER **1**

# The Nonprofit Corporation and Its Directors: What They Do, How They Do It, and for Whom

## The Zoology of the Nonprofit World

### What Does It Mean to Be a Director of a Nonprofit Corporation?

#### A director acts as a part of a board

Anyone serving as a director of a corporation must be aware of what a director is—and isn't. As a body, a board of directors has considerable powers. In most corporations the board plays a substantial part in the beginning or end of any corporate activity, and the board appoints or removes corporate agents, executives, and officers.

In contrast, an individual director, acting alone, has almost no power: rather each director exerts her or his power as one participating element in the board of directors.[1] Nonetheless, the individual director is still legally accountable for corporate actions in certain circumstances and has legally protected rights and duties to participate in the board's decisions and all information related thereto.[2]

#### A director directs, but does not perform, the corporation's activities

The structure of corporations contemplates that corporate actions, as determined by the board, will be carried out by officers, employees and agents—persons chosen, directly or indirectly, by the board of directors. Often a person serving as a director may also wear another hat, such as that of an officer or agent, but corporate theory assumes that neither the board itself nor any individual director, acting solely as a director, carries out day-to-day activities.

#### The directors act on behalf of one or more constituencies

In a business corporation, the director's constituents are, by and large, the stockholders. The stockholders elect the directors. The directors understand that their primary function is to advance the stockholders' wealth, and it is the stockholders, in most instances, who may call the director to account.

In the nonprofit world, identifying a director's constituencies is often not so simple. The persons or entities electing or appointing the nonprofit director, the interests to be served by him or her, and those who may call the director to account can be, and often are, separate parties.

## Who Selects the Directors?

Directors of nonprofit corporations can be selected in three ways.

### Election by members or others

Membership corporations, including, for practical purposes, all mutual benefit corporations, elect directors somewhat as the stockholders elect a business corporation director. Often the members are presented with a slate of candidates for election or re-election at an annual meeting; each member has one vote, and the candidate or candidates having the most votes win. The same basic structure is used where the members are institutions or even one single person or entity. For instance, a hospital may create a subsidiary nonprofit corporation for a particular purpose, with the hospital corporation as the sole voting member electing the subsidiary's directors.

In some cases, the corporation's articles of incorporation or bylaws may provide that a person or group who is not a member of the corporation may appoint one or more of the corporation's directors. For instance, some states permit bondholders or other creditors to vote for directors under certain circumstances.[3]

### Self-perpetuating boards

Many public benefit and religious corporations have self-perpetuating boards of directors, in which the existing board elects—or re-elects—the persons who serve as directors.

### Election by status

A director may serve *ex officio* by virtue of holding another position, such as chief executive of the corporation, or officer of an affiliate organization or constituency group.

## Special Categories of Directors

Frequently a nonprofit board will describe some person as an *honorary, life, emeritus* or *ex officio* director. These designations often cause confusion.

## Honorary directors

An honorary or emeritus director is, almost by definition, not a true director. If a nonprofit corporation's member or board wishes to recognize someone— usually a longtime member of the board—as deserving of special respect, but to be relieved of regular duties as a board member, they are free to do so. However, such an appointment raises three legal issues.

**Status should be provided for in the bylaws.**    It is helpful if not only the method of designating but also the status of honorary directors is described in the bylaws. Otherwise, the distinction between the "regular" and honorary directors can be confusing, for such directors as well as staff and other persons who deal with the board. Especially where the honorary director has recently served as a regular director (such as a board chair who has been bumped up to honorary status), such bylaw clarifications are helpful for all concerned.

**No voting rights.**    Second, although a board may at any time invite any person, including honorary or emeritus directors, to attend any board meeting, such person's presence may not be counted for a necessary quorum, and such person may not vote, even if she or he is allowed to participate in discussion at the meeting. The invitation to attend the meeting confers no voting rights.

**Attorney-client privilege issues.**    The board, in consulting legal counsel concerning matters that the corporation may wish to consider in confidence, must realize that *the presence at a meeting of a non-director (including honorary directors), or his or her receipt of confidential documents, may destroy the attorney-client privilege*—the corporation's right to communicate with counsel while keeping that communication secret even in court.[4]

## Life directors

Life directors usually occupy much the same position as honorary directors and are subject to the same admonitions set forth above. However, if a corporation intends to create one or more full voting directorships with a lifetime term, the board should examine the applicable nonprofit corporation statute—many will not permit it. The bylaws then must clearly define the status of such a director.

## Ex-officio *directors*

*Ex-officio* is the term commonly used to describe a person whose status as a director is tied to the holding of some other office or position (inside or outside the corporation). For example, a hospital may designate whomever is chief of the medical staff as an *ex-officio* director, to serve as long as, and only as long as, she or he is chief of staff. A museum, as a condition of its using park district land, may be required to include the park superintendent as an *ex-officio* director. *Ex-officio* directors may be voting or non-voting, as specified in the bylaws.

Sometimes, however, the term *ex officio* is used to describe someone who needs to be recognized (or appeased) but who is *not* regarded as a fully participating director. For example, the individual may not only be non-voting, but his presence at every meeting may not be expected. All the cautions mentioned with regard to honorary directors (particularly with regard to the attorney-client privilege) apply in such situations, and the ambiguity of the term *ex-officio* dictates that its use should be confined to the situation outlined in the preceding paragraph. It is particularly important, in these cases, that the bylaws define the rights and duties of any *ex-officio* directors.

# The Corporation's Purpose and How It Affects a Director

## All Directors Must Know the Corporation's Purpose and the Persons or Interests It Serves, and Be Prepared to Serve Accordingly

Any person serving or asked to serve as a director must ask: For what purpose is the corporation maintained? What is the constituency that it is serving? It has been said that all organizations exist to maximize something for somebody;[5] the nonprofit corporation is no exception. Defining the something and the somebody is a duty of every nonprofit board and every director. Once it has been determined what the corporation is maximizing and for whom, all persons serving or asked to serve as directors should determine if these aims are compatible with their reasons for serving on the board.

## The Corporate Documents Should State the Corporation's Purpose and Its Constituencies; Actual Corporate Activities Should Be Consistent with Such Statements

### Statements of corporate purposes

In all nonprofit corporations, the corporate purposes should be stated, at least in general terms, in the articles of incorporation and if desired, in the bylaws. The corporate purposes may also be reflected by a mission statement adopted by the board, or by undertakings and activities to which corporate assets and energies are committed. Unfortunately, the foregoing places for inquiry may give inconsistent answers, or no answer at all. Although the articles of incorporation will legally control in the event of conflicts, the purposes stated therein may be as broad as legally allowable and the bylaws may be equally vague.

## Use of mission statements

If a nonprofit corporation has no instrument that clearly details its present purposes, a director should urge the creation of such a document. Even where a nonprofit corporation is conducting a specific program or activity, with a clear consensus among its directors, it is beneficial to describe that activity and its purpose in a brief mission statement. The articles of incorporation and bylaws may define the broad general purposes of the corporation; however, the mission statement should be more specific. As a practical matter, confusion over mission impairs the efficiency of the board in the discharge of its duties. On the other hand, adoption or renewal (such as at an annual board retreat) of a corporate mission statement can rekindle the energies and help focus the attentions of the board members, both individually and collectively.

Mission statements come in varying styles and shapes. An effective mission statement succinctly reflects the board's agreement regarding the corporation's purposes and constituencies. Three examples of how a mission statement may help focus the activities of a nonprofit corporation are described below:

(1) The board of a condominium association usually operates within a fairly tight structure dictated by its declaration and statutory law, but clear choices may have to be made as to the constituency served (all owners? only owner-occupants?) or the corporate purpose (bare structural maintenance? enhanced value through annual improvements?). A mission statement enables the board to reach these decisions with minimum—or greatly lessened—interpersonal controversy.

(2) A local community organization—no matter how small—may have to make choices concerning the constituency served (all residents? only merchants? only youth?) or purposes (all welfare? specific social services?).

(3) The parent corporation of a regional healthcare system may use a mission statement to help guide its planning and strategic decisions, as well as to communicate its commitments to its employees, medical staff, and the community in which it provides services.

The board should re-examine its mission statement on a regular basis. Any vigorous nonprofit corporation will find that demands and opportunities will continually shape and alter what the corporation actually does; the environment in which it acts will change as well. Regular consideration of a mission statement also helps ensure that newer directors both understand the corporation's mission and know that they have been part of the articulation of such mission. Further, a periodic examination will reveal whether the current mission statement is consistent with the articles and bylaws, and if not, what changes in such documents may be required. Tax-exempt nonprofit corporations should also evaluate whether any variations between the corporation's current activities and the statements in its articles and bylaws necessitates a filing with the Internal Revenue Service to confirm the organization's tax-exempt status.

# The Parties to Whom the Director Is Accountable: Understanding the Corporation's Constituencies and Their Deemed Representatives

## All Directors Are Accountable to Defined Classes of Persons or Entities

All nonprofit directors are legally responsible to certain parties. In other words, some classes of persons or entities have the right to question the director's conduct, and even, in extreme cases, to bring him or her into court. By implication, there are others who do not have that right.[6]

## The Accountability of Directors of Mutual Benefit Corporations Is Largely Equivalent to That of Directors of a Business Corporation

We have emphasized that the nonprofit corporation serves to maximize something for somebody, and the director must be able to identify the something and the somebody. In mutual benefit corporations, as a general rule, the somebody involved will be the party or parties who control the tenure of the directors—for example, in a trade association the members usually elect the directors—and those same persons will be the parties who may, in appropriate circumstances, call the board of directors to account. Thus, the directors of most mutual benefit corporations hold a relationship to their members similar to that held by the directors of business corporations to stockholders. Nevertheless, in some circumstances (such as when a mutual benefit corporation considers merging with or selling its assets to a for-profit corporation), the directors of a mutual benefit corporation may be called to account by the state attorney general, or other community representatives, on the theory that some or all of the assets of such corporations are charitable assets that may not be disposed of without state approval.[7]

# The Accountability of Directors of Public Benefit and Religious Corporations

### Direct beneficiaries generally have no legal oversight power over nonprofit corporation directors

From the beginning of public charities, there was a class of beneficiaries of the charitable corporation (for example, the poor of a parish) who were not the parties appointing the director or trustee to office. Further, those beneficiaries were generally deemed incapable of enforcing the director's obligations or were persons who, it was felt, should not have that power. In some cases, moreover, the direct beneficiaries of a nonprofit organization are not people—for example, nonprofits devoted to animal welfare or preserving natural resources. The absence of a mechanism for direct action and oversight by beneficiaries of nonprofit organizations leaves an accountability vacuum. In the United States, this vacuum is filled by the state, generally represented by the state attorney general.

### Attorney general oversight

A state attorney general is generally deemed to speak for the beneficiaries of any entity, such as a public benefit corporation, which has assets that are considered to be held in a charitable trust. In effect, the attorney general becomes the voice of the constituency for whom a charitable corporation was organized.[8] In comparison, except in unusual circumstances, the attorney general does not assert a right to scrutinize activities of mutual benefit corporations.

Traditionally, the attorney general's authority has been understood as giving the attorney general the power to enforce the public's interest in the maintenance of property and funds for the original charitable purpose: to prevent a divergence of such funds for improper purposes and intervene if the persons holding such property attempted to change the purpose, even if the new purpose was a proper charitable activity. As a result, a public benefit corporation planning a major change in the use of its assets may be required to consult the attorney general or join him or her in a so-called *cy pres* proceeding in a court. Statutory provisions have broadened the power of the attorney general in most states to include a general supervision over the solicitation of monies for charitable purposes.[9]

States vary in the degree to which the attorney general is specifically empowered to investigate transactions of nonprofit corporations, such as public charities, which are deemed to hold some or all of its assets in a charitable trust.[10] Many states have adopted laws affirmatively requiring some or all nonprofit corporations to give the state attorney general prior notice and the opportunity to review transactions involving disposition of substantially all of the corporation's charitable assets, particularly in the case of a merger or sale of assets to a for-profit institution.[11]

## Despite Their Importance, Donors Are Not Considered Part of the Nonprofit's Legal Constituency

A director of a public benefit corporation, such as a conventional charity, will note an omission from the list of the persons to whom directors of a nonprofit corporation may be accountable: we have not listed the donors to the corporation as a party with whom the director has a legal relationship. In general, the omission is correct, although obviously the corporation will be sensitive to the concerns of its principal donors. Although there are exceptions, as a general rule, assets acquired by a charitable corporation are no longer subject to the donors' control, unless the donors have specified that the assets be used in a specific manner.[12] The corporation's board of directors may use the donated assets in whatever way they believe appropriate, consistent with the corporation's mission. If donors or others believe such uses are not appropriate, they may petition the state attorney general to review the matter.[13]

## Accountability to Members Responsible for Appointing a Director

Although the attorney general's powers may extend to all public benefit corporations within a given state, many such corporations also have a membership to whom the director may be accountable, to the extent such membership has the power to remove or fail to re-elect the director or to sue directors on the corporation's behalf.[14] If a director is elected by one or more members in order to be able to represent the viewpoint of such members, the director may have—or feel—a duty to such member or members, to make sure that such viewpoint is in fact represented on the board. However, such duty to articulate a member's individual perspective does not change the director's obligation to make decisions and take other actions in accordance with the *corporation's* best interest—irrespective of any individual member interests. The only exception to this rule occurs when the corporation's articles and bylaws specify that certain member interests should be taken into account, such as a requirement that no action be taken that would result in the corporation losing its tax-exempt status.

# Constitutional Considerations Limit the Public Accountability of Religious Corporations

The directors of religious corporations are generally subject to the foregoing considerations. However, because United States constitutional law restricts the role of government in dealing with religious corporations to a minimum enforcement of basic fiscal integrity, oversight is more limited, lest the government intrude on freedom of religion.

See the following checklist (page 14) to review the issues discussed in this chapter.

# Notes

1. A good analogy is that of a representative in Congress, who may, on the floor or through committee, exert immense influence on the actions of government, but is given no function, under our Constitution, when acting alone. But (again paralleling a member of Congress) the individual director has legally protected rights to participate in corporate decisions and has legally recognized rights and duties to be informed concerning corporate transactions.

A one-person board of directors is permitted under some state statutes; where such a board exists, the single director's act is an exercise of the board's powers. The Model Act § 8.03 (and most state statutes) requires a minimum of three directors.

2. *See* Comment to Model Act § 8.01 (describing rights and duties of directors). See also the chapter "Duties and Rights of Nonprofit Corporation Directors" in this *Guidebook*.

3. *See, e.g.,* California Nonprofit Corp. Law § 5124 et seq.; DEL. CODE ANN., tit. 8 § 221; New York Not-for-Profit Corp. Law § 1401(i); OHIO REV. CODE ANN. § 1701.84.

4. *See generally* JOHN WILLIAM GERGACZ, ATTORNEY-CORPORATE CLIENT PRIVILEGE (1997-2000) §§ 5.10 and 5.11 (discussing factors to be considered in determining whether attorney-client confidentiality applies); *see also id.* at § 2.04 (using Kirby v. Kirby to explain why in nonprofit corporations the privilege is considered to attach to directors as part of the corporate entity).

5. Attribution unknown.

6. *See, e.g.,* Cook v. The Lloyd Nolan Foundation, Inc., and Tenet Healthcare, Inc., CV-99-592 (Ala. 2001) (finding that under the state Alabama Nonprofit Corporation Act, the only persons authorized to bring a legal proceeding to challenge an act, conveyance or transfer of property by a nonprofit corporation were members or directors of the corporation, representatives of the corporation and the state attorney general, and that the local district attorney and other community representatives therefore lacked standing to challenge the corporation's actions).

7. *See* James K. Orlikoff and Mary K. Totten, *Governing Conversion Foundations: A Practical Guide for Trustees,* TRUSTEE 51, no. 4 (April 1998), at T1-T4; Gary Claxton, Judith Feder, David Shactman, and Stuart Altman, *Public Policy Issues in Nonprofit Conversions: An Overview,* HEALTH AFFAIRS 16, no. 2 (March/April 1997), at 9-28.

8. *See, e.g.,* CONN. GEN. STAT. § 3-125; Mass. Ann. Laws ch. 12 § 8.

9. *See, e.g.,* Missouri Merchandizing Practices Act § 407.453; New York Executive Law § 171-a.

10. *See, e.g.,* OHIO REV. CODE ANN. § 109.24 (giving the state attorney general the power to "investigate transactions and relationships of trustees of a charitable trust for the purpose of determining whether the property held for charitable, religious, or educational purposes has been and is being properly administered in accordance with fiduciary principles. . . ." and providing that the attorney general "shall institute and prosecute a proper action to enforce the performance of any charitable trust, and to restrain the abuse of it whenever he considers such action advis-

able. . . .”). *See also* RESTATEMENT OF THE LAW, SECOND, TRUSTS (1959) § 391 (“A suit can be maintained for the enforcement of a charitable trust by the Attorney General, or by a co-trustee, or by a person who has a special interest in the enforcement of the charitable trust. . . .”).

11.   *See* TENN. CODE ANN. § 48-62-102(g); *see also* OHIO REV. CODE ANN. § 109.34 (referring solely to nonprofit healthcare corporations).

12.   *See* Newman v. Forward Lands, 430 F. Supp. 1320 (E.D. Pa. 1977) (“. . . someone with a special interest may sue . . .”), citing RESTATEMENT OF THE LAW, SECOND, TRUSTS (1959), § 391. The Restatement makes clear that the donor cannot sue to enforce a charitable trust and is not someone with a “special interest.” The Restatement deals with charitable trusts, not with corporations; however, the principles of accountability for nonprofit corporations that are public benefit corporations are much the same.

13.   *See* Linda Grant, *Acts of Charity; Furious Donors Blame a Lax Board after a Funds Scandal Toppled the Lavish-Living Hand of the United Way,* LOS ANGELES TIMES MAGAZINE, Sept. 13, 1992, 39; *see also* Aramony v. United Way, 28 F. Supp. 2d 147 (S.D.N.Y. 1999).

14.   CAL. CORP. CODE § 5710, 7710, N.Y. Not-for-Profit Corp. Law § 623; *see also* Model Act § 6.30 (1987); DEL. CODE ANN. § 141(k).

# Suggested Questions for Directors Regarding the Nonprofit Corporation and Its Directors

(1) What group of members elected me? If I wasn't elected by a voting membership, how was I elected?

(2) If I was elected by a voting membership, how is that membership defined? Where can I find out: in the bylaws? the articles of incorporation? Are the records of voting membership kept in good order? By whom?

(3) When does my term of office expire? Can I be re-elected? Does my term run until a specific date, or until my successor is chosen?

(4) Can I be removed from my position as director? By whom? On what basis?

(5) Was I selected by some group of members or some entity that differs from the source of tenure of the other directors?

(6) What is our corporation supposed to do and for whom? Is our mission expressed in the articles of incorporation, bylaws and/or a separate mission statement?

(7) Does the corporation have a mission statement? If not, why not? If so, when was the mission statement last reviewed?

(8) What parties or officials can question what we do as directors of the corporation?

# Checklist: The Nonprofit Corporation and Its Directors

*Note:* For purposes of simplicity in these checklists, we describe a corporation with a chair, who presides over the board of directors; a chief executive, who may be a staff person; an executive committee; a nominating committee; and an audit committee. (However, we recognize that in many smaller and other nonprofits, such committee functions may be performed by either the executive committee or the board as a whole.) We also assume a legal counsel—someone, paid or unpaid, having primary responsibility for the corporation's legal affairs. Many corporations, especially larger nonprofits, may have other committees established for specific purposes, such as reviewing staff performance, fixing compensation, monitoring compliance with legal requirements and periodic review of bylaws.

| Subject | To Be Reviewed By Whom | How Often | Comment |
|---|---|---|---|
| 1. Review of the articles of incorporation | a) Full board or committee, with legal counsel<br><br>b) By new directors | a) Periodic review, probably every three years<br><br>b) Upon joining board | Review should include: conformity to corporate mission; compliance with tax and corporate laws; any explicit provisions relating to directors and officers. |
| 2. Review of the bylaws | In general:<br><br>a) Chair, legal counsel, bylaws or other committee<br><br>b) By new directors | In general:<br><br>a) Periodic review, probably every three years<br><br>b) Upon joining board | Review should include conformity to corporate mission; problems possibly arising from changes in program; compliance with tax and corporate laws; any explicit provisions relating to directors and officers, including indemnification, insurance and availability of limitations on liability. |
| a. Does the number directors stated in the bylaws conform to the number actually serving (or the size the board will reach if new directors are elected)? | Chair or chief executive; nominating or bylaws committee | Annually in all cases; always before notice goes out for meeting to elect directors | Consistency of actual board composition with bylaw requirements is a frequent problem, particularly in smaller public benefit corporations. |
| b. Are there officers serving who bear titles or perform functions that are not reflected in the bylaws? For example, is the chief executive's function described therein? | Chair or chief executive; nominating or bylaws committee | Annually in all cases; always before notice goes out of meeting to elect directors | Many public benefit corporations have bylaws describing as "chair" an uncompensated person who simply presides over the board. In many nonprofits, the chief executive's functions are not described in bylaws if he or she is not the president or other corporate officer. |

## Checklist: The Nonprofit Corporation and Its Directors *(Continued)*

| Subject | To Be Reviewed By Whom | How Often | Comment |
|---|---|---|---|
| c. Do the bylaws have a statement of corporate mission or purpose consistent with the articles of incorporation, or other mission statement? | Chair or chief executive; bylaws or other committee | Annually and every time either of these documents is changed | Bylaws may have no statement of purpose and there does not have to be one; but if there is one, it should be consistent with other documents. |
| d. Are there, or should there be Honorary directors? | Chair and chief executive | Probably every three or four years | Voting rights (or lack thereof) should be clearly defined and understood. |
| e. If the corporation has members with voting rights, is there an accurate list of the members consistent with whatever definition of eligibility is contained in the bylaws? | Chief executive or bylaws or other committee | At least annually, and before notice goes out for any meeting where elections are to be held | There is probably no area with greater record-keeping problems than this. Nonprofits, particularly public benefit and religious corporations, will often designate as "members" persons who are simply donors or friends, keeping no accurate records thereof. The rights (or lack thereof) of such persons to vote should be clearly defined and any problems reviewed with legal counsel. |
| 3. Review of a corporate mission statement | Chief executive reporting to board | Probably every three or four years | If there is no mission statement, a board may wish to create one. |
| a. Is there a single mission statement; in what document is it embodied? | Chief executive reporting to board | Probaby every three or four years | There should be a single overall mission statement; separate statements for individual programs may be in order, but they should be consistent. |
| b. Are the corporation's public statements (e.g., brochures, press releases, etc.) as issued during the last year, consistent with the mission statement? | Chief executive | Annually, and as each brochure or press release is issued | Nonprofits dealing with public controversies will often find problems here. |
| c. Has the board reviewed the mission statement and understood the constituency served by the corporation? | Chair, bringing issue to board | Probably every three or four years | Board should always understand that it has a specific constituency or service. |

# Duties and Rights of Nonprofit Corporation Directors

## *Contents*

CHAPTER **2**

# Duties and Rights of Nonprofit Corporation Directors

*In carrying out their functions for the corporation, directors are subject to two primary obligations: a duty of care and a duty of loyalty.*

*The duty of care and the duty of loyalty are the common terms for the standards that guide all actions a director takes. These standards are derived from a century of litigation principally involving business corporations, but are equally applicable to nonprofit corporations.[1]*

## The Duty of Care

The duty of care calls upon a director to act in a reasonable and informed manner when participating in the board's decisions and its oversight of the corporation's management.

The duty of care requires that first, a director be informed; and second, a director discharge his duties in good faith, with the care that an ordinarily prudent person in a like position would reasonably believe appropriate under similar circumstances.[2]

Each of the tasks outlined below requires the efficient allocation of time by the director. The appropriate amount of time required to satisfy a director's duty of care must be decided by the director in his or her reasonable judgment, under the circumstances. Nonetheless, substantial compliance with the elements of care discussed below is commonly expected of the nonprofit director and may be required by law.

### Elements of the Duty of Care

The duty of care requires that a director be informed and exercise independent judgment. The satisfaction of the duty of care may be accomplished in part by the following activities:

#### *Attending meetings and proxy voting limitations*

Regular attendance at meetings of the board of directors is a basic requirement of director service. Generally, directors may not vote by proxy.

**Importance of regular attendance.**    All directors must remember that they act as a group, and therefore regular board meeting attendance is essential. Continuous or repeated absence may expose the director to the risk of not satisfying the duty of care. Moreover, sporadic board attendance by a director may be grounds for the director's removal. Most states permit directors to "attend" a meeting by telephone or use other mechanisms that allow all directors to hear or communicate with each other simultaneously. Therefore, even directors with busy travel schedules should be able to comply with the regular attendance standard.

**Attendance at committee meetings.**    As discussed in Chapter 3, "Committees and Advisory Bodies," boards typically delegate many important functions to committees. A director appointed to serve on a committee of the board is expected to regularly attend such committee meetings, and to be active in the committee's deliberations and other activities. A director must satisfy the duty of care in discharging his duties as a committee member.

**Limits on attendance or voting by proxy.**    Generally, directors cannot designate another person as the director's proxy, to attend or vote at board or committee meetings in the director's place.[3] All directors should understand the reasons for this rule. First of all, whatever reasons a director's constituency may have had for choosing her or him, that choice was the selection of one person to perform a duty, not the grant of a transferable privilege. Secondly, all the other directors are entitled to demand the director's own wisdom and judgment, not that of such surrogate as the director may choose. Thirdly, such deference and accommodation the directors themselves may give to each other in the course of their work usually cannot, as a practical matter, be transferred to purely personal appointees.

If a board of directors encounters significant problems concerning the frequency of a director's attendance, it should consider adopting or recommending bylaws or policies permitting or requiring the removal of directors who regularly miss meetings or attend only portions of meetings. As an alternative, the board could consider creating honorary directorships or advisory councils for such persons.

## Exercising independent judgment

The duty of care requires that each director, no matter how selected, share *equally* in the responsibility of the board to act in the best interests of the corporation. Each director should exercise her or his independent and informed judgment on all corporate decisions. While such judgment may be informed by the director's individual experience and affiliations, and even knowledge of the viewpoints of any entity that contributed to his appointment, the director's decision must only be based on what is in the corporation's best interest. No director should vote solely on the basis of what another director thinks, even if that director has special expertise; each director must use his independent judgment to evaluate any position taken by another director, the corporation's staff or an outside expert.

**Each director must judge what is in the corporation's best interest, irrespective of other entities with which the director is affiliated or sympathetic, or to which the director owes his board appointment.**     The law conceives of a board of directors as an entity, each member of which shares the same rights and the same duties and is accountable to the same constituency. Even if a director is specifically nominated or appointed by a particular group, or is chosen in part because of an association with a certain subset of the organization's members or beneficiaries, each director shares the same fiduciary duty to act in the best interest of the entire organization.

There are situations in which a board of directors may be explicitly structured to provide for representation of certain interests. For example, a trade association may have a board of directors composed of men and women who are selected by separate regions or states. A university alumni association may have a board on which each of the schools of the university is represented by directors elected from the alumni of that particular school. This can create confusion in the director, with respect to how to address situations in which the interests of his or her constituency and the interests of the corporation are actually or potentially different. In bringing to the attention of the board the particular sensitivities and concerns of his or her constituency, a director may aid the whole board in fulfilling its duty of care, and add wisdom to the whole board's deliberations. Nonetheless, the director's duty of loyalty lies with the interests of the corporation, not to any constituent group. (See the discussion in the section "The Duty of Loyalty" below.)

**Directors may give weight to the views of directors or others having special expertise, but must make an independent decision on any questions presented for board or committee determination.**     The reason for having more than one director is to ensure that differing viewpoints have the opportunity to be heard, and that directors with different talents, experiences, and perspectives share their views and together decide on what course of action is in the corporation's best interests. While it is natural, and often appropriate, for a director to seriously consider the viewpoints of another director who has special expertise or knowledge on a matter being discussed, it is part of each director's duty of care to evaluate all views and information presented to the board or board committee, and to make an independent judgment regarding the proper course of action.

## Having adequate information
To function effectively, a director needs to be adequately informed.

**Assuring the adequacy and clarity of information.**    To satisfy the duty of care in an effective manner, a director needs to have an adequate source of information flow. This information is generally supplied by the corporation's management and other staff. To the extent that it is not adequate, a board or an individual director will have to determine what additional information is needed. Needless to say, the director should carefully read the information supplied. If the information is highly technical, lengthy or otherwise difficult to comprehend, the board should request an executive summary or other version of the information, which is in a more understandable form. In addition, a board member should ask questions at the board meeting as necessary to clarify the information or help assure the director that he or she has fully understood it. If a director has a special expertise with respect to a certain kind of information, he or she may assist the other board members by asking such clarifying questions, or in pointing out specific items to the rest of the board. (However, such director should try to avoid stating opinions in such a way that other directors are tempted or pressured to "rely" on the director's opinion without engaging in independent analysis). (See the discussion in the section "Directors May Give Weight to the Views of Directors…" above.)

**Sources of board information.**    In some small nonprofit entities, such as neighborhood improvement bodies or condominium associations, the board itself may be its own primary source of information. With larger organizations, however, the board will inevitably use and rely on information prepared by the corporation's officers and agents. This means that the corporation's staff will inevitably have a significant effect on the board's decisions since the staff must select much of the information the directors receive. Even when a director has total and justified confidence in the suppliers of information, he or she should be at least aware that for every piece of information received, other information may have been determined to be not necessary for the board's consideration.

Especially in heavily regulated areas or other areas that are significant to the organization's existence and mission, the director should evaluate whether he or she needs additional information to fulfill the director's duty and to best serve the organization. If for any reason any member of the board thinks that the information provided to the directors is inadequate in any respect, he or she should not hesitate to request further information from the staff or other sources. Since boards tend to become accustomed to the *status quo*, new board members can often serve a valuable function by calling the board's attention to the question of whether the board should be receiving different or additional information in certain areas.

# Reliance

In the ordinary course of business, a director may act in reliance on information and reports received from regular sources that the director reasonably regards as trustworthy.

A director may rely upon the reports, communications and information received from a committee or from any officer, employee or agent, if the director reasonably believes the source to be reliable and competent. The Model Act, as well as many state nonprofit codes, expressly recognizes the concept of reliance on others. A director is entitled to rely on information, opinions, reports, or statements, including financial statements and other financial data, if prepared or presented by:

### Officers and employees

A director may rely on information provided by officers or employees of the corporation whom the director reasonably believes to be reliable and competent in the matters presented. If the information is provided in written form, the director must have independently reviewed or evaluated the information before relying on it.[4]

### Experts retained by the corporation

A director may rely on legal counsel, public accountants, or other persons retained by the corporation, as to matters the director reasonably believes are within the person's professional or expert competence.

### Board committees

A director may rely on information provided by a committee of the board of which the director is not a member as to matters within the committee's jurisdiction, if the director reasonably believes the committee merits confidence.

### Religious authorities presenting information to religious corporations

A director of a religious corporation may rely on information provided by religious authorities and ministers, priests, rabbis, or other persons whose position or duties in the religious organization the director believes justify reliance and confidence and whom the director believes to be reliable and competent in the matters presented.[5]

These general rules of reliance *never* apply if the director has personal knowledge that would make reliance on the information provided by any of the above persons unwarranted.[6] In such circumstances, relying on such information would not constitute "reasonableness" or good faith on the part of the director. Moreover, a director having knowledge that brings into question the reliability of any information presented to the board may have a duty to share such knowledge with the other board members.

# Delegation

The board of directors, as such, does not operate the day-to-day business of the corporation. In delegating that function to others, it must adopt appropriate policies and procedures that ensure effective oversight of the actions of the corporation's management and other corporate agents.

### General rule: the directors oversee, but do not directly engage in the corporation's day-to-day operations

The board of directors is not expected to operate the corporation on a day-to-day basis. Even under statutes providing that the business and affairs of a corporation shall be "managed" by the board of directors, it is recognized that actual operation is a function of management, that is, the officers and agents of the corporation.[7] In conventional corporate theory, the responsibility of the board is limited to overseeing corporate operations. This principle does not relieve the board of its monitoring responsibilities; however, it does mean that directors are not personally responsible for actions or omissions of officers, employees or agents of the corporation as long as such persons have been prudently selected and the directors have relied reasonably upon such officers, employees, or agents.

### Adoption of appropriate monitoring and control procedures

Directors and prospective directors of nonprofit corporations, especially those in highly regulated areas such as health care, should be aware of the kind of legal claims to which their corporation may be vulnerable, based on trends in government enforcement actions or private litigation involving similar organizations. Directors should evaluate whether the corporation has appropriate policies and procedures in place to ensure that the corporation complies with applicable laws.[8] (For a more detailed discussion of how a board can become aware of the legal environment of its corporation, see Chapter 11, "The Legal Environment of the Nonprofit Corporation.")

### Evidencing specific delegations of authority to officers

While in the for-profit world, a corporation's board often makes clear written delegations of authority to the chief executive and other officers, this is often not the case in the nonprofit world. The board may wish to adopt bylaw provisions, or a general resolution, setting forth the scope of management authority delegated to the chief executive officer (who may then be free to sub-delegate portions of such authority). Formalizing the scope of delegated authority may be particularly useful in small nonprofit corporations, where lines of responsibility may be easily blurred.

### Directors with multiple "hats"

When a member of the board occupies both the role of a director and that of an officer, employee, or other agent, corporate law treats that person, while acting in his or her capacity as an agent, just as the law would treat such a person who is not serving on the board. It is therefore essential that such person (and the other directors) always be aware of which "hat" the director is wearing at any particular time.

### *Delegations of director authority to members or other persons*

The Model Act, as well as many state laws, permits a nonprofit corporation's articles of incorporation to specify exceptions to the general management authority of the board.[9] In such cases, the articles or bylaws may name other parties, such as the corporation's members, a representative assembly, or a board-appointed committee, who are specifically responsible for certain corporate management decisions that would ordinarily fall to the board of directors. Depending on the jurisdiction and the nature of the delegation, the directors of such corporations may be partially or wholly relieved of their fiduciary responsibilities in such specified areas (while the alternate decision-maker may become correspondingly subject to fiduciary obligations to the extent of its specified authority). It is incumbent upon any director to make sure that he clearly understands the extent to which such article or bylaw provisions serve to release him of the fiduciary duties that would ordinarily apply.

### *Delegation to an executive committee*

Many nonprofit corporations make extensive use of an executive committee to make board-level management decisions. Such delegation of board authority may be both appropriate and practical, especially if the size of the board is very large or if it meets only a few times a year. Even fairly active boards may appropriately make use of an executive committee. However, the scope of such delegations of board authority to an executive committee should be clearly set forth in the corporation's bylaws and/or in board resolutions. In addition, directors who do not sit on the executive committee should understand the extent to which the board has (and has not) delegated its fiduciary duties to the executive committee. Such directors should understand that they still retain a duty of oversight over the executive committee. The executive committee is accountable to the board, and the board members should receive sufficient information regarding executive committee decisions to be able to evaluate whether delegations of authority to the committee are appropriate. (See further discussion in the section "Description of Common Standing Committees" in Chapter 3, "Committees and Advisory Bodies.")

# Discharging the Duty of Care:
# Some Practical Suggestions

In all but the smallest and simplest corporations, the corporation's needs for the board's attention will often exceed the time the board has to furnish this resource. Hence, well-run nonprofit corporations will adopt certain procedures, including those set forth below, to enable the board and its individual members to use their time efficiently.

## Regular Schedule of Meetings

The board of directors should meet on a regular basis. The schedule of board meetings should be fixed at the beginning of each year, so that each board member can place the meetings on his or her calendar well in advance, and thus assure attendance. While the appropriate frequency (monthly, quarterly, etc.) of scheduled board meetings will depend on the size of the corporation, the geographic nature of its constituency, budgetary considerations and other considerations unique to each corporation, the need for a regular schedule of meetings applies to all nonprofit corporations. Without such regular schedule, the board is more vulnerable to claims that it has not adequately fulfilled its duties of oversight of the corporation. Because decisions regarding the management of the corporation occur on a regular basis, some person or body other than the board is likely making management decisions in the board's absence. By allowing such situation to occur, the board members may have effectively, and inappropriately, transferred board power to persons other than the board.

## Meeting Agenda and Committee Reports

Although the items discussed will vary, most boards find it helpful to have a standard form of meeting agenda, to ensure the board routinely addresses issues important to the corporation. Such agenda should include reports from the executive committee (if any), and from all other active committees, regarding significant actions taken since the last board meeting.

## Action by Written Consent

The Model Act as well as many state statutes permits the directors to act without a meeting, by unanimous (or in some states, less than unanimous) written consent.[10] Such a procedure may frequently be appropriate in the transaction of routine business, or for the approval of specific actions that have already been fully discussed at prior board meetings. Directors should, however, be cautious about the ratification or authorization of major activities or decisions without a meeting or other opportunity for the board as a whole to raise questions and fully evaluate the ramifications of the action. The use of consents should not be a substitute for regular meetings.

# Regular Schedule of Information

As much information as practical should be provided on a regular schedule.

### Schedule of reports to be provided to the board

Information should be provided to the board of directors in a regular and timely manner, so that the board will have a realistic opportunity to review and consider it. The board's information needs will be more easily and efficiently satisfied if the directors establish a regularly scheduled system of reports and data for those corporate activities that are sufficiently repetitive to be predictable to all parties. Such information will include financial reports, program reports, and the like. Just as with infrequent board meetings, when information is provided only sporadically, directors will find it much more difficult to satisfy their duty of care on the corporation's behalf. Furthermore, in almost all such situations, *some* board member is receiving information, and thus inequalities within the board's knowledge base may be created. Regularity of information distribution is important to the entire board's ability to be informed regarding significant corporate matters.

### Distribution of information in advance of board meetings

Directors should require distribution of as much material as possible in advance of a board meeting (preferably by the weekend before the meeting). As noted above, certain types of reports—particularly financial reports—should be furnished on a regular schedule, whether monthly, quarterly, or semi-annually.

### Practical limitations on staff time to prepare required reports and other information

The board's need for regular reports and other information must necessarily be balanced by its recognition of any limitations on staff time to prepare the information. The preparation of meaningful data for a board meeting consumes significant amounts of time, and particularly in small organizations, may take away from time needed for operational activities. The board should be mindful of this in defining the information it requires. The board—as a whole or through its chairman or other representative—should discuss with its staff the most efficient way to provide the board with necessary information while not impeding the staff's operational responsibilities.

# Rules of Procedure and Minutes

The board should adopt rules of procedure appropriate to its size, the constituencies represented on the board and the diversity of its membership. Minutes of the board should be prepared regularly, and should note the names of the persons attending the meeting, all votes taken, and how each director voted.

Any working board will work out its own standard procedures for board meetings and the degree of formality, or lack thereof, used in submitting motions, amendments to resolutions, recording votes, etc. However, matters of importance should always be acted on by formal resolution. The corporation's minutes should be prepared on a regular basis by a director or other individual with the ability to accurately record and produce in a timely manner the minutes of each meeting. At a minimum, minutes of board meetings should note the names of all directors and other persons who attended each meeting, and the outcome of each vote taken (specifically noting the names of the directors who voted for, against, or abstained). Further, when the board or committee is acting on a matter involving a conflict of interest for, or compensation or other benefit to, a director or executive officer, the minutes should recite the documentation and information relied on by the board or committee in making its decision. For tax-exempt corporations, such minutes and documentation can be used to establish a rebuttable presumption of reasonableness for transactions covered by the IRS's "excess benefit" rule. (See the discussion of the excess benefits rules in the section "Intermediate Sanctions: Excise Tax on Public Charities' Excess Benefit Transactions" in Chapter 4, "Taxation.")

Board committees should also prepare minutes, particularly when acting by authority delegated by the full board.

# The Business Judgment Rule

Even where a corporate action has proven to be unwise or unsuccessful, a director will generally be protected from liability arising therefrom if he or she acted in good faith and in a manner reasonably believed to be in the corporation's best interest, and with independent and informed judgment.

### *Availability of the business judgment rule to prevent second-guessing of board decisions*

A director exercising good-faith judgment will usually be protected from liability to the corporation or to its membership under the Business Judgment Rule.[11] The Business Judgment Rule provides that a court, in an action brought by the corporation or its internal constituency, will not re-examine the actions of a director in authorizing or permitting a corporate action if such director's action was undertaken in good faith, in a manner reasonably believed to be in the best interests of the corporation, and based on the director's independent and informed judgment. The doctrine basically is a statement by the courts that it is inappropriate for them to second-guess corporate management decisions. This legal concept is well established in the case law applying to business corporations. It has also been recognized as applicable to the directors of nonprofit corporations.[12] However, because the doctrine is less well established in the nonprofit context, courts may be less willing to afford directors protection of the Business Judgment Rule when individuals are harmed, or other "bad facts" are present.[13]

### Exceptions to availability of the rule

The Business Judgment Rule defense will not be applied in situations where basic breaches of duty by the director (such as criminal activity, fraud, bad faith, willful and wanton misconduct) are present.[14] In addition, for public charities, business decisions that would result in significant reduction or cessation of operations (such as the decision of a nonprofit health system to close down a money-losing hospital) may be challenged by the state attorney general on grounds that such action would violate the directors' duties to maintain the functions of a charitable trust.[15]

## Satisfying Other Legal Requirements

In discharging the duty of care, a nonprofit board director should be mindful of the variety of legal requirements to which the corporation may be subject. For example, organizations that use volunteers should be aware of the variety of legal issues that can arise in connection with volunteers, as discussed in the *Guidebook* chapter "Employees." (As noted in Chapter 11, "The Legal Environment of the Nonprofit Corporation," an awareness of the corporation's legal environment gives the board the opportunity to ensure that there are appropriate policies and procedures in place to avoid or address legal problems.)

## The Duty of Loyalty

The duty of loyalty requires directors to exercise their powers in good faith and in the best interests of the corporation, rather in their own interests or the interests of another entity or person.

By assuming office, the director acknowledges that with regard to any corporate activity the best interests of the corporation must prevail over the director's individual interests or the particular interests of the constituency selecting him or her. The basic legal principle to be observed here is a negative one: *The director shall not use a corporate position for individual personal advantage.* The duty of loyalty primarily relates to:

• conflicts of interest;
• corporate opportunity; and
• confidentiality.

# Conflicts of Interest: General Principles

Directors of nonprofit corporations may have interests that conflict with those of the corporation. The duty of loyalty requires that a director be conscious of the potential for such conflicts and act with candor and care in dealing with such situations.

Conflicts of interest involving a director are not inherently illegal nor are they to be regarded as a reflection on the integrity of the board or of the director. It is the manner in which the director and the board deal with a disclosed conflict that determines the propriety of the transaction.

## Conflicts of interest are not unusual

Since nonprofit corporations generally look to populate their boards with civic, business and community leaders, it is to be expected that from time to time that a director of a nonprofit corporation will encounter situations in which a proposed corporate action will in some way relate to or affect the director's other activities and affiliations.

## When is a conflict of interest present?

A conflict of interest is present whenever a director has a material personal interest in a proposed contract or transaction to which the corporation may be a party. This interest can occur either directly or indirectly. The director may be personally involved with the transaction, have an employment or investment relationship with an entity with which the corporation is dealing, or have a family member who is either personally involved with the transaction or has a relationship with an entity that is involved in the transaction. A conflict of interest may result from a director performing professional services for the organization. For example, a banker, insurance agent, attorney, or real estate broker may benefit from employment by the organization. *The board should not assume that a conflict cannot exist for a director who receives no direct monetary or other tangible benefit from a transaction with the corporation.* As discussed below, some personal interests of directors may result in the directors experiencing a conflict between their own interests and those of the corporation. In the nonprofit world there are also common possible conflicts of interest arising from a director's simultaneous service on the boards of other (for-profit or nonprofit) corporations; it is therefore important that a director disclose such affiliations in general, as well as any specific circumstances in which a conflict between his role as a director for one corporation creates a conflict with respect to his director position with another corporation.

## Determining whether a personal interest is a conflict of interest

It is improper for a director to use his or her position to advance a personal interest. At the same time, the very reasons why a particular director is selected may relate to that director's concern for, and knowledge of, the particular business of the corporation. The following examples of personal interests illustrate that such interests may or may not be considered a conflict of interest, based on the circumstances:

- A director of an art museum may have—and probably should have— definite opinions as to the priority, in new purchases, of contemporary American painting versus old masters. The director's opinion and preferences present no conflict.
- If the art museum director was generally a collector of contemporary painting and the museum was faced with a particular possible acquisition in that field of art (which acquisition might then increase the recognition or value of pieces in the director's own collection), the director's personal interests might require disclosure.
- A director of a trade association might have been selected because of her familiarity with the impact of Pacific Rim competition on the products of the association's members. Her urging, based on her experience, that the association advocate a particular tariff bill would present no problem even if the director's own company would benefit along with others.
- If the trade association director's own company was one of the relatively small group of manufacturers affected by Pacific imports, but most of the association's members were untouched thereby, a decision to divert association assets and influence on behalf of that minority might present a material conflict.

### Dealing with conflicts: disclosure and approval requirements under nonprofit corporation laws and IRS rules

The law recognizes that conflicts of interest will occur. It deals with conflicts not by treating them as inherently immoral or illegal, but rather by prescribing the methods whereby affected directors should disclose conflicts and how a board of directors should proceed in the face of such situations. Under the Model Act, as well as many state nonprofit corporation laws, a director's conflict will not result in a deemed breach of the director's duty of loyalty, or render void the transaction under which the conflict arose, if the corporation can show that certain requirements were met, such as:

(1) The transaction was approved by a disinterested majority of the board or in some cases a board committee (or by another disinterested party as specified by the statute), after full disclosure by the affected director of the material facts regarding the transaction and the director's interest therein; and/or

(2) The transaction was fair to the corporation at the time it was entered into.[16]

In addition, as discussed in the section "Intermediate Sanctions: Excise Tax on Public Charities' Excess Benefit Transactions" in Chapter 4, "Taxation," the

IRS has specified certain procedures for approving transactions with a corporation's "insiders" that can establish a rebuttable presumption of reasonableness under the IRS' excess benefits/intermediate sanctions rules.

**When is it appropriate to approve a transaction in which a director is interested?**    Provided there has been appropriate disclosure and evaluation of transactions involving a conflict of interest, there are many situations in which such a transaction not only *can* but also, in the best interests of the corporation, probably *should* be approved. For instance, a board may legitimately choose to deal with a company affiliated with a director or other insider, because of greater familiarity with the supplier's reliability or the supplier's favorable pricing. In some cases, a company's affiliation with a director may result in the corporation receiving better service or prices than can be obtained from other commercial sources. Nonetheless, the corporate records must still show that the affiliation was appropriately disclosed, and that the board made its decision to do business with the director's affiliated company based on the fairness of the transaction and the best interests of the corporation

**Conflicts of interest policies and disclosure statements.**    In light of state and other laws that relate to how a board should handle the identification and evaluation of conflicts of interest involving directors and other insiders, it is good corporate practice for nonprofit corporations to adopt and adhere to a written conflict of interest policy. For instance, as noted in Chapter 4, "Taxation," the IRS is increasingly encouraging the adoption of a conflicts of interest policy containing provisions consistent with its model policy. The IRS model policy includes the requirement that directors and other persons having potential influence over the corporation fill out annual statements disclosing all of their significant affiliations, as well as contacts with entities doing business with the corporation. In other contexts, the presence of and adherence to a conflicts of interest policy can serve as evidence that it was the corporation's regular practice to seek to identify and resolve potential conflicts. For instance, adherence to a conflicts of interest policy could make the difference in a court determining whether the Business Judgment defense was available to a corporate decision involving an insider, since the Rule only applies to decisions made by directors who made reasonable efforts to obtain all material information. (See Appendix C.)

**Making a record of conflict disclosures and resolution.**    Whenever a conflict of interest situation arises, the corporate minutes or other records should document the nature of the disclosure given regarding the conflict, as well as the board's proceedings to evaluate the relevant transaction in light of the conflict. In addition, related party transactions may have to be disclosed in the notes to the corporation's audited financial statements, and in its annual tax filing (such as Form 990) to the IRS.

**Duty of disclosure.**    As noted above, the Model Act, as well as many state nonprofit corporation statutes, upholds the validity of a transaction authorized even when a director had an undisclosed interest, as long as the transaction was "fair" to the corporation. (Note, however, that in some states, such as California, fairness is only one of several factors—including disclosure—that must be satisfied in conflict situations.) Nonetheless, directors should be aware that *lack of disclosure of a conflict exposes both the affected director and the rest of the board, to greater risk.* In the event of litigation, the non-disclosing director, and, in some instances, even the disinterested directors who supported the transaction will have the burden of proving after the fact that the transaction was fair. Disclosure also enables the other members of the board to evaluate the proposed transaction not merely in terms of fairness, but also for its impact on the public image of the corporation.[17]

**Content of disclosure and participation in board discussions by interested director.**    Generally, the disclosure of a conflict of interest should include the existence of such interest and its nature (e.g., those arising from financial or family relationships, or professional or business affiliations, etc.) and should be made in advance, before any action is taken by the board concerning the matter. It is generally prudent—and may be required by state law or the corporation's conflicts policy—that the interested director be absent from that part of the meeting when the matter is being discussed except when her or his information may be needed. A director having a conflict should make sure that his or her absence from discussion and abstention from a vote relating thereto is duly noted in the meeting minutes.

In some cases a director may have an interest in a transaction but be unable, because of duties running to others, to disclose the nature of the interest. In such a case, the director should at least state that such an interest exists, consider leaving the meeting, or at least abstain from the discussion and not vote thereon. Where the conflicting interest presents so difficult a problem that even the above measures are impossible, the director should consider resigning.

**Quorum and voting requirements.**    State law and other applicable laws (as well as the corporation's bylaws or conflicts of interest policy) may specify whether an interested director can be counted in determining whether a quorum exists at a meeting at which the board considers the conflict of interest transaction. Legal standards and corporate procedures may also address whether an interested director may vote on the transaction in which he or she has an interest. Generally, a director, even if interested, may be counted for the purpose of determining the presence of a quorum. However, such director may not be permitted to vote, or such director's vote may not be allowed to be counted in determining whether there were sufficient votes to approve the transaction.

**Action by board after discovering an undisclosed conflict.**    A board of directors who discovers that it has acted upon a proposal in ignorance of an undisclosed interest therein should promptly reexamine the issue, with an appropriate record of such scrutiny.

## Corporate Opportunity

Before a director engages in a transaction which the director reasonably should know may be of interest to the corporation, the director should disclose the transaction to the board of directors in sufficient detail and in adequate time to enable the board to act or decline to act with regard to such transaction.

In certain circumstances, a director is obliged to treat a business opportunity as a "corporate opportunity" which must first be offered to the corporation before the director can take advantage of it outside of his role as a corporate director. The duty to treat a potential transaction as a corporate opportunity arises when a director learns of a prospective transaction or business opportunity which would be attractive to the director or the director's business apart from his role as a director, but which is also a transaction that would plausibly fall within the corporation's present or future activities. The requirement of a director's good faith, as well as statutory requirements in some states,[18] generally requires that the director should affirmatively present the opportunity to the board before participating in the transaction outside the corporation.[19] Although legal requirements as to these transactions vary from state to state, a director should, for her or his self-protection, and as a matter of good corporate practice, make a clear record of such disclosure and request that the board's abstention (if any) from exercise of the opportunity be explicit and of record. Further, even if entering into such a transaction would not breach the director's duty of loyalty, the applicable director should consider any appearance of impropriety that could be created.

# Confidentiality

A director should not, in the regular course of business, disclose information about the corporation's legitimate activities unless they are already known by the public or are of public record.

In the normal course of business, a director should treat as confidential all matters involving the corporation until there has been general public disclosure or unless the information is a matter of public record or common knowledge. The individual director is not a spokesperson for the corporation and thus disclosure to the public of corporate activities should be made only through the corporation's designated spokesperson, usually the chief executive or the board chair or, in large organizations, a public relations officer. This presumption of confidential treatment should apply to all current information about legitimate board or corporate activities.[20]

# Directors' Rights

As a corollary to all the previously described director duties, the director has rights appropriate to the discharge of such duties.

## Management Access

Within the bounds of reason, board members should feel free to contact the chief executive, the board secretary, or similar staff person, to obtain information needed to fulfill the board's duties. Board members should be more restrained in contacting other members of management and should be cognizant of management's role, of not interfering with it, and of not undercutting the chief executive or other officers. Requests for such access to information or management staff are most effective (for both management and the board) if requested at board meetings or pursuant to committee work or other delegations of authority from the board. If directors also serve as volunteers or receive services from the organization, they should be especially careful when in those other roles to not make demands or requests of staff that would be inappropriate for other volunteers or clients of the organization. All board members should benefit from equal access to management staff and the information management can provide.

## Books and Records

A director has a right to inspect, for reasonable purposes and at reasonable intervals, the corporation's books and records and to be provided with requested data derived there from. A board member may reasonably require that her or his accountant or attorney have access to such data.

## Notice of Meetings

All directors should be given ample advance notice of all board and committee meetings that the director is expected to attend.

## Right to Dissent and to Have Dissent Recorded

There are two circumstances in which a director may register dissent regarding actions to be taken at a board meeting. First, any director may dissent from the holding of a board meeting for which the proper notice has not been given or other procedural requirements have not been satisfied. In such a circumstance, the board member should state either upon arriving or prior to voting on a specific matter that he objects to the transaction of some or all business at the meeting, because of non-compliance with notice or other applicable procedures. If the director does not so object, his presence at the meeting is deemed to be a waiver of any improper notice or other procedural requirement.[21]

Second, a director has the right not only to vote against any matter put forth for vote at a board meeting, but also to have the minutes of the meeting record that he dissented from the action approved by other members of the board.[22] This right is important in the event that the action is ever challenged. A director who voted against an action later found to be improper will not generally be subject to liability relating to such action, assuming no separate violation of fiduciary duty on his part (such as failure to disclose material information relating to the proposed matter to the other members of the board). However, the dissenting director needs to be able to prove, through the voting detail recorded in the meeting minutes, that he did in fact dissent.

## Minutes

All directors should be given a copy of minutes of all meetings of the full board and any committee exercising board powers. Except for the minutes of the executive committee, which generally acts in place of the whole board, and except for the minutes of committees of which he or she is a member, a director usually will be satisfied with a review of only the summarized reports of committees that are submitted to the whole board. However, a review of other minutes can be a useful way of keeping informed, and a director has a right to receive them on request.

## When a Special Duty Applies: The Director with Knowledge of Illegal Activities

A director may not ignore what he or she believes to be illegal activity. When a director believes that an activity being engaged in by or on behalf of the corporation (whether or not clearly approved by the board of directors) may be illegal, he or she should proceed as follows:

## Contact Chief Executive or Board Chair

If the subject activity is ongoing, or is about to take place, the issue should be drawn to the attention of the chief executive or board chair with a demand for action or investigation; and if he or she fails to respond, the issue should go to the full board.

## Dissent and Consult with Personal Counsel

If, after a board discussion, an activity that still appears to be illegal is not repudiated, or if the activity is a past event of which the director was previously unaware, the director's dissent should be clearly recorded in the minutes; the director may wish to consult his or her counsel to determine if further disclosure outside the corporation is required, or if she or he should resign.

# When Is a Director of a Nonprofit Corporation Considered to Be a "Trustee" with Duties beyond Those Normally Attributed to Directors?

Even if the governing members of a nonprofit corporation are referred to as a board of trustees, they are not subject to a different or higher standard of care compared to nonprofit boards of directors. The use of the word trustee to refer to a member of a nonprofit corporation's governing board does not in and of itself change the duties of the members of such board, which are the same as those described above for directors. However, in certain circumstances, a member of a nonprofit board (whether called a director, trustee, or other term) may legally be required to comply with the higher standards of a trustee.

## When a Director May Be Considered a Trustee

Persons who are considered trustees of a trust are subject to stringent standards of conduct. For instance, whereas most state nonprofit corporation laws treat director conflicts of interest as a problem to be dealt with by certain guidelines and disclosures, the law of trusts generally regards a trustee's self-dealing as inherently voidable, regardless of motives or objective fairness. Furthermore, the trustee's power to delegate may be narrowly limited, much more so than a corporate director. Although the law does not consider a director of a nonprofit corporation to be a trustee in most situations, in some circumstances, directors may be held to the generally higher trustee standards, such as in the following situations:

- The corporation holds an endowment fund designated for specific purposes, which may require the directors to invest and manage the endowed funds separately.
- The directors are responsible for carrying out the terms of a gift or bequest.
- An employer corporation maintains employee benefit plans, thereby triggering, in certain circumstances under both state and federal law, obligations analogous to those of a trustee with respect to such plans.
- A public benefit or religious corporation seeks to change its purpose or function, but public or community representatives challenge such action on the basis that the assets of such corporations are generally deemed to be held in trust for the purposes set forth in the corporation's governing documents, and that the proposed change is inconsistent with such purposes. In some states, the directors may not be permitted to effect the change in corporate purpose or use of corporate assets until approved by the attorney general, or by a court in a *cy pres* proceeding.

## When a Director or Trustee Is Not a Trustee under the Law

Some nonprofit corporations, particularly in the public benefit field, may call their directors trustees without intending to confer any special powers or impose any special duties in so doing. Directors of public benefit and religious corporations (this issue rarely arises for mutual benefit corporations) should make sure they understand under what circumstances they could legally be considered to be trustees. For example, funds held by a corporation in acknowledged trusts must be identified and treated separately on the corporation's balance sheets, and the board must see to it that an appropriate officer (and counsel and the corporation's accountant) is acquainted with the terms of the relevant trust instrument. In any other circumstance in which a board is faced with an assertion that it should be held to a trusteeship standard with respect to a certain matter, the matter should be discussed with the corporation's counsel, in order to give the board clarification of its role under the specific circumstances.

See the following checklist (page 42) to review the issues discussed in this chapter.

# Notes

1. *See* Model Act §§ 8.30 and 8.31.
2. In determining the degree of care that a director should exhibit, the law generally sets forth an ideal, such as the care of "an ordinarily prudent person in a like position under similar circumstances" (see the Model Act § 8.30(a)), or the care that a person in a like position under similar circumstances reasonably believes is appropriate (see the Model Business Corporation Act, § 8.30(b), as revised effective September 30, 1997). In describing a director's standard of care, the recent revision of the Model Business Corporation Act eliminated the reference to an "ordinarily prudent person," a phrase that has a special meaning under tort law, but may have a different meaning in the context of a director's duty of care. The ABA Nonprofit Corporations Committee has recently begun a revision of the Model Act. This revision effort will consider whether to conform the Model Act's articulation of a director's standard of care to the new formulation used by the Model Business Corporation Act. Currently, however, many states follow the existing "ordinarily prudent person" standard as stated in the current Model Act. *See, e.g.,* ALA. CODE § 10-2B-830(a)(2); CAL. CORP. CODE § 5231.

   The Model Act Comment to § 8.30 states "[t]he concept of 'under similar circumstances' relates not only to the circumstances of the corporation but to the special background, qualifications, and management experience of the individual director and the role the director plays in the corporation." Nonetheless, all directors may be expected to exhibit a minimum level of competence and responsibility, regardless of skill, experience or ability.
3. *See, e.g.,* DEL. CODE ANN. § 141 (declaring that directors cannot act by proxy). However, in at least one state, a nonprofit corporation director may give advance written consents or opposition to an action to be considered at a board meeting. *See* N.D. Nonprofit Corporation Act, § 10-33-40.
4. However, as the Official Comment 7 to the Model Act § 8.30 states, "[i]n order to rely on a report a director must have read it, been present at a meeting where it was presented or otherwise have evaluated it."
5. *See* Model Act, § 8.30(b).
6. *See* Model Act, § 8.30(c).
7. *See* Model Act § 8.01, Official Comment (stating that directors, although considered to "manage" the corporation, may delegate management authority to officers).
8. In the In Re Caremark International Inc. Derivative Litigation case, 698 A.2d 959 (Del. Ch. 1996), the Delaware Chancery noted that a board's failure to assure that there was an adequate information and reporting system to provide senior management and the board with timely and accurate information regarding legal compliance might, in some circumstances, be viewed as a violation of a director's duty of care.
9. *See* Model Act, § 8.01(b); COLO. REV. STAT. § 7-128-101; GA. CODE ANN. § 14-3-801.
10. *See* § 53-8-97 NMSA (allowing directors to act without a meeting).
11. The Business Judgment Rule, as applied to business corporations, is discussed in detail in BLOCK, BARTON & RADIN, THE BUSINESS JUDGMENT RULE, 5th ed. (Aspen Law & Business, 1998). See also the discussion in DANIEL L. KURTZ, BOARD LIABILITY: GUIDE FOR NONPROFIT DIRECTORS 49-59 (Moyer Bell, 1988), regarding applicability of the Business Judgment Rule to nonprofit corporations.
12. *See* Oberly v. Kirby, 592 A.2d 445, 462 (Del. 1991) ("A court cannot second-guess the decisions made by wisdom of facially valid decisions made by charitable fiduciaries, any more than it can question the business judgment of the directors of a for-profit corporation."). Although cases explicitly mentioning the Business Judgment Rule in a nonprofit context are few, the standards used by the courts in nonprofit cases are often clearly derived from the business context. *See, for example,* Beard v. Achenbach Mem. Hosp. Ass'n., 170 F. 2d 859 (10th Cir. 1948).
13. *See* Lisa A. Runquist, *The Night the Sky Fell: Directors of Nonprofits Continue at Risk,* Vol. 15, No. 2 BUSINESS LAW NEWS 15 (Spring 1994) [available at runquist.com], discussing the California Supreme Court's decision in *Francis T. v. Village Green Owners Association,* 42 Cal. 3d 490 [1986], holding that the business judgment rule protection provided for under the California Corporations Code is not a bar to individual director liability for action taken as a board member, if the action created an unreasonable risk of personal injury to third parties—in a case brought by the owner of a condominium who was assaulted and robbed by an intruder, after the condominium board ordered the owner to stop using exterior lights she had installed outside her unit following numerous burglaries in the complex.

14.   *See* Stern v. Lucy Webb Hayes National Training School for Deaconesses & Missionaries, 381 F. Supp. 1003, 1012-1014 (D.D.C. 1974).

15.   See Chad Bowman, *AG Launches Probe of Catholic West after Charitable-Trust Allegations by Union*, BNA's HEALTH LAW REPORTER 9 (no. 40): 1565, regarding California attorney general investigation of hospital closure; see also Deanna Bellandi, *The Watchdogs Are Biting: State Attorney General Asserting Authority over Not-For-Profit Hospital*, MODERN HEALTHCARE, January 29, 2001, at 22; and *Lawsuit Seeking to Preserve Acute Care Set for Trial on AG's Charitable Trust Claims*, BNA's HEALTH CARE DAILY REPORT, March 2, 2001; both discussing a Florida attorney general lawsuit against Intracostal Health Systems, a two-hospital nonprofit health system that had proposed to move all acute-care services out of a money-losing hospital and shift such services to its "sister" hospital three miles away.

16.   *See* Model Act § 8.31, Official Comment. Under the Model Act, as well as the laws of many states, a conflict of interest transaction need only be fair to the corporation at the time entered into to avoid treatment of the transaction as void or a potential breach of the duty of loyalty by the conflicted director. *See, e.g., id.,* and Ohio Nonprofit Corp. Law, § 1702.301; KY. REV. STAT. ANN. § 273.219. However, some state nonprofit laws are more stringent, with fairness to the corporation being only one of several necessary elements necessary to avoid characterization of a conflict of interest transaction as void and one that may subject the interested director to liability. *See, e.g.,* Cal. Nonprofit Corp. Law, § 5233(d)(2).

17.   *See* Linda Grant, *Acts of Charity: Furious Donors Blame a Lax Board after a Fund's Scandal Toppled the Lavish-Living Hand of the United Way*, LOS ANGELES TIMES, September 13, 1992, at 39.

18.   *See generally*, IND. CODE ANN. § 23-17-13-2.

19.   Valle v. North Jersey Automobile Club, 141 N.J. Super. 568, 359 A.2d 504 (App. Div. 1976).

20.   Some public benefit corporations face demands for open meetings of their boards; in some cases, mixed public-private activities may impose that duty. Such practices are infrequently required as a matter of law; however, if open meetings are adopted as a practice, specific rules as to confidentiality, whether or not legally mandated, will have to be developed. *See* JAMES C. BAUGHMAN, TRUSTEES, TRUSTEESHIP AND THE PUBLIC GOOD: ISSUES OF ACCOUNTABILITY FOR HOSPITALS, MUSEUMS, UNIVERSITIES & LIBRARIES, 52, 155 (Quorum Books/Greenwood Press, 1987).

A somewhat different issue is raised by the many statutes governing condominiums, which require that all board meetings (with narrowly defined exceptions) be open to owners, *e.g.,* 765 ILL. COMP. STAT. 605/18.5(4). In such cases, of course, the board meets in the presence of those to whom it is accountable.

21.   *See* Model Act, § 8.23.

22.   Otherwise, a director who is present at a board meeting at which action is taken may be presumed to have assented to the action, *see, e.g.,* Ill. General Not For Profit Corporation Act of 1986, § 108.65(b).

# Suggested Questions for Directors Regarding Director Duties and Rights

(1) How often does our board meet? Is this according to a regular schedule?

(2) How frequently do I attend regular board meetings?

(3) What information is given to me in advance of each board meeting? Is it relevant to decisions to be reached at the meeting?

(4) Am I satisfied with the information I have received? As to quantity? As to subject? As to reliability? Is it too little? Is it more than I can really analyze between my receipt of it and the board meeting?

(5) Is there any information submitted to me that I feel is incomplete or untrustworthy? How do I deal with this problem?

(6) Who manages, in the day-to-day sense, the business of the corporation?

(7) Do I have an interest—personal or business—that conflicts with the interests of the corporation?

(8) Has an occasion arisen where I should disclose that interest?

(9) Do I know of a conflict involving another director? Did she or he disclose that problem?

(10) Does our corporation have a policy on conflict disclosure? Is it in writing? Do we sign a disclosure statement relating to this subject?

(11) What contact do I have with the chief executive of the corporation? Is it solely at board meetings? Should it be solely in that context?

(12) What contact do I have with subordinate staff members? Am I interfering too much?

(13) What notice is given as to board meetings? When?

(14) When do I receive the agenda and materials for board meetings? Do I have time to examine and consider them before voting thereon? Do I, in fact, read them?

(15) When do I receive minutes of prior board meetings? Do I read them? Do I see minutes or reports of committee meetings? When?

(16) Do I know of illegitimate or illegal acts of the corporation or its officers? What should I do about such acts?

(17) Was I chosen to serve on the board as a representative or delegate of a particular constituency? What am I expected to do for that constituency?

# Checklist: Duties and Rights of Nonprofit Corporation Directors

*Note:*    For purposes of simplicity in these checklists, we describe a corporation with a chair, who presides over the board of directors; a chief executive, who may be a staff person; an executive committee; a nominating committee; and an audit committee. (However, we recognize that in many smaller and other nonprofits, such committee functions may be performed by either the executive committee or the board as a whole.) We also assume a legal counsel—someone, paid or unpaid, having primary responsibility for the corporation's legal affairs. Many corporations, especially larger nonprofits, may have other committees established for specific purposes, such as reviewing staff performance, fixing compensation, monitoring compliance with legal requirements and periodic review of bylaws.

| Subject | To Be Reviewed By Whom | How Often | Comment |
|---|---|---|---|
| **A. The Board's Record of Service** | | | |
| 1. What is the record of each director's attendance at board meetings? | Chair, chief executive, nominating committee | Before submission of nominations for election; from time to time during year | Regular attendance serves to maintain an active board of high morale. |
| 2. What members of the board have missed half the meetings during last 12 months? | Chair, chief executive and nominating committee | Before submission of nominations for election; from time to time during year | If the number is large, see below. |
| 3. Does the board have, or should it examine having, a provision for removal of a director who fails (without adequate excuse) to reach a minimum record of attendance? | Chair, chief executive and nominating committee | Whenever there is review of bylaws | Sometimes the simple proposal of such a bylaw will trigger appropriate resignations. Even if actual removals are accomplished by requested resignations, a bylaw provision may be desirable. |
| 4. How many board meetings took place in the last 12 months? Were all the meetings called for in the bylaws actually held? | Chair and chief executive | At least annually | The optimum number of board meetings is to be determined by needs, but a quarterly meeting schedule is recommended as a minimum. |
| 5. Is there any feeling on the part of the members of the board that this number of meetings is inadequate for effective oversight of the corporation's business? | Chair and board | Annually | This question is closely related to the committee structure of the corporation. |
| 6. Should the number of meetings be reduced? | Chair and board | Annually | |
| 7. Would more adequate oversight be obtained by delegating more duties to committees? | Chair and board | Annually | See Chapter 3, "Committees and Advisory Bodies." |

## Checklist: Duties and Rights of
## Nonprofit Corporation Directors *(Continued)*

| Subject | To Be Reviewed By Whom | How Often | Comment |
|---|---|---|---|
| 8. How many directors have contributed funds to the corporation? Have all done so? What is the average? | Chief executive and nominating committee | Annually, and before any re-election or renomination of directors | |
| 9. What has been the attendance record of the members of the corporation's committees? | Chief executive and nominating committee | Annually, if committees are elected or appointed on a schedule, before such election or appointment | Attendance records at committees should be part of director's record reviewed for any re-election decision. |
| **B. The Board's Procedures** | | | |
| 1. What material is distributed *in advance* of board meetings? Does it include: | Chair and chief executive | As a general matter, periodically by chair; as to particular meetings, chief executive | A regular minimum schedule of items should go out before all meetings. |
| a. Minutes of the last meeting? | Full board | All regular meetings | Always |
| b. Current financial statements? | Full board and audit committee | All regular meetings | Always |
| c. Current reports of committees? | Full board | At each meeting of board | Committees should report in writing, as well as orally. |
| d. Summaries of decisions to be made? | Full board | Before each meeting | All directors should be urged to study decisions before meeting. In addition to such summary, relevant documents should be provided for the directors' advance review. |
| e. Copies of resolutions proposed for adoption | Full board | Before each meeting | Having these resolutions distributed in advance enables the board to focus on the precise matters to be considered by the board and results in increased efficiency. |
| **C. The Corporation's Policies on Conflicts** | | | |
| 1. Do we have a conflict policy statement which all directors and officers are expected to execute? | Full board | Annually | If there isn't one, there should be. |

*(Continued)*

## Checklist: Duties and Rights of
## Nonprofit Corporation Directors *(Continued)*

| Subject | To Be Reviewed By Whom | How Often | Comment |
|---|---|---|---|
| a. Should it be reviewed for substantive content? | Legal counsel and audit committee; then full board | Annually | Review by full board should test its understanding of statement. |
| b. Was it, in fact, signed by all directors? | Audit committee | Annually and at point at which each new director joins board | Statement should be re-executed every year. |
| c. How does the corporation deal with conflicts that arise between the execution dates of a regular conflict statement? | Chief executive reporting to board | As often as conflicts arise; review of totality annually | Full and prompt reporting is essential. |
| 2. Was there a meeting at which a director disclosed a conflict of interest regarding a decision? | Legal counsel and audit committee | The disclosure should precede or be simultaneous with the decision | Corporate minutes must record this event. |
| a. If so, was there an adequate record in the minutes of that disclosure? | Legal counsel and audit committee | As often as such disclosure occurs | Corporate minutes must record this event. |
| b. Was there a vote on the issue to which the director had a conflict? | Legal counsel and audit committee | As often as such disclosure occurs | Corporate minutes must record this event. |
| c. If so, was there a quorum (as defined by the statute of incorporation) for such vote? | Legal counsel and audit committee | At meeting in question | State statutes vary as to how quorum and proper votes are determined in these situations. |
| d. Was there a vote of an adequate number of disinterested directors? | Chair, legal counsel | At meeting in question | Resolution should pass without needing vote of conflicted director. |

## CHAPTER 3

# Committees and Advisory Bodies

## Contents

# Committees and Advisory Bodies

*The directors of a nonprofit corporation will frequently discharge their duties through committees composed, wholly or in part, by members of the board. The directors should understand what functions can be delegated to committees, what responsibilities the board has concerning committee activities and the degree to which directors can rely upon information provided by committees. The directors should also understand the difference between committees of directors and certain kinds of advisory or auxiliary boards or other bodies composed of non-directors.*

## Board Committees: Introduction

Committees are usually necessary for the efficient discharge of the board's work.[1] Indeed, many boards would find it impossible to discharge their responsibilities without the use of committees. A director should understand the different types of committees available to the corporation, and the extent to which the board may delegate authority to committees to act on behalf of the board. For example, in some states, only board members may serve on a committee that has board-delegated powers. The purpose, powers and limitations of any committee should be clearly stated in the corporation's bylaws or by resolution recorded in the minutes of the board. These documents should define the membership, term of office, and method of appointment.

## Advisory and Auxiliary Bodies: Introduction

In comparison to board committees, advisory or auxiliary boards, councils or other bodies are generally composed of non-directors (although they may include former directors) and largely work independently of the board. Such boards may provide additional support to the corporation's mission and provide useful insight to the corporation's board. Directors should be aware, however, that such advisory boards and auxiliary groups may be regarded by the public as agents of the corporation. Board members should make sure there are effective procedures both for exercising oversight for advisory and auxiliary boards and directing such boards to report back periodically to the corporation's board concerning their activities and recommendations.

# The Types of Board Committees

For analysis in this *Guidebook*, we divide board committees into two categories:

## Special Committees

These committees are temporary or *ad hoc* groups established for a limited purpose. Most special committees will be created by board resolution as the need arises, and are often limited in their duration.

## Standing or Permanent Committees

These committees are permanent, and may be described or provided for in the corporation's bylaws or board resolutions. Standing committees may make recommendations, oversee operations, and study specific areas of activity and the like. Depending on the bylaws or resolutions creating them, they may have power to bind the corporation. Such power may be extensive (as in the case of executive committees) or fairly limited. A common standing committee is the executive committee, which generally has extensive power to act on behalf of the corporation between board meetings. Other common standing committees include: a nominating committee; finance/audit committee; compensation committee; investment committee; personnel/human resources committee; planning committee; public relations committee; programming committee; and capital campaigns and grants committee. Although the circumstances of each nonprofit will dictate what kinds of standing committees are appropriate, most nonprofit corporations should, at a minimum, consider the merits of a nominating committee and an audit committee. (For further discussion of common standing committees, see the section "Descriptions of Common Standing Committees" below.)

# Special Committees

Special committees are appointed by a board of directors to perform limited functions.

## Purposes of Special Committees

Special committees can be either advisory—with no power to bind or act for the corporation—or created for a certain purpose with limited powers. The board of directors may, from time to time, create committees to investigate or recommend actions of a special nature. Special committees may be formed to negotiate the purchase of a building, plan a reception, approve drafts of documents, evaluate a major transaction, assess the fairness to the corporation of a transaction between the corporation and a director or officer, or for some similar purpose. They may also be asked to represent the corporation in dealing with another group or meeting. Special committees can also be delegated special powers to act as agents or to act in place of the board in appropriate situations. For instance, the corporation's bylaws or an applicable law may require the delegation of decision-making authority to a committee of "disinterested directors" to decide sensitive issues involving other board members or key management, such as indemnification, compensation arrangements or conflict of interest transactions.

## Special Committees of Non-Board Members

Of course, a board of directors may, at any time, retain persons, entities, or organizations to investigate a problem and report to it, or to serve as agents of the corporation in some matter. Thus, even a committee of total outsiders, named to perform some specific function, can be formed at the discretion of the board of directors, except that in most states, the board may not delegate any board-level power to such non-director committees.

The board should note, however, that even when a special committee has either no authority, or strictly limited authority to bind the corporation, parties outside the corporation may be entitled to rely on the *apparent* authority of the committee, and both the committee and the board should be alert to this danger.

# Standing Committees: General Issues

Most nonprofit corporations find it necessary, in order to fulfill their duties, to have permanent standing committees of the board.

## Board Use of and Reliance on Committees

The board of directors may discharge its duties for a particular class of issues through a committee created to assemble information and make recommendations concerning such specific corporate activity. A board member who does not serve on a specific committee is entitled to rely on such committee in the normal course of business,[2] unless the director has some reason to know that the committee's report is deficient.[3]

## Committee Creation: Bylaw Description or Board Resolution

Because the work product of the committee can form part of the record of the board's action in regard to an issue, the committee's formation, purpose, and authority to act on behalf of the corporation should be stated in detail in the bylaws or in the board resolution creating the committee. Directors should recognize that in a dispute concerning a committee's purpose and the scope of its duties, the resolutions and minutes recording the committee's creation may be examined long after their adoption.

## Committee Exercise of Board Authority

Committees empowered to exercise board authority in a wide scope of activities must, first of all, be formed consistently with applicable provisions of the corporation's articles of incorporation and bylaws and the state nonprofit corporation law. Under the Model Act, executive or other committees may be authorized to exercise the board's authority in general or specific respects, except that the board may not delegate to committees the authority to take certain actions defined by law, such as approving the distribution of assets, dissolution or merger, the sale of substantially all the corporation's assets, or amendment of the corporation's articles or bylaws.[4]

## Committee Size

As with the board itself, committees should be selected and managed so as to maximize the efficiency of the directors in discharging their duties. In general, smaller groups are more efficient—three to seven is an optimal size—and large committees can be unwieldy. Awarding committee memberships as "perks" or to assuage egos is a sure prescription for poor performance. However, the committee must contain enough people to carry out the committee's mission and to provide representation from all whose concerns shall be examined in the committee's work. As is frequently the case in the nonprofit field, there may be a conflict between the corporation's need for diversity in committee membership and for efficiency in its operations. The bylaws or the resolution appointing the committee should specify the size of the committee, by requiring a particular number or by setting forth a permissible range.

## Conflicts of Interest

All standards regarding directors' duty of loyalty and conflicts of interest apply to members of board committees (see the section "Conflict of Interest: General Principles" in Chapter 2, "Director Duties and Rights"). Indeed, they apply with somewhat greater force, since a conflict involving a single member of a small committee directly may affect whether a director not serving on that committee may reasonably believe that the committee's recommendations merit confidence.

# Descriptions of Common Standing Committees

## Executive Committee

Many nonprofit corporations will find that the efficient discharge of their work requires the creation of an executive committee able to exercise, between board meetings, most of the power the board could exercise.

Nonprofit corporations often find it expedient to have an executive committee. Most executive committees are composed of directors of the corporation who are also officers, and perhaps also a small number of other directors. The purpose of an executive committee is to create a group that is able to act for the board between its regular meetings and in situations in which an assembly of a quorum of the board would be impractical or impossible. Such an executive committee, in an organization of more than purely local nature, should generally consist of directors geographically close to the corporation's center of operations, except to the extent others are able to participate effectively long-distance, through telephone conferences or similar communications equipment. At each board meeting, the board should be informed of any actions taken by the executive committee since the last previous meeting.

If the executive committee exercises a substantial amount of the power of the board, the board as a whole should periodically evaluate whether the board is meeting its fiduciary obligations through such delegations, and whether the board effectively oversees and has the opportunity to provide input regarding executive committee decisions. The board should also review the amount of board-level power that the executive committee typically delegates to the corporation's chief executive or other officers (apart from any such officer's role as a director or executive committee member), to ensure that board power is not routinely exercised by officers rather than the board and its committees. As noted in the section "Committee Exercise of Board Authority" above, the board should be aware that state law generally places limits on the powers that a nonprofit board may delegate to an executive or other committee.

A large board that delegates a significant amount of power to its executive committee should also periodically evaluate whether the corporation would benefit from having a smaller board that meets more frequently, thereby enabling the full board to participate in many decisions typically handled by the executive committee. Nonetheless, for many nonprofits, the use of the executive committee mechanism is an appropriate and efficient use of board resources, by identifying board representatives who are able to make decisions when needed on the board's behalf.

# Nominating Committee

Good corporate practice suggests the appointment of a nominating committee in order to strengthen the corporate mission and identify board candidates having the range of qualities desired for an effective board.

## Importance of nominating committees

A nominating committee is almost always a standing committee,[5] yet is rarely regarded as a body whose diligence or negligence is legally reviewed. Nevertheless, the process used to determine board nominations obviously is of great importance to the corporation's future and its ability to carry out the corporation's mission. The board of directors has a duty to ensure that a nominating committee is organized and operated in a manner that is likely to generate quality candidates for open board positions.

A nonprofit corporation's mission may require racial and gender diversification or other specific qualifications in the corporation's governing body. Similarly, certain diversity, qualifications or status among the corporation's board may be necessary in order to be considered for government and other funds. Even apart from such specific demands, the nominating committee should formalize and develop procedures for determining who should have positions on the board itself and on committees. The presence of a nominating committee also helps to ensure that important board decisions regarding the selection of directors (and perhaps also officers and committee members) will not be handled on a default basis by management alone.

### Developing criteria for board nominees

The nominating committee should define explicit criteria and qualities for board membership, and have the full board approve such list. Such criteria may include knowledge of the corporation's business or industry; skills needed on the board (e.g., legal, financial, fund raising); association or familiarity with corporation's constituencies, prior successful board experience, evidence of commitment to the corporation's mission, experience with facing similar challenges as those currently facing the corporation, and the ability to satisfy the time commitment required for board service. The nominating committee may also identify personal qualities desirable for board members, such as a sense of humor, good listening skills, ability to effectively (and diplomatically) articulate views contrary to those of other board members, and willingness to support board decisions in which his or her views are in the minority.

### Other powers: recommendations for removal of directors, board size, and composition and functions

The nominating committee may also have responsibility for recommending removal of a director prior to the expiration of a director's term of office, based on inappropriate acts or the director's inattention to his duty. It may have broader-ranging functions, such as evaluating the optimum size of the board, the age profile of board members, the merits of inclusion (or exclusion) of management officers on the board, and the types and functions of board committees.

### Composition

Ideally, the nominating committee should be composed of directors who do not participate in management and are free of relationships, both business and personal, that could interfere with their exercise of independent judgment. This will help provide both the appearance and the reality of objectivity. In addition, it may be prudent to rotate the members of the committee from time to time. A compromise should be reached between the need to draw on the corporation's present activities, history, and experience, and the need for fresh insights into the corporation's present and future mission.

## Audit Committee

Good corporate practice suggests the need of a committee to review and guide accounting and audit practices. Such a committee should be comprised solely of non-management directors.

An audit committee has responsibilities concerning the corporation's auditing, accounting and control functions. Depending on the size and activities of the nonprofit, the organization may hire an outside accounting firm to compile, review or audit the corporation's financial books and records. Federal and state laws or regulation may require a formal audit by a certified public accountant. The audit committee serves as a liaison between the corporation and the outside accountants. In order to retain objectivity of the audit process, employees of the corporation, even if serving on the board of directors, should not be members of the audit committee. Thus, the audit committee should be composed entirely of independent directors. In addition, to be able to evaluate effectively the financial matters related to the corporation, each audit committee member should be or be willing to become financially literate, including the ability to read and understand the corporation's financial statements and the kind of financial issues typically faced by the corporation.[6]

The audit committee's duties usually include choosing services needed in financial management, reviewing reports and determining adequate procedures and controls, reviewing financial performance and approving the annual budget for submission to the board. Sometimes a review of legal compliance is included within the duties of an audit committee. Any additional duties should be undertaken with caution, for if the committee becomes involved in operational matters, it may jeopardize its essential independence from management. In order to adhere to the proper limits, the duties delegated to the committee should be spelled out very specifically, after consultation with and the concurrence of the outside accountant. This definition of duties can be accomplished either by bylaw provisions or board resolution.

## Compensation Committee

It is useful for many nonprofit corporations to establish compensation committees to evaluate the appropriateness of compensation for the chief executive and other key individuals.

A nonprofit board should consider whether it should have a standing compensation committee. Whether a separate committee is formed for this function or it is assigned to another committee, the corporation should clearly organize the review of staff qualifications and compensation, and, in particular, the compensation of the chief executive. Since such a task involves the receipt and evaluation of confidential and sensitive data, it should be assigned to a separate standing committee, if the size of the board is large enough to make this possible. The entire board should be aware of the total compensation package for the chief executive and for other key individuals; however, in order to avoid conflicts of interest, approval of such compensation may need to be delegated to a committee. (As noted in the section "Procedures for Establishing Reasonableness" in Chapter 4, "Taxation," the IRS's excess benefit rules provide a presumption of reasonableness if certain financial transactions with insiders (known as "disqualified persons") are approved by disinterested members of a board or board committee, and certain other procedures are followed.)

# Investment Committee

For nonprofit corporations that maintain an endowment or significant cash reserves, good corporate practice (and the demands of the Uniform Management of Institutional Funds Act), suggest appointing an investment committee.

## Standard of care under UMIFA

The Uniform Management of Institutional Funds Act (UMIFA), which has been adopted in most states, provides rules governing the investment of a charity's assets. Section 6 of UMIFA requires that a board having responsibility for management of charitable funds:

> ...act with the care, skill, prudence, and diligence under the circumstances then prevailing that a prudent person acting in a like capacity and familiar with these matters would use in the conduct of an enterprise of like character and with like aims to accomplish the purposes of the institution. In the course of administering the fund pursuant to this standard, individual investments shall be considered as part of an overall investment strategy.

UMIFA further provides that in exercising its judgment, the board must consider the long- and short-term needs of the institution in carrying out its purposes, its present and future financial requirements, expected total return, general economic conditions, the appropriate level of risk, appropriate levels of income, growth and long-term net appreciation, and the probable safety of the funds. Rather than involving every director in the analysis necessary and appropriate for management of investments in accordance with applicable legal standards, most charities with significant fund balances find it most efficient to appoint an investment committee.

## Investment policy

An investment committee that intends to satisfy the UMIFA standard of care should first develop an investment policy that considers the charity's short-term, mid- term and long-term financial needs, and its tolerance for risk. The policy as written should be reviewed regularly and approved by the investment committee and the full board. That policy should not be static; it should be reconsidered at least annually, in light of the changing needs of the organization, economic conditions, and any other factors that may affect the corporation's tolerance of risk and need for income. It is important for the investment committee to reassess that policy from time to time with appropriate professional counsel.

Following the development of an investment policy, the investment committee should determine appropriate asset-class allocations needed to satisfy the policy objectives. Here again, the committee should consult with professional investment counsel in determining proper allocations. Finally, after determining appropriate asset-class allocations, the individual asset decisions should be made. The decision should not be made in a vacuum. Rather, the investment committee should make this determination in light of its other investments and the total portfolio's consonance with the standards of the investment policy. Particular attention should be paid to the portfolio's overall level of compensated risk.

# The Composition of Committees

The appropriate composition of a committee will depend upon the type of committee involved. Executive committees may be composed primarily of directors who are also officers; in contrast, nominating and audit committees should consist primarily or entirely of non-management directors.

The Model Act requires that all committee members be members of the board of directors.[7] Some state statutes permit non-directors to serve on committees, although such committees may be limited to serving only in an advisory capacity. The extent to which a committee should consist solely or predominantly of directors, or may be appointed without any directors at all, depends upon the purpose of the committee and the authority given it. In most cases, state law or good management may require that at least a majority of the members of a standing committee be directors.

# Committee Procedures, Minutes, and Reports

The procedures, records and operations of committees should be as clearly defined as those of the board itself.

The distinction between the board of directors' procedures and those of a committee will depend somewhat on the size of the corporation and the individual committee. The committees of large nonprofit boards may be of substantial size and therefore require, for orderly and efficient procedure, a degree of formality that would be inefficient (and possibly ridiculous) in smaller committees. The need for formality is increased if the directors are not routinely acquainted with each other, and the board or committee meetings may be the only occasion when any interpersonal contact is achieved. In such situations, meetings conducted according to fairly structured rules may be necessary. Nonetheless, committees may provide a more flexible way for the board to fulfill specific functions.

Committee members are entitled to notices of meetings, quorum requirements, access to records, clear resolutions in the event of controversy, and a right to record dissent. Informality of discussions should not amount to or imply an infringement of the committee members' rights in this regard.

All committees should maintain minutes of meetings and other records appropriate to their purposes. The more a board relies on a committee in the discharge of the board's duty of care, as in reliance upon the judgment and actions of an investment committee, the more such committee should maintain fully detailed minutes and records, and make regular reports to the board. Executive committees and other standing committees should submit minutes to the board in detail roughly comparable to those of the board itself. On the other hand, it may be sufficient for the board to require that a special committee prepare only a report.

# Advisory and Auxiliary Boards

## Use of Advisory and Auxiliary Bodies

A frequent device used in nonprofit corporations, particularly in the public benefit field, is to appoint one or more advisory or auxiliary boards, councils, or committees, composed of community leaders, volunteers, and other supporters and community representatives. Such bodies differ from board committees in generally being composed entirely of non-directors, and in lacking the ability to exercise power on behalf of the board. Such advisory and auxiliary bodies are also distinguished from committees in that such advisory and auxiliary groups act with a high degree of independence from the board.

The establishment of advisory and auxiliary bodies may be useful in enabling a nonprofit board to enlist the interest and activity of individuals who would be too numerous or too busy to serve on the board directly. For example, a public benefit corporation may use an advisory council as a mechanism for involving the community leaders who are unable to give the time commitments necessary for board service, but whose insights and names will aid the organization in fund raising or political arenas. In some cases, an advisory board may be advantageous for start-up nonprofits, as a means to assure donors and the community that the actions of the new organization are subject to some form of independent review. Advisory boards may also be established in connection with a merger or consolidation of nonprofit organizations, allowing the new organization to take advantage of the continued contributions and insight of persons who formerly served as directors of one of the merged organizations, while keeping the consolidated board to a manageable size. Advisory or auxiliary boards having either indefinite or limited duration may prove useful in a variety of other circumstances. Despite the usefulness of such advisory or auxiliary groups, the board should be aware of legal implications of the creation and maintenance of such groups.

## Legal Status of Advisory and Auxiliary Bodies

First of all, corporate law, in general, does not give an advisory or auxiliary board any particular status (unless it is a separately-incorporated auxiliary) and its members do not have the same legal duties, responsibilities, and powers that have been outlined in this *Guidebook* as applicable to the board of directors. For that reason, the board of directors should make sure there exists some document (whether titled charter, bylaws, regulations or other name) outlining the purposes and powers of the advisory or auxiliary group, and indicating the group's legal relationship to the establishing organization.

At the same time, any group or individual publicly acknowledged to be connected with the corporation in some manner can, in some circumstances, be considered an agent of the corporation. Thus, the advisory or auxiliary group's actions, even if unauthorized, could be found to be binding against the corporation. Because the group's advisory or unofficial status may not be clear to the public, statements or actions of such a group or individual may, at least in the public's eye, be attributed to the board of directors or the corporation. In addition, members of such a board or group may face the same kinds of conflicts of interest experienced by directors. None of these problems are insoluble, but they do call for scrutiny and attention.

## Relationship of Board to Advisory Bodies

With respect to advisory bodies, the board should recognize that, having purported to seek advice from a body outside the corporation's regular structure, the board then has at least a moral obligation to give such advice at least some measure of consideration, perhaps through a formal process followed at the board or committee level. Directors should further recognize that, unlike the regular committees of the board whose efficient functioning may lessen the burdens of the board, an advisory organization may increase those burdens by placing on the board an obligation to review its recommendations.

## Relationship of Board to Auxiliary Organizations

With respect to auxiliary organizations, the board should exercise some level of oversight, since the auxiliary will be acting publicly in the name of the corporation or the institutions it operates. If the auxiliary functions as a division of the nonprofit, the chief executive or other corporate officer should oversee the auxiliary and report to the board regarding auxiliary operations. In addition, the corporation should establish a mechanism for periodically recognizing the contributions made by the auxiliary group. The board or a committee should also afford the auxiliary periodic opportunities to report on its activities, and give or seek advice relating to the operations of the corporation or the auxiliary.

## Defining Scope of Activity of Advisory and Auxiliary Bodies

When creating an advisory or auxiliary body, the board must first define the purposes of the advisory or auxiliary group and determine how the board of directors will exercise oversight of the group's activities. Second, the role of the advisory group in relation to the corporation's staff should be defined in the same documents and decisions that create the group. Advisory and auxiliary board members should not be allowed to demand more staff time than is appropriate to the group's role. Moreover, particularly when the advisory or auxiliary group relates to a successful and/or growing function, the board should be alert to the danger that the group and its related staff may develop a level of independence that fails to recognize that the group is still ultimately subject to the board's control. While such events are not unknown in the public benefit field, they can be avoided through appropriate structuring of the group at the outset and continued oversight thereafter.

## Limitations on Rights of Members of Advisory and Auxiliary Boards and Liability Protection

The bylaw or board resolution creating the advisory or auxiliary board should designate the criteria for membership therein, the term for which such board members are appointed and the power of some corporate officer, director or the board itself to remove members of the advisory or auxiliary group. In general, the members of an advisory or auxiliary group have no vested right to serve, no immunity from removal, and no right to renewal of appointment. The board should be careful, however, to make sure that no resolutions or communications imply the creation of such rights. In addition, as part of the board's review of its directors and officers insurance (D&O insurance), indemnification rights, and other liability protections (see the discussion in Chapter 10, "Director Liability Risks and Protections"), the board should determine what protections can and should be afforded to advisory and auxiliary group members.

See the following checklist (page 62) to review the issues discussed in this chapter.

# Notes

1. *See* DANIEL L. KURTZ, BOARD LIABILITY: GUIDE FOR NONPROFIT DIRECTORS 10–13 (Moyer Bell, 1988).
2. Model Act § 8.30(b).
3. Model Act § 8.25 Comment. See the section "Reliance" in Chapter 2, "Director Duties and Rights."
4. Model Act § 8.25.
5. Some statutes specifically provide for a nominating committee; *see* PA. CONS. STAT. ANN. § 5725(e) (Purdon, 1991).
6. *See Report and Recommendations of the Blue Ribbon Committee on Improving the Effectiveness of Corporate Audit Committees,* 54 BUS. LAW. 1067 (May 1999).
7. Model Act, § 825.

# Suggested Questions for Directors Regarding Committees and Advisory Bodies

(1) What committees does our board have? What powers does each committee have?

(2) Is there an executive committee? What are the limitations on its power to act?

(3) Do we have a nominating committee?

(4) Who monitors the corporation's accounting and financial reports? Is there an audit committee? Who serves on it?

(5) Is there a committee that reviews staff performance and compensation?

(6) If the corporation has investments, does it have or need an investment committee?

(7) How do committees report to the board?

(8) What auxiliary groups or advisory boards are associated with the corporation? How does the board monitor and recognize the activities of such groups?

# Checklist: Committees and Advisory Bodies

*Note:* For purposes of simplicity in these checklists, we describe a corporation with a chair, who presides over the board of directors; a chief executive, who may be a staff person; an executive
committee; a nominating committee; and an audit committee. (However, we recognize that
in many smaller and other nonprofits, such committee functions may be performed by either
the executive committee or the board as a whole.) We also assume a legal counsel—someone, paid or unpaid, having primary responsibility for the corporation's legal affairs. Many
corporations, especially larger nonprofits, may have other committees established for specific
purposes, such as reviewing staff performance, fixing compensation, monitoring compliance
with legal requirements and periodic review of bylaws.

| Subject | To Be Reviewed By Whom | How Often | Comment |
|---|---|---|---|
| **Committees** | | | |
| 1. What are the committees of the corporation? | Chair, chief executive, full board | Annually | A review of bylaw provisions relating to committees should be performed simultaneously. |
| 2. Which committees have power to bind the corporation? | Chair, chief executive, full board | Annually | The board should periodically review whether it is delegating too much, or too little, authority to committees. |
| 3. Which committees, with or without power to bind the corporation, deal with major parties or interests outside the corporation? | Chair, chief executive, full board | Annually | Even committees or committee members without *actual* authority to bind the corporation could have *apparent* authority in the view of outside parties. |
| 4. Which committees simply report or advise the board? | Chair, chief executive, full board | Annually | The board should periodically review the use and usefulness of advisory committees. |
| 5. Do we have a nominating committee? | Chair, chief executive, full board | Annually, in preparation for annual meeting; before each meeting at which a vacancy is to be filled | An effective nominating committee must discuss board evaluation and board needs with full board prior to annual meeting. |
| 6. Should there be provisions limiting the number of consecutive terms a director may serve? Or a maximum age for directors? | Nominating or bylaws committee, reviewing proposed changes with legal counsel, and reporting to board | Probably every three or four years | Nominating committee should, as a regular function, analyze years of service of each director, maximum age, and average age of board. No bright-line tests apply to all cases, but decisions on these issues (including the decision to make no changes) should be conscious. |

## Checklist: Committees and Advisory Bodies *(Continued)*

| Subject | To Be Reviewed By Whom | How Often | Comment |
|---|---|---|---|
| 7. Should there be a board having staggered terms, so one-half or one-third of the board is chosen each year? | Nominating or bylaws committee, reviewing proposed changes with legal counsel, and reporting to board | Probably every three or four years | Many nonprofits use a staggered board to ensure continuity of board operations. |
| 8. What committee reviews staff compensation? | Chair, chief executive, full board | Annually | This function should be formally assigned even if no separate compensation committee is created. |
| 9. Does the committee that decides compensation matters report to the board in executive session? | Chair, chief executive, full board | Annually | Discussion of staff salaries should always be held outside of the presence of staff, without need for a special resolution to that effect. |
| 10. Does the corporation have or need an investment committee? Is the corporation subject to the Uniform Management of Institutional Funds Act? | Chair, chief executive, chief financial officer, and full board | Every two or three years | The board should periodically review and assure that investment committee members understand their responsibilities. |

# Taxation

## *Contents*

# Taxation

*A director should understand the basic application of federal and local tax law to the corporation. This chapter outlines the principal federal income tax issues of the more common nonprofit corporations.*

## Introduction

A director should have a general understanding of the tax status of the corporation. The director should know, for example, if the corporation is exempt from federal income tax, and if so, under what section of the Internal Revenue Code (the Code); if the corporation is exempt from local real estate or other taxes; and, in a general way, what is required to maintain such exemptions.

Taxation is a technical field, and a director's obligations do not require a detailed knowledge of the various tax statutes and regulations. Most nonprofit corporations have, or should consider having, their tax reporting handled by outside professionals, either accountants or attorneys. The function of the board, in oversight of these persons, is part of the oversight that the board exercises generally. Moreover, the reader should be aware that federal tax law and the interpretation of its provisions is subject to change; therefore, while the issues discussed herein are areas requiring a director's attention and are likely to remain relevant to the operations of tax-exempt corporations, specific rules may change over time.[1]

The subject is a broad one, but this chapter will outline only the principal federal income tax issues of the more common nonprofit corporations. And, despite the importance of local tax issues, we do not address state and local tax law; space constrains us. However, directors must understand that federal tax-exempt status does not automatically confer exemption from state and local taxes.[2]

## Qualifying for Exemption from Federal Income Tax

Most nonprofit corporations are exempt from the federal income taxes applicable to corporations. However, corporations do not automatically qualify for exemption from federal income taxation simply because they are nonprofit.

A director should not assume that because the corporation is nonprofit it is exempt from any income tax whatsoever. Tax-exempt status is a privilege, not a right, which is conferred on an organization that meets and continues to meet certain requirements set out by the Code. Other than churches and very small organizations, organizations seeking exemption under Code § 501(c)(3) described in this chapter, must obtain IRS approval of their applications for exemption. The IRS lists 31 types of tax-exempt organizations in IRS Publication 557, *Tax-Exempt Status for Your Organization*, along with brief descriptions defining their activities.[3] This list is set forth in Appendix B in this *Guidebook*.

A director should understand that exemption from federal income tax does not necessarily permit donors to the corporation to deduct gifts to it. The IRS permits donors to deduct gifts to tax-exempt corporations *only* if the corporation qualifies under § 501(c)(3). Payments to other types of tax-exempt corporations may be deductible by the donor only if the payment qualifies as a trade or business expense. While the ability to attract tax-deductible charitable contributions is essential for many organizations, it is not a primary or significant source of income for others. Directors should periodically evaluate whether the corporation is qualified under the appropriate category, or whether conversion to a different category or creation of an affiliate of a different category should be considered.

# Corporations Exempt from Tax under § 501(c)(3)

Most public benefit and religious corporations, and any such corporation wishing deductibility of gifts as charitable contributions, will seek exemption under Code § 501(c)(3).

For a corporation to be exempt under § 501(c)(3) it must be organized and operated for a charitable purpose.

A nonprofit corporation may qualify for exemption from federal income tax as a § 501(c)(3) organization if it is organized and operated exclusively for charitable, religious, educational, literary, or scientific purposes.[4] These general categories conform roughly to the traditional trust and corporate law definitions of "charity."

## Particular Advantages of § 501(c)(3) Status

In addition to exemption of the corporation itself from most federal income taxes, § 501(c)(3) organizations enjoy certain unique advantages. Contributions made to them are tax-deductible by the contributors, up to the limits imposed by Code § 170(b).[5] In addition, some § 501(c)(3) corporations may finance their exempt activities by issuing tax-exempt bonds, enabling these organizations to lower their borrowing costs. Other benefits may include exemption from state real property and sales and use taxes and reduced postal rates for mailings.

## General Requirements

To achieve and maintain exemption under § 501(c)(3) the corporation must comply with explicit restrictions.

In order to be tax exempt under § 501(c)(3) a corporation must be *organized and operated* exclusively for exempt purposes. It must not allow any net earnings to inure to private individuals, as described in the section "Limitations on Private Benefit and Private Inurement" below. It also must not carry on substantial activities to influence legislation and must not participate, in *any* way, in any political campaign, as described in the sections "Limitations on Lobbying" and "The Absolute Prohibition on Political Campaign Activities" below.[6] Furthermore, with limited exception, the IRS must approve an application for such exemption, as described in more detail in the section "Obtaining Tax-Exempt Status" below.

The requirement that the corporation be organized exclusively for exempt purposes means that the articles of incorporation (and any amendments thereto) must contain appropriate restrictions on the corporation's purposes, activities and use of assets, including ultimate disposition of assets upon a dissolution of the corporation. A director should bear this in mind in considering any amendments to the articles. It is not sufficient that the corporation merely operate in an appropriate manner.

## Limitations on Unrelated Business Activities

The conduct of unrelated business activities may not disqualify an otherwise exempt § 501(c)(3) corporation if the unrelated activities do not constitute the organization's primary purpose; however, the corporation may be taxed on income from the unrelated activity.

A § 501(c)(3) corporation may engage in some activities that are not related to its exempt purposes. For example, the corporation may own property that it leases to commercial tenants when the property is not needed by the corporation. Such activities will not disqualify the corporation from tax-exempt status so long as the corporation's unrelated activities do not constitute the corporation's primary purpose.

Income derived from certain unrelated activities may be subject to federal tax. See the discussion in the section "Unrelated Business Income" below.

## Limitations on Private Benefit and Private Inurement

The activities of a § 501(c)(3) corporation must not be for the benefit of a shareholder or individual.

A § 501(c)(3) corporation is not operated for charitable purposes if it serves a private interest. This is the general standard applicable to all charitable corporations and simply incorporates into the Code the trust law standards of a charity. Further, in order for the corporation to be recognized as a § 501(c)(3) organization "no part of the net earnings of" a corporation may inure "to the benefit of any private shareholder or individual." Private benefit or private inurement may occur, for example, when a § 501(c)(3) corporation pays for goods or services in sums in excess of their fair market value, when assets of a corporation are given to or used for the benefit of an individual who gave less than fair consideration for the same, or when an individual or corporation is paid by the exempt organization on a percentage of the tax-exempt organization's net income. As discussed below in the section "Intermediate Sanctions: Excise Tax on Public Charities' Excess Benefit Transactions below," the payment of other than fair market value for items or services may also raise excess benefit transaction excise tax issues.

## Limitations on Lobbying

A corporation will not qualify as a § 501(c)(3) organization if it devotes a substantial part of its activities to lobbying, propaganda or attempting to influence legislation. Section 501(h) of the Code provides a safe harbor for certain corporations that wish to regularly engage in some lobbying. Although § 501(h) clarifies the scope of permitted activities, it can impose strict penalties on the corporation and its directors if these safe harbor limits are exceeded.

As a general rule, a corporation will not be considered to be engaging in substantial lobbying if *less than five percent* of its activities are devoted to such activity. Whether or not more than five percent constitutes a substantial amount of activities is determined based on all the facts and circumstances.

Certain qualifying organizations may file a special election under § 501(h) of the Code to allow them to spend up to a specified dollar amount (which may represent a larger percentage of total activities) for lobbying without fear of adverse tax consequences from such activities. While persistent lobbying in excess of that permitted by § 501(h) will lead to a loss of both the protection of the § 501(h) safe harbor and a loss of the corporation's basic tax exemption, isolated instances of lobbying in excess of permissible amounts will not cost the organization its tax-exemption. Instead, an excise tax will be applied against the organization. *In addition, penalty taxes may be imposed on any officer, director, or responsible employee of the organization* involved in the excessive lobbying activities. In some cases, the definition and measurement of lobbying activities will be easier than in others; for instance, as discussed in Chapter 6, "Supervision of Internet Activities," lobbying activities on the Internet pose challenging questions both for tax-exempt organizations trying to comply with § 501(h) and the IRS.

## The Absolute Prohibition on Political Campaign Activities

A § 501(c)(3) corporation cannot support, participate or intervene in any election for public office.

A § 501(c)(3) corporation will lose its tax-exempt status if it participates or intervenes in a political campaign on behalf of, or in opposition to, a candidate for public office, through financial support, endorsements, or other actions directly or indirectly advocating the election or defeat of a candidate. In addition it will be subject to an excise tax of 10 percent of such political expenditures. Unlike the restrictions on lobbying, the prohibition on political activities is absolute, and applies to any such activities, no matter how small. There are *severe penalties imposed on the corporation and, in some instances, its directors*, if prohibited political activities continue.[7]

# Special Rules Relating to § 501(c)(3) Corporations: Public Charities and Private Foundations

All § 501(c)(3) corporations are regarded as private foundations unless they demonstrate that their activities or the nature of their financial support conform to certain defined exceptions. Private foundations are subject to various restrictions and excise taxes not applicable to other § 501(c)(3) corporations (commonly referred to as public charities).

The Code classifies certain § 501(c)(3) organizations as "private foundations," in contrast to "public charities," the latter being the term commonly used to refer to those § 501(c)(3) organizations that are not private foundations, although this term does not appear in the Code. A director should understand that all § 501(c)(3) corporations are treated as private foundations unless they can demonstrate that they meet one of the definitions of a public charity, as described below. Since private foundations are subject to greater restrictions and certain excise taxes not applicable to public charities, a § 501(c)(3) corporation should make sure that the classification of the organization as a public charity or private foundation is properly determined and maintained. This *Guidebook* gives this question only a brief overview.

# Definition of Public Charity

A corporation can avoid the additional taxes and restrictions imposed on private foundations if it falls within one of the enumerated types of organizations classified as public charities as listed in IRS Publication 557. Typical public charities include churches, educational organizations, and hospitals. A corporation not falling within one of the categories listed in IRS Publication 557 may still avoid classification as a private foundation if it qualifies as a "publicly supported" organization or a "supporting organization." To qualify as either type of organization, certain specific tests must be met. These very detailed tests are beyond the scope of this *Guidebook*. A more complete discussion can be found in IRS Publication 557.

# Restrictions and Taxes on Private Foundations

Private foundations generally are subject to a two percent excise tax on their net investment income (including capital gains). Private foundations are also subject to several other restrictions that may result in various taxes and penalties, including:

- restrictions on self-dealing between private foundations and their substantial contributors and other individuals described as "disqualified persons," including their directors and trustees;
- minimum requirements for distribution of income and principal for charitable purposes, as described below;
- a potential tax upon termination of private foundation status; and
- a potential excise tax on non-charitable grants.

## Self-dealing rules

The prohibitions on self-dealing reach a broad range of transactions between a private foundation and a "disqualified person," including:

- the sale, exchange or leasing of property;
- the lending of money or other extensions of credit;
- the furnishing of goods, services or facilities;
- the payment of unreasonable compensation or expenses;
- the transfer to, or use by or for the benefit of, a disqualified person of the private foundation's income or assets; and
- payments to government officials.

In determining whether a transaction is restricted or prohibited by the self-dealing rules, it does not matter whether the transaction results in a benefit or a detriment to the private foundation or whether the transaction is "fair." (In this respect, the self-dealing prohibitions differ from the intermediate sanctions imposed on public charities.) An act of self-dealing includes both direct and indirect transactions between a private foundation and a disqualified person. The Code does, however, permit certain exceptions to the self-dealing rules, including, for example, the payment of reasonable compensation. *Any transaction between a private foundation and a disqualified person should be reviewed by counsel or an appropriate committee to assure the self-dealing rules are not violated.* Violations of the self-dealing restrictions may result in severe penalties and substantial legal complications.

## Distribution requirements

A private foundation must distribute annually a minimum amount for charitable purposes, which is roughly five percent of non-charitable (e.g., investment) assets. The required distribution may take the form of a direct payment for charitable purposes, such as payment of expenses incurred in conducting a charitable activity, an acquisition of assets to be used in performing the organization's exempt purposes, or a contribution to another charitable organization.

If a private foundation satisfies its distribution requirements by making charitable contributions to other § 501(c)(3) exempt organizations, the foundation's responsibilities may not end at the time the contribution is made. Except where the contribution is made to a public charity or to certain operating foundations, the private foundation must take steps to assure that the contribution is, in fact, subsequently used by the receiving organization to accomplish exempt purposes. Some private foundations, in very limited circumstances, may avoid this requirement.

## Limitation on excess business holdings

The Code imposes limitations on the ability of a private foundation to hold an ownership interest in another business entity, such as a corporation or a partnership.

## Liability of foundation managers

Excise taxes generally are imposed against a private foundation that violates any of the private foundation rules. In some cases, moreover, excise taxes may be imposed against "foundation managers," substantial contributors to the foundations, and, with respect to self-dealing, other "disqualified persons." Persons considered foundation managers include officers, directors, or trustees of a private foundation, and employees of the foundation who have authority or responsibility over the matter resulting in the tax.

# Section 501(c)(4) Organizations: Civic Leagues and Social Welfare Organizations

A nonprofit corporation operated exclusively for the promotion of social welfare may seek exemption under § 501(c)(4). Exemption under this section will not confer charitable contributions deductibility for donors to the corporation, but may enable it to avoid the restrictions of private foundation status, and the restrictions on lobbying and other political activity.

A nonprofit corporation that is operated exclusively for the promotion of social welfare may qualify as a § 501(c)(4) organization and thus be exempt from federal income tax. In addition to the lack of deductibility as charitable contributions, contributions or dues paid to a § 501(c)(4) corporation are subject to the same tax treatment limitations as discussed with respect to trade organizations in the section "Tax Treatment of Contributions or Dues to a § 501(c)(6) Corporation" below.

## Definition of Social Welfare

A corporation is operated exclusively for the promotion of social welfare if it is operated primarily to further the common good and general welfare of the people of a community, such as by bringing about civic betterment and social improvement, and no part of its net earnings inures to the benefit of any private shareholder or individual. In addition, a § 501(c)(4) corporation must benefit the community as a whole. Thus, a corporation will not qualify under § 501(c)(4) if its activities benefit only its membership or a select group of individuals. Examples of the types of organizations that may qualify for § 501(c)(4) status are civic associations and volunteer fire companies, or organizations engaged in crime prevention, etc.

A § 501(c)(4) corporation may not, as its primary activity, conduct a business with the general public in a commercial manner.

## Comparison of § 501(c)(3) and § 501(c)(4) Exemption Status: Which Is Better for Your Corporation?

Although the requirements for § 501(c)(3) and § 501(c)(4) appear to be similar, a corporation may more easily satisfy the requirements of § 501(c)(4). First, it may benefit a smaller or more specific group or community than would qualify a corporation for charitable status under § 501(c)(3). Second, a § 501(c)(4) organization may engage in a greater amount of social activities, a greater amount of lobbying activities, and some, as opposed to no, political activities.

Note, § 501(c)(3) status is preferable to § 501(c)(4) status if tax-deductible contributions or tax-exempt financing is important to the organization. However, § 501(c)(4) status may be more advantageous if:

- lobbying will be a substantial part of the corporation's activities;
- freedom to support or oppose candidates for public office is sought; or
- the organization would be subject to the restrictions imposed on a private foundation (as discussed above) if the organization were exempt under § 501(c)(3).

However, if an organization was once exempt as a § 501(c)(3) organization, but has lost its exemption because of lobbying or political campaign activities, it cannot then convert into a § 501(c)(4) organization.[8]

# Section 501(c)(6) Organizations

Nonprofit business leagues, chambers of commerce, trade associations, boards of trade, and professional football leagues may qualify as § 501(c)(6) organizations.

## Requirements for Exemption

A § 501(c)(6) corporation is an association of persons having a common business interest, the purpose of which is to promote such interest and no part of the net earnings of which inures to the benefit of any private shareholder or individual (such as members). These corporations must improve the business condition of the industry in general, rather than benefiting individual members by supplying such members with such things as management services, or improving the economy and convenience of conducting individual businesses. The corporation may satisfy this requirement if, as a whole, it represents all components of an industry or line of business within a particular geographic area. The corporation generally may not, however, be in competition with another group within the same industry or line of business, although members within the corporation may compete with each other.

There are certain examples of common activities worth noting that may affect a corporation's compliance with § 501(c)(6). On one hand, activities such as conducting an advertising campaign to promote an industry (rather than particular individuals) and publishing a trade publication for the benefit of an industry generally are considered activities that promote a particular line of business and, hence, are permissible activities. On the other hand, activities such as operating a real estate multiple-listing service and supplying management services and supplies to members have been found to benefit the members individually, rather than promote the industry or line of business as a whole. A § 501(c)(6) corporation may engage in some business activities that do not promote an industry or line of business, subject to the rules relating to Unrelated Business Income (UBI) discussed in the section "Unrelated Business Income" below, so long as such activities are not substantial.

## Tax Treatment of Contributions or Dues to a § 501(c)(6) Corporation

As a general rule, contributions or dues payable to a § 501(c)(6) organization may be deductible as trade or business expenses except to the extent they are used to

(a) participate in a political campaign on behalf of any candidate for public office;
(b) engage in certain types of lobbying; or
(c) attempt to influence legislation that is not of direct interest to the taxpayer's business.

A § 501(c)(6) organization that incurs lobbying or political expenditures is required to notify its members of a reasonable estimate of the portion of their dues allocable to those expenditures. If the organization fails to provide such notice, or otherwise elects not to provide such notice, the organization must pay a proxy tax based on the amount of the expenditures.

It should also be noted that § 501(c)(6) contributions cannot be deducted as charitable contributions.

## Obtaining Tax-Exempt Status

With few exceptions, most § 501(c)(3) corporations must obtain IRS recognition of tax-exempt status and they hold such status only when and if such recognition is applicable. Other tax-exempt organizations (i.e., § 501(c)(4), § 501(c)(6) and other corporations qualifying for exemption under § 501(c) of the Code) should consider obtaining IRS recognition to ensure their tax-exempt status, but are not required to do so.

If a corporation is, in fact, organized and operated in accordance with the applicable requirements to qualify for tax exemption under § 501(c) of the Code, the corporation may claim tax-exempt status without the need for an IRS ruling to that effect, *unless* exemption under § 501(c)(3) is sought. Section 501(c)(3) corporations generally are required to obtain recognition of their tax-exempt status by the IRS as a condition to the tax exemption. Section 501(c)(3) corporations that are not subject to the application requirement are (1) churches and certain other church-related corporations, and (2) corporations (other than private foundations) normally having annual gross receipts of not more than $5,000. In addition, certain corporations do not have to apply directly to the IRS for recognition of exemption under § 501(c)(3), because they are covered by a group exemption letter issued to a central organization. Other corporations should consider obtaining IRS recognition to ensure their tax-exempt status.

# Unrelated Business Income

Any exempt corporation may be subject to a tax on UBI, if it regularly carries on a trade or business that is unrelated to its exempt purpose. If its unrelated business activities are more than insubstantial, the corporation may lose its tax exemption.

The Code permits an exempt organization to engage in some activities that are not related to its exempt purposes. Such activities are permissible so long as the exempt corporation's unrelated activities remain insubstantial when compared to the corporation's exempt activities. Whether an activity is considered substantial is based on all the facts and circumstances, including the amount of income derived from the activity, the expenses devoted to the activity, and the staff time devoted to such activity. No one factor is controlling.

While the Code imposes a tax on certain income generated from the conduct of an "unrelated trade or business," certain passive-types of investment income, such as rents, dividends, and interest are generally excluded from taxation. If the corporation has significant unrelated activities, a director should have a basic understanding of the types of activities that produce UBI to assure that the organization's unrelated business activities do not become substantial and that procedures are in place to monitor and properly report such activities to the IRS.

## Definition of Unrelated Trade or Business

An *unrelated trade or business* is any trade or business that is *regularly carried on, the conduct of which is not substantially related to the corporation's exempt pur-*

*poses*. For example, a tax-exempt corporation may sell advertising in its otherwise educational publications.

An activity is *regularly carried on* if the activity is conducted with the frequency and continuity comparable to commercial activities of for-profit ventures.

An activity is *substantially related* (i.e., not unrelated) to the corporation's exempt purposes if the activity contributes importantly to the accomplishment of the corporation's exempt purposes other than through the production of income. The need for the funds generated by the activity does not make it substantially related.

The Code excludes several types of activities from the definition of *unrelated trade or business*. An activity will not be treated as an unrelated trade or business if:

- substantially all of the work is performed by volunteers;
- it is carried on primarily by a § 501(c)(3) organization for the benefit of its members, students, patients, officers, or employees;
- it consists of selling merchandise, substantially all of which has been donated;
- it relates to the distribution of low-cost articles ($7.60 in 2001, indexed for inflation) in connection with charitable solicitations; or
- the business consists of a legal bingo game, in a State where bingo games are ordinarily not conducted on a commercial basis.

## Types of Income Excluded from UBI

The Code excludes the following types of income from UBI unless such income is debt-financed:[9]

- dividends, interest, payments with respect to securities loans and annuities;
- royalties;
- most rents from real property;
- insubstantial rents from personal property when leased with real property; and
- gain from the sale of capital assets.

In addition, certain research income is excluded from UBI.

## Use of a Taxable Subsidiary

As noted above, an exempt corporation may conduct an insubstantial amount of unrelated activities itself. It is not necessary to establish a separate taxable corporation for such activities. However, an exempt corporation may choose to create a taxable subsidiary through which to conduct unrelated activities, especially if such activities would otherwise become substantial and thereby jeopardize the corporation's exempt status, or for non-tax reasons, such as the desire to limit the corporation's liabilities.

If a taxable subsidiary is formed, the subsidiary itself will be taxed on the income from the activities, but dividends paid by the taxable subsidiary to the exempt parent generally will not be UBI. However, the tax-exempt parent of a taxable subsidiary should be aware that for all such subsidiaries in which the parent nonprofit holds more than a fifty percent ownership interest, the tax-exempt corporation's receipt of rent, royalties, interest, and other types of income may be taxable as UBI. (This is in contrast to the usual rule, under which a tax-exempt corporation's receipt of rent, royalties, interest, and similar kinds of "passive" income is not taxable as UBI, provided that such income is received from an entity unrelated to the tax-exempt corporation.)

The use of a taxable subsidiary requires careful tax planning as, in general, decisions made in the process are usually irrevocable. For example, future transfers of property from the taxable subsidiary to the exempt corporation and the eventual liquidation of the subsidiary may result in certain adverse tax consequences. For further discussion of issues to be considered by tax-exempt corporation directors regarding use of taxable subsidiaries, see Chapter 5, "Creation of For-Profit Subsidiaries and Joint Ventures."

## Advertisements versus Sponsorship Acknowledgements

### *Acknowledgements versus advertisements*

Directors of tax-exempt entities should understand the difference, both in terms of donor deductibility and UBI treatment, between revenues received from sponsors, for which the tax-exempt organization provides public acknowledgement (such as in event banners, program brochures or public announcements) and revenues received in exchange for advertising. Revenues received from corporate sponsors who are then publicly acknowledged by the tax-exempt organization—in a statement that recites only basic and "fact neutral" information about the sponsoring organization, such as its name, address and telephone number—are generally deductible by the sponsor as a tax-exempt contribution. Provided the event being sponsored is substantially related to the tax-exempt corporation's purposes, such revenues would not be subject to taxation as UBI. In contrast, revenues received by a tax-exempt corporation for advertisements placed in a publication—such as an ad for a dance apparel store in the program for the annual recital of a local ballet school—would be considered payment for advertising and not be deductible as a charitable contribution by the apparel store.[10] In this example, if the apparel store also underwrote a portion of the recital costs, and was acknowledged as a corporate sponsor in that regard, the store could deduct the portion of its payment to the school that exceeded the regular cost of the ad. In such case, the payment by the sponsor may not be considered fully tax-deductible as a charitable contribution. Moreover, depending on the context (e.g., was the payment made in connection with an activity that is "regularly carried on" by the organization, or was it a for a discrete event, such as the annual recital?), the money paid for advertising by the for-profit may be considered taxable UBI.

### Different treatment of advertisements in periodicals

If advertising revenue is considered taxable as UBI to the tax-exempt organization, the amount of UBI tax payable will depend on whether or not the ad revenue was generated from an advertisement in a periodical publication, such as a monthly newsletter or magazine, or in a non-periodical publication. Ad revenue that is UBI will be taxed at a lower rate if the ad appeared in a periodical. However, in some cases, it is difficult to determine whether a publication is a periodical for which the lower UBI tax calculation would apply. The general rule is that advertising within material that appears on a regular periodic schedule, within a standard format, is likely to be considered a periodical, whereas material that appears perennially with regular updates (like a brochure) would not.

# Special Reporting Requirements

## Non-Charitable Contributions

The director must understand that exemption from federal income tax does not necessarily mean that donations to the corporation are deductible as charitable contributions and, if deductibility is not available, the corporation must disclose this fact—including disclosures on dues statements.

Any tax-exempt corporation or political organization that is not eligible to receive charitable contributions—i.e., any corporation other than a § 501(c)(3) corporation—is required to disclose to its donors "in a conspicuous and easily recognizable format" in all fundraising solicitations, whether in written or printed form, by television or radio, or by telephone, that contributions to it are not deductible as charitable contributions for federal income tax purposes.[11] A dues statement or solicitation of a § 501(c)(4) or § 501(c)(6) organization counts as a fundraising solicitation for this purpose.

## Charitable Contributions

Any contribution to a charitable organization of $250 or more may only be deductible as a charitable contribution to the donor if such donor receives contemporaneous substantiation from the charitable organization as to the receipt of the donation.

While technically a charitable organization is under no requirement to provide substantiation of a charitable contribution of $250 or more to a donor, the fact that the donor will not receive a charitable contribution deduction without such substantiation imposes a practical requirement on the charity to provide such information. In general, the substantiation should be supplied by the charity contemporaneously with the receipt of the contribution and, additionally, describe the property donated and state whether any goods or services were provided in connection with the contribution. Detailed guidance concerning the substantiation requirements is contained in IRS Publication 1771.

## Charitable Contributions in Return for Items of Value

If a donor receives an item of value in return for a contribution to a § 501(c)(3) corporation, the Code requires that the donor's deduction be limited to the difference between the amount contributed and the fair market value of the goods or services received by the donor. For example, if a donor contributes $100 and receives a ticket to a symphony concert or a dinner that would normally cost $60, the donor is entitled to deduct $40. In addition, the Code requires that the charity receiving such contribution (provided such contribution is in excess of $75) provide substantiation to the donor indicating the fair market value of the goods or services received in return for the contribution.

Failure to make this disclosure could result in fines against the charity.[12]

## Disclosure of Annual Returns and Exemption Applications

Both annual information returns and IRS exemption applications must be made available by the tax-exempt organizations for public inspection or in copy form.

Tax-exempt corporations must make their annual tax information returns and their IRS exemption applications, and related documentation and correspondence, available for public inspection at their principal offices and at all regional offices. (The corporation may, however, withhold the names and addresses of its contributors if it is a public charity and may also withhold any information in the exemption application relating to trade secrets, patents, processes, or styles of work, if the IRS determines that public disclosure of such information would adversely affect the organization.) Such organizations are also required to provide copies of these items to individuals requesting such items, but may charge reasonable copying fees to the requestor. However, organizations that post copies of their tax returns, exemption applications and related documents on the Internet (whether on their own Web site or a compilation site such as GuideStar), are relieved of the obligation to provide physical copies of such documents to requesting individuals. See the section "Sales of Good and

Services" in Chapter 6, "Supervision of Internet Activities" for further discussion of Internet postings of Form 990s.

Corporation personnel who have a duty to comply with the public inspection requirements and fail to comply may be subject to penalties. Criminal penalties may be imposed on any person who willfully and knowingly furnishes false or fraudulent information.

# Intermediate Sanctions: Excise Tax on Public Charities' Excess Benefit Transactions

Effective generally for transactions occurring on or after September 14, 1995, the IRS may impose an excise tax on "disqualified persons" who engage in "excess benefit transactions" with § 501(c)(3) public charities and § 501(c)(4) corporations. In addition, the IRS may also impose an excise tax on any "organization manager" of such a tax-exempt organization that knowingly approved the excess benefit transaction. The IRS may impose such "intermediate sanctions" for transactions that previously could have been punished only with revocation of an organization's tax-exempt status.

Section 501(c)(3) organizations that are private foundations are subject to the range of restrictions and taxes described in the section "Restrictions and Taxes on Private Foundations" above. The intermediate sanctions for excess benefit transactions impose taxes that are similar to the private foundation self-dealing taxes, on transactions with § 501(c)(3) public charities and § 501(c)(4) corporations. One significant difference, however, is that intermediate sanctions are imposed only on transactions that are not at fair market value (hence the term "excess benefit" transactions), while the private foundation self-dealing rules apply to any covered transactions whether or not at fair market value.

## Potential for Imposition of Intermediate Sanctions for Excess Benefit Transactions

Every member of a board of directors of a § 501(c)(3) public charity or § 501(c)(4) organization should be aware of the possibility of financial sanctions that could be imposed on board members, officers, and related persons as a result of transactions that the IRS determines provide "excess benefits" to a related ("disqualified") person.

An excess benefit transaction is a transaction, such as the payment of compensation or the transfer of property, in which a disqualified person receives more than fair market value from the exempt organization or pays the exempt organization less than fair market value for property or services received. The tax imposed on the disqualified person is twenty-five percent of the excess benefit amount. If the excess benefit transaction is not corrected (for example, through repayment), a second-tier tax of 200 percent of the excess benefit amount can be imposed. However, if a transaction does not involve a disqualified person, directly or indirectly, no excess benefit transaction excise tax may be imposed by the IRS.

The IRS defines the term *disqualified person* as any person who, at any time during the five-year period ending on the date of such transaction, was in a position to exercise substantial influence over the affairs of the organization. The term also includes a member of the family of an individual described in the previous sentence and any entity in which disqualified persons in the aggregate control thirty-five percent of the voting interests. For most § 501(c)(3) and § 501(c)(4) organizations, the disqualified persons will generally include directors/trustees, officers, and top-management employees. Whether a person has substantial influence over the affairs of the organization, however, is a facts and circumstances test. Accordingly, the definition is potentially much broader than the aforementioned categories. For example, it may include substantial contributors, depending on the facts and circumstances.

## Taxes on Directors, Officers, and Other Managers

In addition to imposing an excise tax on disqualified persons that engage in excess benefit transactions, the IRS has the authority to impose excise taxes on "organization managers" that knowingly approved an excess benefit transaction. An organization manager includes any officer, director, or trustee of an applicable tax-exempt organization, or any individual having the powers or responsibilities similar to those of officers, directors, or trustees or the organization. The tax is ten percent of the excess benefit amount, up to a collective maximum of $10,000 per transaction.

## Procedures for Establishing Reasonableness

In determining whether there is an excess benefit transaction, the reasonableness of compensation and the fair market value of transactions are determined under existing tax law standards. However, there is a rebuttable presumption of reasonableness if the transaction with a disqualified person is approved by an independent board or committee thereof, comprised of individuals without a conflict of interest, who obtained and relied upon appropriate data as to comparability, and documented the basis for their determination. Even without this presumption, benefits provided to disqualified persons are not excess benefit transactions if it can be demonstrated that they are part of a fair market value exchange of goods or services. In this connection, however, payment of personal

expenses and benefits and non-fair-market-value transactions benefiting disqualified persons can only be justified as compensation for services if it is clear
that the organization intended and made the payments as compensation for
services at the time the payments were made.

The enactment of intermediate sanctions does not alter the actual standards
of conduct for tax-exempt organizations; instead, it simply provides another
mechanism for enforcement of existing standards. In particular, the intermediate sanctions legislation does not eliminate revocation of exempt status as a
penalty for organizations that commit egregious or repeated violations of the
laws governing exempt organizations.

A full discussion of the excess benefit transaction excise tax is beyond the
scope of this publication. Nonetheless, § 501(c)(3) and § 501(c)(4) organizations are encouraged to consult with their legal advisors to establish procedures
that will protect parties with whom the organization deals, and its
directors/trustees, officers, and other organization managers, from the potential
imposition of significant personal excise taxes.

See the following checklist (page 88) to review the issues discussed in this chapter.

## Notes

1. Our discussion, even of these limited areas, is based upon the law as it stood upon the date
of writing of this chapter. The Internal Revenue Code (Code) is usually amended in some manner
with each session of Congress, and the IRS periodically issues new rulings and interpretations that
change the general understanding of tax law provisions. As a result, some statements contained
herein may be incomplete or inaccurate when they meet the reader's eyes. Nonetheless, the issues
addressed are relatively permanent.

2. Although many states rely on federal tax-exempt status in determining exemption from
state income tax, some require separate filings. In addition, the requirements for exemption from
real property and sales taxes typically may be more stringent. Generally, only certain § 501(c)(3)
organizations (and usually not all of them) will qualify for such exemptions, but the criteria vary
from state to state.

3. As shown in the list provided in Appendix B, § 501(a) of the Code recognizes thirty-six
categories of tax-exempt organizations, but the list includes some entities that are not corporations and hence are outside our concern. Three significant types of tax-exempt organizations not
included in the appendix are trusts held under qualified pension plans, state and local government
instrumentalities, and political organizations.

4. An organization also may qualify under § 501(c)(3) if it is organized for testing for public
safety; fostering national or international amateur sports competition (if no part of its activities
involve providing athletic facilities or equipment); or preventing cruelty to children or animals.
These ways of qualifying as a § 501(c)(3) organization are self-explanatory.

5. The limits on deductibility imposed by § 170(b) range from twenty percent to fifty percent of an individual contributor's income. A discussion of these limits is outside the scope of this
*Guidebook*. See, however, IRS Publication 526, *Charitable Contributions*.

6. These requirements are set forth in detail in IRS Publication 557.

7. Churches are not exempt from challenge when they engage in political activities; despite
the general reluctance of most government officials to challenge actions of religious organizations, the IRS has not hesitated in this regard (e.g., the revocation of tax-exempt status of Branch
Ministries, Inc. [Church at Pierce Creek] and the affirmation of revocation by the district and
appellate courts).

8.  I.R.C. § 504(a) (1990).

9.  I.R.C. § 514 provides a special exception for real property acquired by certain "qualified organizations," including educational institutions and pension trusts. However, interest, rents, royalties and annuities paid by controlled for-profit subsidiaries to their exempt parent generally will not be excludable from income. To the extent that income is excluded from UBI, any related deductions also are excluded from the computation of tax.

10.  *See* I.R.C. § 513(i).

11.  I.R.C. § 6113. The rule does not apply to (a) organizations with annual gross receipts of $100,000 or less, or (b) any letter or telephone call if the communication is not part of a coordinated campaign soliciting more than ten persons during the calendar year.

12.  IRS Publication 1771 provides a good summary of the IRS position on this issue.

# Suggested Questions for Directors Regarding Taxation

(1) Is the corporation on whose board I serve exempt from federal income taxation?

(2) If it is, under what section of the Code is it exempt?

(3) If it is exempt under § 501(c)(3), is it a private foundation?

(4) If it is a private foundation, do I understand the special limitations that status imposes? Do the board and staff understand them?

(5) If we aren't exempt under § 501(c)(3), do we make clear to our donors that they cannot deduct their contributions to us?

(6) Who prepares our tax returns?

(7) What were the corporation's activities and mission as described to the IRS in applying for an exemption ruling? Is this description still an accurate portrayal of what we do?

(8) Do I know how much legislative activity we have engaged in? How much are we allowed under our particular exemption?

(9) If we are exempt under § 501(c)(3), do I understand the scope of activities covered by the absolute prohibition on electioneering by the organization?

(10) Have we put procedures in place to ensure that transactions potentially subject to intermediate sanctions are reviewed and documented to the extent we determine appropriate?

(11) What activities, if any, of our corporation may result in Unrelated Business Income?

(12) Who on our staff monitors this matter? Do our independent accountants do so?

# Checklist: Taxation

*Note:*   For purposes of simplicity in these checklists, we describe a corporation with a chair, who presides over the board of directors; a chief executive, who may be a staff person; an executive
committee; a nominating committee; and an audit committee. (However, we recognize that
in many smaller and other nonprofits, such committee functions may be performed by either
the executive committee or the board as a whole.) We also assume a legal counsel—someone, paid or unpaid, having primary responsibility for the corporation's legal affairs. Many
corporations, especially larger nonprofits, may have other committees established for specific
purposes, such as reviewing staff performance, fixing compensation, monitoring compliance
with legal requirements and periodic review of bylaws.

| Subject | To Be Reviewed By Whom | How Often | Comment |
|---|---|---|---|
| 1. If our corporation is exempt from federal income tax, under what section of the Internal Revenue Code is it exempt? | Legal counsel | Annually | Whole board should understand basic nature of the corporation's specific exemption. Information on this subject should be in the director's manual. |
| 2. If it is exempt under Section 501(c)(3), is the corporation a private foundation, a private operating foundation, or a public charity? | Legal counsel, then full board | Annually | Board should understand the privileges or limitations imposed by the applicable provisions of the Code on the corporation's particular type of activity. |
| 3. If the corporation is exempt under Section 501(c)(3) or Section 501(c)(4) and is not a private foundation, has the corporation established procedures to identify potential excess benefit transactions and obtain the rebuttable presumption of reasonableness where appropriate? | Chief executive, legal counsel | Annually | Boards should determine the level of scrutiny that will be applied to various types of transactions depending on the likelihood that the party is a disqualified person and the significance of the transaction. |
| 4. If the corporation is exempt under Section 501(c)(3), have we engaged in activities that are limited (in the case of lobbying) or prohibited (in the case of participating in an election) by virtue of our 501(c)(3) status? | Legal counsel, then full board | Annually, and during discussion of any major change in contemplated political activities | This is a field of tax law with frequent new interpretations. Section 501(c)(3) organizations should closely monitor activities to assure compliance. For instance, as discussed in Chapter 6, "Supervision of Internet Activities," whether links from a tax-exempt organization's Web site to an organization that |

*(Continued)*

## Checklist: Taxation *(Continued)*

| Subject | To Be Reviewed By Whom | How Often | Comment |
|---|---|---|---|
| 4. *Continued* | | | engages in substantial lobbying activity constitutes lobbying by the organization is an issue being reviewed by the IRS. |
| 5. If the advocacy activities of the corporation are restricted but not prohibited (as in the case of lobbying), have we compared the actual activities undertaken with the restrictions of applicable tax law? | Chief executive, legal counsel | Annually | If such activities are substantial and continuing, the corporation's books should be organized to quantify such activities. |

# Creation of For-Profit Subsidiaries and Joint Ventures: Tax-Exemption and Other Issues

## *Contents*

CHAPTER 5

# Creation of For-Profit Subsidiaries and Joint Ventures: Tax Exemption and Other Issues

*The board of a nonprofit corporation may decide that the corporation's mission and goals would be served by engaging in an activity that does not easily fit within the corporation's current structure. If such activity is one that is typically engaged in by nonprofit organizations, the board may establish a nonprofit subsidiary or affiliate. However, if the activity is one that will generate taxable income, or is typically conducted by for-profit rather than nonprofit organizations, the board may consider establishing a for-profit subsidiary, or entering into joint-venture arrangement with a for-profit entity. Set forth below is a summary of many of the issues that a nonprofit board should consider before establishing a for-profit subsidiary or entering into a joint venture with a for-profit organization.[1]*

## Engaging in New Activities, either within the Corporation or through a For-Profit Subsidiary

A nonprofit, tax-exempt corporation may find that in order to fulfill its corporate mission, it would be useful to engage in an activity that is outside the general range of activities for which it was organized and is operated. For example, a health care corporation or museum may desire to operate a cafeteria or gift shop, or a community organization may find it has an opportunity to buy used computers and re-sell them to low-income residents. Similarly, a corporation that owns and operates low-income housing may desire to provide housing management services to similar corporations. The revenues derived from such activities may be of a kind not generally treated as exempt from taxation. Nevertheless, the nonprofit's board may believe that engaging in the activity will further its exempt purposes. When a corporation's board considers engaging in such a non-exempt activity, the directors should bear the following considerations in mind:

### Furtherance of Exempt Purposes

Generally, the non-exempt activity should only be engaged in if it is consistent with the corporation's mission and exempt purposes. The organization could jeopardize its tax exemption if a substantial amount of its activity is deemed to be "unrelated" to the corporation's tax-exempt purpose. In the IRS's view, an activity is treated as unrelated to a § 501(c)(3) corporation's tax-exempt purposes unless it is "substantially related" to such exempt purposes, by "contributing importantly" to the accomplishment of the exempt purposes.

## UBI

If the non-exempt activity is unrelated, in the IRS's view, to the corporation's exempt purposes, the revenue from the activity may be subject to taxation as unrelated business income (UBI) and reported on Form 990-T. However, some forms of unrelated revenue are exempted from taxation, including investment income and passive income, as well as: revenues derived from unrelated activities that are performed entirely by volunteers; are primarily conducted for the benefit of members, students, officers or employees; or involve resale of primarily donated items.

## Substantiality of Non-Exempt Activity

An unrelated, non-exempt activity may be conducted within the corporation as long as it would not constitute a "substantial" part of the organization's overall activity. As a rule of thumb, an activity is likely to not be considered substantial if revenues from the activity are less than twenty percent of the organization's overall revenues—although higher percentages may be permitted in certain circumstances, and lower percentages are recommended for tax-exempt corporations classified as "supporting" organizations under § 509(a)(3) of the Internal Revenue Code.

# Advantages of Establishing Separate For-Profit Subsidiaries

If a proposed non-exempt activity is of a kind that is likely to be viewed by the IRS as unrelated to the corporation's purposes, the board may decide to place the activity in a separate, for-profit subsidiary, rather than maintaining it within the corporation's structure. Some of the factors that nonprofit boards tend to weigh in favor of establishing a for-profit subsidiary include the following:

(1) The amount of the unrelated activity, or the income generated thereby, could become substantial and thus threaten the corporation's tax-exemption if conducted within the corporation.

(2) The non-exempt activity requires a substantial devotion of management time and attention, or requires a significant number of employees.

(3) The activity entails a level of business risk that should be segregated, to the extent possible, from the assets or endowment of the charitable organization.

(4) The management of the activity requires a kind of expertise not generally present in the corporation's management officers or board.

(5) It will be easier to recruit management staff for the non-exempt activity if the activity is contained in a separate organization rather than within the confines of the nonprofit corporation.

(6) The non-exempt activity is best performed in a corporate environment that is less hierarchical, or otherwise distinct from that of the nonprofit.

(7) The board prefers that the revenues and expenses of the non-exempt activity not be reflected on the income statements and balance sheet of the exempt corporation (note, however, that most often an organization owning the stock of a subsidiary must include the subsidiary's financial statements in its own consolidated financial statement).

(8) It is considered desirable or necessary to be able to offer stock or stock options to senior management or other employees associated with the non-exempt activity, in order to recruit and incentivize the performance of such employees.

(9) The board wants to maximize the revenue generated from the subsidiary, but to avoid the activity being deemed a substantial activity of the exempt corporation itself (and thereby threaten the corporation's tax-exempt status).

# How to Establish a For-Profit Subsidiary

Once the board has decided to establish a for-profit subsidiary, it will need to decide how the new corporation will be organized, and the extent and nature of control that the nonprofit corporation will exert over the for-profit.

## Who Will Serve on the New Corporation's Board?

If the nonprofit owns more than fifty percent of the stock of the for-profit, it usually will have the power to elect a majority of the for-profit's directors. The board of the nonprofit should determine who will serve as the new corporation's initial board of directors, and whether certain director positions should be filled, *ex officio*, by persons who hold certain officer or director positions with the nonprofit. For instance, the board of the nonprofit could specify that its chairperson, chief executive and/or chief financial officer will serve *ex officio* on the for-profit corporation's board, or that one or more of the nonprofit's board members will also serve on the for-profit corporation's board.

## Who Will Serve as the Corporation's Officers?

Depending on the activities of the for-profit, the nonprofit parent may desire to have some degree of overlap between the officers of the nonprofit and its for-profit subsidiary. For instance, when organizing the for-profit subsidiary, the parent nonprofit board may require the subsidiary's bylaws to provide that the chief executive of the nonprofit will serve, *ex officio*, as the president of the for-profit subsidiary. This will ensure that the chief executive of the nonprofit parent is kept informed regarding all material operational issues affecting the subsidiary. Alternatively, the nonprofit, as shareholder, can elect directors of the subsidiary who will appoint officers acceptable to the nonprofit.

## Other Oversight Mechanisms

The parent board should evaluate what other mechanisms it will use to oversee the operation of the subsidiary. In addition to any director and officer overlap between the parent nonprofit and the for-profit subsidiary, the parent board should determine how often it desires to receive reports on the subsidiary's operations, and incorporate such reports on the parent board's agenda. The board may also wish to provide for shareholder approval or veto power over significant corporate actions—such as the adoption of budgets. The board should be aware of which corporate actions (such as merger, substantial asset sale, and dissolution) typically require approval by a majority or higher number of shareholders. On the other hand, although the parent nonprofit can and should oversee the for-profit subsidiary, the nonprofit should not participate in the subsidiary's day-to-day operations; otherwise, the activities of the for-profit may be attributed to the nonprofit by the IRS or other parties.

## Tax Implications

Any revenue generated by the for-profit subsidiary, if it is a corporation, will be subject to taxation at the corporate level, although dividends or royalties to the tax-exempt shareholder would frequently be tax-exempt in its hands, similar to other passive income. (See the discussion in the section "Types of Income Excluded from UBI" in Chapter 4, "Taxation."). Any losses experienced by the for-profit corporation may be offset by the gains from that corporation's other activities.

## Other Organizational Issues

Nonprofits that establish a subsidiary will generally find that it is most appropriate to establish such entity under the laws of the state in which the nonprofit is itself incorporated. However, nonprofit corporations may sometimes find it useful to take advantage of favorable provisions in the corporation laws of another state (such as Delaware), by forming the subsidiary under the laws of such other state, and registering the subsidiary as a foreign corporation doing business in the nonprofit corporation's state. The corporation's legal counsel can assist the nonprofit's board and officers in assessing whether the use of a foreign corporation offers any significant advantages to offset the administrative inconveniences of organization under a different state.

# Creation of Joint Ventures with For-Profits

Nonprofit, tax-exempt corporations may also find it useful in certain circumstances to enter into joint ventures with individuals or for-profit entities. The nonprofit board should make sure that the joint venture is not structured or operated in a manner that would constitute an undue benefit to its for-profit partner or other for-profit entities.[2] A tax-exempt corporation that is a prospective partner in a joint venture (whether organized as an limited liability company (LLC), partnership or corporation) must take care to structure the joint venture, and the nonprofit's role therein, in a manner that minimizes the risk that the nonprofit's participation might put the organization's tax-exemption in jeopardy or generate unexpected UBI.

Even if the tax-exempt corporation's participation in a for-profit joint venture is only a small part of the tax-exempt's total activities, the tax-exempt should exercise a level of control over the venture's operational issues that will assure that the venture operates in furtherance of the tax-exempt organization's charitable purposes. This is particularly true in the case of LLCs or joint ventures structured as partnerships. With such "pass-through" entities, the IRS attributes the acts of the partnership (or LLC) entity as being the actions of the joint-venture partners.[3] To evaluate whether a tax-exempt corporation's participation in the joint venture is in furtherance of tax-exempt purposes, the IRS will look at such issues as:

(a)  Does the nonprofit appoint a majority of the joint-venture's governing body?

(b)  Does the for-profit partner (or partners) have a veto power over significant corporate actions?

(c)  Will a for-profit entity (whether a partner, a partner's affiliate or unrelated third party) manage the operations of the joint venture? If so, what is the term of the management contract? How are the management fees determined?

(d)  Do the governing documents of the joint venture explicitly provide that the joint venture will be operated consistently with the charitable purposes of the tax-exempt partner? Does the tax-exempt partner have the ability to require the joint venture to put charitable purposes ahead of economic objectives?

(e)  Will the compensation paid to the joint venture's officers and vendors (especially the for-profit partner or any affiliate) be reasonable in light of the services and/or goods provided?

(f)  Will the joint venture use space financed by the tax-exempt bonds? If so, have the implications of such "bad use" on the tax exemption of the bonds been considered?

# Taxation of Joint Venture Revenue

Any income generated by the joint venture will be subject to tax at the joint venture level, if the joint venture is a "regular" (or C) corporation. However, joint ventures structured as tax "pass-through" entities—that is, partnerships and LLCs—will not be taxed at the entity level. If the joint venture is appropriately structured to further the purposes of the tax-exempt partner, the tax-exempt organization's share of joint venture revenue (that is, LLC/partnership revenue allocations) should be exempt from taxation, and not treated as UBI. Joint venture interests in S corporations present special issues. Although S corporations are generally pass-through entities, the statutes specifically provide that all of an exempt S corporation shareholder's allocated income is UBI.

The UBI rules are complex. As an illustration, joint venture income that is passive (such as rents, royalties and interest) would not ordinarily be taxed to the nonprofit when "passed through." However, any otherwise nontaxable joint venture income will be taxed to the nonprofit (at least in part) if the venture is debt-financed or if the nonprofit acquired its joint venture interest with debt. Any nonprofit contemplating a joint venture with for-profit entities should thoroughly explore the structure with tax counsel. (See the section "Unrelated Business Income" in Chapter 4, "Taxation.")

See the following checklist (page 102) to review the issues discussed in this chapter.

# Notes

1. For a detailed discussion of legal issues that arise in partnerships and joint ventures involving nonprofit corporations, see generally, Michael I. Sanders, *Joint Ventures Involving Tax-Exempt Organizations* (John Wiley & Sons, 2000).

2. The IRS is giving increasing scrutiny to nonprofit joint ventures with private individuals or for-profit entities. *See* I.R.S. Rev. Rule 98-15. *See also IRS Says Charities Must Control Joint Ventures*, DON KRAMER'S NONPROFIT ISSUES 11 (April, 1998), at 11.

3. *See* Redlands Surgical Services v. Commissioner, 113 T.C. No. 47 (1999), *aff'd per curiam*, 87 AFTR2d Par. 2001-642 (March 15, 2001).

# Suggested Questions for Directors Regarding For-Profit Subsidiaries and Joint Ventures

(1) Is the corporation contemplating engaging in any new business activities or joint ventures?

(2) If so, is such activity substantially related to the corporation's nonprofit purposes?

(3) Do we know if the new activity or joint venture will generate unrelated business income (UBI)?

(4) What are the reasons for or against putting a new activity in a taxable subsidiary, or conducting it with a partner through a joint venture, rather than conducting the activity through a division within the corporation?

(5) If the board wants to establish a taxable subsidiary, who will serve as the subsidiary's officers and directors? How will the nonprofit parent board exercise oversight on the subsidiary?

(6) In what state should a subsidiary or joint venture be established?

(7) For joint ventures to be engaged in by a tax-exempt nonprofit, what controls has the organization put into place to assure that the venture operates in furtherance of the nonprofit partner's charitable purposes?

(8) How will the joint venture be organized (general partnership, LLC, corporation, etc.)? What are the advantages of such form over another alternative?

(9) Will the joint venture use space that was financed by tax-exempt bonds?

(10) Who is the organization's proposed joint venture partner? Will this partner (or co-venturer) provide goods or services to the joint venture? What controls are in place to assure that the other joint venturer does not profit from the venture at the expense of the venture or the nonprofit partner?

# Checklist: For-Profit Subsidiaries and Joint Ventures

*Note:*    For purposes of simplicity in these checklists, we describe a corporation with a chair, who presides over the board of directors; a chief executive, who may be a staff person; an executive committee; a nominating committee; and an audit committee. (However, we recognize that in many smaller and other nonprofits, such committee functions may be performed by either the executive committee or the board as a whole.) We also assume a legal counsel—someone, paid or unpaid, having primary responsibility for the corporation's legal affairs. Many corporations, especially larger nonprofits, may have other committees established for specific purposes, such as reviewing staff performance, fixing compensation, monitoring compliance with legal requirements and periodic review of bylaws.

| Subject | To Be Reviewed By Whom | How Often | Comment |
|---|---|---|---|
| 1. Are there any new activities planned by the corporation that might be best conducted through a for-profit subsidiary or joint venture? | Full board and chief executive | At least annually | The chief executive should recommend, and the board should decide, if any such activities should be kept within the corporation or placed in a separate entity. |
| 2. For existing taxable subsidiaries and joint ventures, how often is the board apprised of financial and business issues for such entities? | Full board and chief executive | At least quarterly, with detailed reviews at least annually | |
| 3. Are the activities and organizational form of existing subsidiaries or joint ventures consistent with the organization's nonprofit purposes? | Full board, chief executive, legal counsel | At least annually | The board should monitor the evolution of such affiliates' activities to ensure consistency with the organization's purposes. |
| 4. How much UBI, if any, have subsidiaries or joint ventures generated for the nonprofit? | Full board, chief financial officer | At least annually | |
| 5. Does a joint venture partner provide management or other services or goods to the joint venture? If so, does such partner derive any revenues in excess of those that would be paid to an unrelated party on an arms'-length basis? | Full board, chief executive officer, chief financial officer | Quarterly, with detailed reviews annually | Management contracts with for-profit joint venture partners are subject to close scrutiny for private inurement and other tax-exemption concerns. |

CHAPTER **6**

# Supervision of Internet Activities

## *Contents*

CHAPTER **6**

# Supervision of Internet Activities

*The law applying to activities on the Internet is still evolving. Lawmakers, regulators and judges across the country are in the process of determining how various laws written for the traditional economy fit the virtual world of the Internet. While this chapter is designed to alert nonprofit corporation directors to some of the major legal implications of Internet activity, specific statements may become inaccurate, or less accurate, over time. (For instance, it can be expected that the IRS will make, and periodically revise, pronouncements on many of the topics discussed below.) Nonprofit boards should make sure that their corporation's Internet activities are reviewed by legal counsel on a regular basis, to ensure compliance with changing legal standards.*

## Potential Hazards, and Benefits, of Maintaining a Web Site and Using the Internet

The Internet offers a highly convenient and cost-effective tool for communicating a nonprofit corporation's purposes and conducting some of its activities. However, use of the Internet may implicate a number of legal issues applicable to nonprofit corporations generally. Some of the more significant of such general laws are discussed below. Although it may be unlikely that any one nonprofit would simultaneously (if ever) encounter all of the issues discussed below, a broad range of potential issues is presented here in order to alert directors to the wide variety of legal issues that could be raised by different forms of Internet activity.

## But First, a Few Definitions

The *Internet* is a global network connecting millions of computers that send, receive, and store information. No single entity owns or administers the Internet or controls all of the information it contains. Instead, the computers and small computer networks that make up the Internet are owned and operated by government and public institutions, nonprofit organizations and private entities.

Individuals can access the Internet through a variety of sources, including universities, governmental institutions, the military, large companies, and commercial Internet service providers.[1]

The *World Wide Web*, or *Web*, is a popular way to access the information on the Internet. The Web is made up of a series of documents stored in different computers all over the world. The documents may contain text and images, like a page in a magazine, as well as sounds or video.

A *link* on a web site may appear as text or an image on which a web site visitor clicks, and is then carried over, or linked to a web site maintained by another entity. If a *framing link* is made, the new web site appears in a box on the screen displaying the initial web site; otherwise, once the link is made, the first web site disappears from the user's screen.

# Fund Raising

## Charitable Solicitation Registration Requirements

### General rule

Most states and many local governments require nonprofit organizations and their fund-raisers to register before soliciting contributions in that jurisdiction. Such jurisdictions have regulations relating to telephone and mail solicitations from organizations that are not physically located in the solicitation area.[2] A majority of the states that require charitable solicitation registration accept the Unified Registration Statement form for charitable solicitations, which was developed to ease the burden on charitable organizations of filling out multiple different registration forms.[3]

### Application to the Internet

Most jurisdictions are just beginning to determine what constitutes sufficient presence over the Internet to require registration under the jurisdiction's charitable solicitation laws. Any organization that raises funds over the Internet should be sure that it keeps abreast of the evolving standards that apply to such fund raising.

The Internet allows nonprofits to communicate with a large audience of potential new donors, generally at less expense than traditional fund-raising methods. Many nonprofits have identified this opportunity and developed web sites that describe their organizations' purposes, activities, upcoming events, contact information and more. They may also include statements that directly solicit contributions. For example, some nonprofits provide a form on their web sites that enables donors to make contributions on-line, using their credit cards.

At the time this chapter was written, a few state and local agencies had contacted charities with web-based fund-raising solicitations and indicated that registration under the state's charitable solicitation law was required. Currently, it is unlikely that most jurisdictions would require registration of nonprofit organizations that only maintain a passive web page that merely provides information on the organization but does not request donations. In contrast, registration may be required if a nonprofit actively solicits donations by e-mail to persons located in the jurisdiction or permits donors to make contributions by providing their credit card numbers on the organization's web site. The registration requirements are less clear for nonprofits that provide the opportunity for donations to be made over the Internet via their web site, but which do not otherwise actively solicit donations in specific jurisdictions. Directors should expect both that the rules in this area will continue to be refined, and that different jurisdictions may take different approaches.[4] Accordingly, directors should periodically check with counsel whether its web site or other Internet activity subjects the organization to the charitable solicitation laws of different jurisdictions—both in and out of the United States.

Questions that are likely to be relevant to the issue of whether an organization's Internet activities is deemed to make it subject to regulation in a particular jurisdiction include the following:

(1) Must individuals take the initiative to go to the organization's web site, or does the organization contact prospective donors (such as through e-mail) and request that they log on to the web site and make a donation?

(2) Does the organization's web site have a mechanism for corresponding (by e-mail or regular mail) with persons who express an interest in the organization after visiting the web site?

(3) Does the organization's web site have a mechanism for accepting contributions by donors who provide credit card information?

(4) How much money is raised in a particular jurisdiction through Internet activities?

# Acknowledgments of Contributions Made by Donors

### *General rule*

Federal tax law requires a donor contributing $250 or more to a charitable corporation to obtain a written receipt for the contribution before filing a federal income tax return in order to claim a charitable contribution deduction for the donation.[5] Similarly, charitable organizations that receive contributions of more than $75 in connection with the provision to the donor of a certain amount of goods or services—such as a seat at a table for a charity dinner (*quid pro quo* contributions)—must provide the donor with a written statement estimating the deductible portion of the contribution, above the value of the goods or services the donor received.[6] These requirements apply regardless of whether the contribution is made in person, over the telephone, through traditional mail or over the Internet. See the section "Charitable Contribution" in Chapter 4, "Taxation."

### Application to the Internet

Charitable corporations that allow contributions to be made over the Internet should be sure the corporation has a system in place for acknowledging such contributions that complies with current IRS acknowledgement requirements. As of this writing, the IRS has announced that it will revise IRS Publication 1771 to make clear that an acknowledgment provided by e-mail, or that can be provided off the organization's web site, will satisfy this donation acknowledgement requirement.

## Allowing Other Organizations to Raise Money for the Corporation

### General rules

**Registration requirements.**   A nonprofit organization may use an individual or other organization to generate donations. Such individual or group may need to register under the charitable solicitation rules of the jurisdiction in which donations are solicited.

**Fund raiser as agent of the tax-exempt corporation.**   If the individual or group is not itself tax-exempt, the fund-raiser must qualify as an agent of the tax-exempt entity in order for the donor's contribution to be tax-deductible. If the fund-raiser is considered the organization's agent, contributions to such agent are deductible in the same way that direct contributions are deductible. In contrast, if a non-tax-exempt fund-raiser is not the agent of a tax-exempt organization, contributions to the fund-raiser will not be tax-deductible to the donor.

**Fund raising resulting from sales by taxable entities.**   Another way that a tax-exempt organization may raise funds is through an arrangement to receive a percentage of the sales of goods sold by a taxable entity to supporters of the tax-exempt organization. For instance , a taxable entity may volunteer, or agree, to make donations to the tax-exempt entity based on purchases made by organization supporters on a certain day or during some other time period. Similarly, for-profit stores may sell to nonprofits coupons or "scrip" for store products, at a discount to face value. Under such an arrangement, for example, a local grocery store may agree with a tax-exempt preschool to honor coupons for groceries bought by supporters of the school. Such coupons may be purchased at a discount by the school, and resold at face value to school supporters. The net income made from the sales is generally not considered UBI, if the coupon sales are not an activity "regularly carried on" by the school, or if it is carried on by volunteers. However, the payment for such purchases or scrip is not deductible by the purchasers as tax-exempt contributions.

Under other arrangements between a for-profit merchant and a nonprofit corporation, a merchant (such as a credit card company) may pay to a nonprofit institution (such as a nonprofit college) a percentage of sales made by a credit card depicting the college, its name and logo. In such cases, the percentage of sales payments may be eligible to be treated as a royalty for the use of the institution's name and image, and not taxed as unrelated business income (UBI). As noted in the section "Types of Income Excluded from UBI" in the chapter "Taxation," royalties for use of an intangible (such as a corporation's name or logo) are generally considered exempt from treatment as UBI; however, if such payments were instead to be characterized as payment for a service (i.e., the referral of customers), then such income would be considered UBI.

## Internet applications

The Internet has spawned a number of creative fund-raising mechanisms. Directors of nonprofit organizations that receive donations through web sites maintained by for-profit entities should obtain legal advice regarding whether the contributions were generated in a manner consistent with IRS rules on deductibility.

**Web sites acting as agents of tax-exempt organizations.**   Some web sites purport to raise funds for many charities at once. They are promoted as offering donors convenience and detailed information about potential donees. Some such donation web sites are not themselves operated by tax-exempt charitable organizations, so contributions made through these sites are not deductible by donors unless the donation web site operator is an agent of the nonprofit. Nonprofit boards should ensure that the terms of any agreement they enter with a donation web site operator establishes an appropriate agency relationship if users of the site are going to be promised deductibility for their contributions.[7]

On a more fundamental level, nonprofit boards should establish a mechanism for evaluating when and whether to allow such donation web sites to serve as their fund-raising agents. For instance, before granting permission to a donation web site to use the corporation's name, the charity should investigate the history of the web site, its operators and its operations. Other questions to ask include the following:

- If the web site deducts an administrative fee before passing on the donations, is the fee reasonable?
- How long does it take for donation payments to be processed by the site and then payment to be made to the nonprofit?

**Fund raising through sales by for-profit entities: Internet merchant affiliation and charity malls.**   Certain Internet sites have programs under which a tax-exempt organization receives a payment as a result of sales made by the for-profit over the Internet. In exchange for this payment, the nonprofit generally either provides a link from its web site to that of the participating for-profit, or the for-profit refers to the participating nonprofit on its own web site and promises to donate money to support its mission.[8] As discussed above, the structure of such programs can have different UBI implications. Moreover, the IRS has questioned whether the payment by a vendor of a percentage of sales from customers referred by a tax-exempt organization to the vendor's web site can ever be considered "substantially related" for UBI determination purposes.[9]

A unique on-line variant of the merchant affiliation model is a web site that brings together consumers, for-profit retailers, and nonprofit corporations in a program that is similar to affinity credit cards. Visitors to such a charity mall web site designate a preferred charity and then shop at affiliated on-line retailers through links on the charity mall's web site. For each item a shopper buys through the charity mall, the retailers donate a specified percentage of the purchase price to the shopper's preferred charity through the charity mall operator. Because shoppers initiate these donations and charities are therefore not involved in sales that are unrelated to their exempt purposes, it is generally believed that charities can treat the money they receive through charity malls as donations and not UBI. However, donors should generally not be unable to deduct donations attributable to purchases they make through charity malls because they receive items of equal value in return for their payments to retailers.

Some Internet charity mall operators claim that their programs have a special structure that allows donors to deduct donations. In these programs, when a donor makes a purchase through the charity mall, the operator offers the donor a rebate on the purchase. The operator holds the rebate in an account for the donor, and the donor has the option to either receive the money or donate it to the charity through the operator. Because the donor has the choice to keep or donate the rebate, the IRS allows the donor to claim a charitable contribution deduction.[10] Before participating in a charity mall, or if a nonprofit learns that a charity mall is making donations to its organization an option for mall-site shoppers, the nonprofit should investigate the operations and operator of the charity mall to make sure that it will not be associated with a questionable program or group. (See discussion in the section "Web Sites Acting as Agents of Tax-Exempt Organizations" in Chapter 4, "Taxation.")

# Acknowledging a Nonprofit's Corporate Sponsors versus Providing Advertising for a For-Profit Corporation

## General Rules

### *Acknowledgements versus advertisements*

The distinction between sponsorship acknowledgements and advertisements may be subtle. Simple references to an organization sponsor by name, address and phone number would generally be characterized as acknowledgements, and the funds paid by the sponsor in connection with the activity with which the acknowledgement is associated would be considered a tax-deductible contribution. In contrast, references to a sponsor's products or services that include an endorsement or statements about the relative quality of the sponsor's goods or services would be likely treated as advertisements (at least to the extent of the fair market value of comparable ads provided by the tax-exempt organization).[11] In addition, the money paid to the for-profit may be considered taxable UBI to the nonprofit, if paid in connection with an activity that is "regularly carried on."(See the section "Advertising versus Sponsorship Acknowledgements" in Chapter 4, "Taxation.")

### Different treatment of advertisements in periodicals

As noted in the section "Advertising versus Sponsorship Acknowledgements" in Chapter 4, "Taxation," payments received for an individual ad placed in a nonprofit's periodical publication will be subject to less UBI tax than an ad placed in a non-periodical. However, it may sometimes be difficult to determine whether a publication is a periodical for which the lower UBI tax calculation would apply. The general rule is that material that appears on a regular periodic schedule, in a standard format, is likely to be considered a periodical, whereas material (such as a brochure) that is continuously available but subject to updating from time to time, is not likely to be considered a periodical.

## Internet Applications

### Acknowledgements versus advertisements

For-profit companies may be interested in appearing on a nonprofit corporation's web site as a sponsor or as an advertiser. As noted above, if the information about a for-profit company that appears on a nonprofit corporation's web site is considered a sponsorship acknowledgment ("The maintenance of XYZ Charity's web site is made possible through the support of Acme Widget and Gizmo Corporation, located at 1200 Main Street."), payment made by the sponsor is likely deductible as a charitable contribution, and the revenue received from the for-profit corporation in connection with the posted message would not be subject to tax. However, if the information about a for-profit corporation that is posted on the nonprofit corporation's web site is considered an advertisement ("Need widgets or gizmos—fast? Call Acme Widget and Gizmo Corporation, a full-service provider of widget and gizmos since 1999, at area code 222, 333-9999, or order on-line at www.widgetsnow.biz."), the revenues received from the for-profit corporation in connection with such information will be subject to taxation as UBI.

Because of the novel nature of certain Internet applications, the acknowledgement/advertisement distinction is not always obvious. For example, the

IRS at one time suggested that a simple displayed link to a sponsor's web site is not an advertisement, even though an individual who clicks on the link will then be presented, through the for-profit's web site, with information on the company's products and services and how to purchase them. In contrast, the IRS indicated that a nonprofit that a runs a banner display for a for-profit organization's web site that shows information about a for-profit company's products, but does not provide a link to the for-profit's web site, may be considered an advertisement.[12]

More recently, the IRS has solicited comments on the significance of links in the preamble to the proposed regulations on corporate sponsorship, which were published in the spring of 2000.[13] The regulations made clear that an acknowledgment of a sponsor may include the street address of the sponsor's place of business and/or the sponsor's telephone number.[14] A link is essentially an Internet address combined with a tool the user may employ, solely at the user's discretion, to go to the linked site. There appears to be no basis for treating the link differently than a street address or telephone number.

### Internet periodicals

Whether material containing advertisements published by a nonprofit corporation on the Internet can be considered a periodical for purposes of more favorable UBI tax calculation rules can be a difficult determination. The IRS has indicated that the UBI rules for periodical advertising income will not be available for Internet advertisements run by a nonprofit unless the advertisement appears in on-line materials that are "prepared and distributed in substantially the same manner as a traditional periodical,"[15] with an editorial staff, marketing program and budget that is independent of the administrator of the rest of the organization's web site. Under these rules, an advertisement that appears on a nonprofit web site would not generally be considered to be "published in a periodical," even if the web site is periodically updated.

# Association (Links) with Taxable Entities

## General Rule: Only Incidental Promotion of Taxable Entities

Tax-exempt corporations may lose tax-exempt status by promoting, or appearing to promote private interests of individuals or taxable entities, except as an incident to the tax-exempt organization's purposes.

# Internet Applications

## Web site links with web sites of taxable organizations

The nature of the Internet is to create easy-to-use links between otherwise unrelated material. Corporate sponsors and other for-profit companies may wish to establish links with a tax-exempt corporation's web site (either by placing a link on the for-profit's web site to the nonprofit's site, or having the nonprofit's site contain a link to the for-profit corporation's web site). While a link to a for-profit corporation on a tax-exempt corporation's web site may take up very little space, the existence of the link can create the impression that the tax-exempt corporation supports or is involved with some or all of the activities described on the for-profit corporation's web site. Further, links to the sites of corporate sponsors may (or may not) be deemed to be advertisements subject to taxation as UBI. (See the section "Acknowledging a Nonprofit's Corporate Sponsor versus Providing Advertising for a For-Profit Corporation" above.)

Tax-exempt organizations maintaining web sites are well advised to develop a policy for determining which linkage requests it will honor and which it will reject.

Nonprofit boards should consider several issues as they develop and apply their linkage policies.[16] The policy should include a procedure for screening proposed links to ensure that they further the nonprofit's charitable purposes and satisfy its requirements for exemption. For instance, tax-exempt organizations should reject requests by political candidates to establish links with particular campaign sites, to avoid the appearance of making political endorsements and protect their tax-exempt status.

When a link goes to a site maintained by another nonprofit, the linkage policy should also provide for an evaluation of the § 501(c) status of the proposed linking organization, to assess the potential for attribution of the linking organization's activities to the nonprofit. For example, if the web site of a nonprofit that works to preserve wetlands contains a link to an environmental advocacy group that conducts substantial lobbying, should the existence of the link cause the advocacy group's lobbying to be attributed to the nonprofit? (See further discussion of this issue in the section "Implication of Links to Lobbying Organization web sites" below.)

In addition, a linkage policy should include a procedure for responding to the discovery of links on a for-profit corporation's web site to the nonprofit's site that were created without the nonprofit's permission. If the linking organization would not meet the approval requirements set forth in the established policy, the nonprofit may want to have communications to record the fact that the nonprofit on the destination end of the link does not approve or condone what the linking organization is saying or doing, and, if appropriate, requests that the link be removed.

# Lobbying

## General Rule

As noted in the section "The Absolute Prohibition on Political Campaign Activities" in the chapter "Taxation," organizations that are exempt from federal income taxation under § 501(c) are prohibited from devoting more than an "insubstantial" part of their activities to lobbying. To avoid the subjective vagaries of what insubstantial may mean—for instance, as determined by percentage of organizational revenue, percentage of volunteer time or other resources, or the impact of the activities conducted—tax-exempt organizations (other than churches and other religious organizations) may take advantage of the election under § 501(h) of the Code. This Code section provides objective measures for determining permissible levels of lobbying, based on the organization's annual spending on its exempt purposes, and with different limits for "grassroots" and "direct" lobbying. (For more information about the § 501(h) election, see the discussion in the section "Limitations on Lobbying" in Chapter 4, "Taxation.")

## Internet Applications

### Benefits of § 501(h) Election

The Internet provides great potential for a nonprofit to increase the scope and effectiveness of its lobbying activity while satisfying the IRS limitations on lobbying by tax-exempt corporations. Lobbying activity can be conducted over the Internet (through web sites and electronic mail) at a very low cost, especially compared to the cost of traditional mail or personal lobbying visits. For example, legislative alerts or calls to action can be posted at the organization's web site, referenced by links to other sites, and/or e-mail communications can be sent directly to the nonprofit corporation's list of supporters. The time and economic costs of these communications are typically trivial compared to mail or traditional broadcast mechanisms. As noted in the section "Lobbying: General Rule" above, the amount that a nonprofit can spend on lobbying is limited to an insubstantial amount. Tax-exempt corporations that would like to maximize the potential for lobbying using the Internet (alone or in conjunction with more traditional lobbying activities), while not jeopardizing their tax-exempt status, may wish to make the election permitted under § 501(h). Such election can be extremely beneficial to a nonprofit corporation by providing a mechanism for calculating a specific "safe harbor" maximum dollar amount that the corporation may spend on lobbying activities. (See the section "Limitations on Lobbying" in Chapter 4, "Taxation.")

### Allocation of costs of e-mail and web site postings

Despite the fact that lobbying through e-mail or web site postings can save considerable expense over traditional mail or fax communications, it is currently unclear how costs should be allocated for such Internet lobbying activities. Making an appropriate allocation of costs of Internet lobbying is essential in order to ensure that the nonprofit does not exceed the applicable spending limit if a § 501(h) election has been made (or remains within the insubstantial range for organizations that have not made the § 501(h) election). Costs to be allocated may include hosting and maintenance of web sites. Until the IRS provides specific guidance in this area, nonprofits should consult with their accountant regarding appropriate measures of the cost of such activities.

### Implications of links to lobbying organization web sites

Tax-exempt nonprofits should exercise caution before creating or permitting links on the nonprofit's web site to a web site for a lobbying organization. It is not yet clear under what circumstances, and to what extent, a link on a nonprofit organization's web site to the web site of an organization that engages in lobbying would be considered lobbying by the nonprofit. It can be expected that the IRS will be taking positions on this issue in the future; therefore, directors of nonprofits for whom this issue may be relevant should make sure that the organization routinely receives updated advice in this area.

# Political Activity

## General Rule

As noted in Chapter 4, "Taxation," tax-exempt organizations are prohibited from supporting candidates for political office or otherwise intervening in political campaigns. (See the section "The Absolute Prohibition on Political Campaign Activities" in Chapter 4, "Taxation.")

# Internet Applications

## *Implications of links to political campaign or candidates web sites*

Tax-exempt nonprofits should avoid creating or permitting links on the nonprofit's web site to web sites for selected political campaigns or candidates for political office. In some instances, providing strictly nonpartisan information, including links to sites maintained by all the candidates in a race, may be consistent with federal tax law requirements, but a nonprofit should get legal advice before pursuing such an approach. In a letter to the Federal Election Commission, IRS Assistant Chief Counsel Mary Oppenheimer was careful to say that whether links constitute campaign intervention is a question of facts and circumstances.[17] Ms. Oppenheimer wrote to the FEC after it issued proposed rules that would not treat links as an expenditure in support of a candidate as long as the party providing the link on its site receives no compensation in return for creating the link.[18] The IRS has requested comments on whether the existence of a link to a political campaign web site would in all or some cases be deemed to violate the prohibition against involvement by § 501(c) corporations in political campaigns.[19] The IRS is expected to provide further guidance in this area in the future; however, because of the absolute prohibition on involvement in political activities, tax-exempt corporations should be extremely careful to avoid any implication of intervention in political campaigns through Internet links.

# Avoiding Copyright and Trademark Infringement

## General Rule

Like other entities, nonprofit corporations should take appropriate steps to safeguard any intellectual property (such as copyrights, trademarks and service marks) developed or owned by the corporation, while ensuring that its activities and those of its employees and agents do not infringe on the intellectual property of others. Thus, it should place copyright symbols and notices as appropriate on original written material, and use trade/service mark symbols and notices wherever such marks are used.

## Internet Applications

### Protection of the nonprofit's copyrights and trademarks on the Internet

If a nonprofit corporation intends to post material that it has developed and copyrighted on its web site, it should also post notices to site visitors that inform them of the copyright status and the corporation's intent to pursue those who violate its copyright. The corporation should also consider providing copyright notices at the bottom of each screen.

The organization should take similar steps to protect its trademarked names and logos, especially if these are highly valued assets. Technological advances are likely to bring improved methods to assist a nonprofit corporation in protecting its trademarks and logos for this purpose; therefore, the nonprofit board should make sure that intellectual property protection mechanisms are periodically evaluated to take advantage of such improvements.

### Avoiding infringement of the copyrights and trademarks of others

The directors of a nonprofit organization should make sure that the corporation's employees and volunteers who engage in Internet activity on behalf of the corporation understand that certain activities, when done on the Internet, may constitute infringement of another organization's copyright or trademark, although an analogous "physical world" activity does not raise infringement issues. For example, whereas clipping a newspaper article from an actual newspaper and posting it on an office bulletin board would not generally be deemed to be copyright infringement, cutting the article electronically from an electronic copy of the paper and posting it on a page of the corporation's web site without proper authorization may well constitute copyright infringement.[20]

# Sales of Goods and Services

## General Rules as Applied to Typical Activities

### Sales in stores or through catalogues, sales tax and foreign business registration requirements

Some nonprofit organizations, such as museums, maintain stores in which goods related to the nonprofit corporation's activities can be purchased. Others sell products through catalogues. Whether the sale of such goods constitutes an unrelated trade or business is generally assessed on an item-by-item basis, with sales of certain items being deemed "related" (and therefore not treated as UBI) and others being "unrelated" (with revenues from such items taxable as UBI). In addition, if there are a substantial amount of sales of products to persons in states other than the state in which the nonprofit is incorporated, the nonprofit may be required to register in such other states as a foreign corporation doing business in the state. Sales to non-U.S. residents may require similar business registration.

In general, such stores are required to collect and remit state and local sales and use taxes on their product sales. State and local sales and use taxes also must be collected and remitted on catalog sales, *if* the seller has a physical presence in the states to which the items are shipped. As a practical matter, a catalog seller may be required to collect and remit such taxes for the states in which it or any of its property is located, and in any state in which its employees or representatives engage in business on its behalf.

## Auctions and trade shows

Many § 501(c)(3) corporations raise money through annual charity auctions. Charities that conduct traditional auctions generally do not pay UBIT on the income they receive from donors, provided that the auction is not "regularly carried on" or the auctioned items are all donated. Similarly, trade organizations (such as the ABA) that are exempt from federal taxation under § 501(c)(6) of the Code may raise money through trade shows that coincide with one or more meetings of the organization's membership. The trade organization receives revenue by renting space to exhibitors and receiving underwriting contributions from corporate sponsors. As with charitable auctions, such trade show revenue is generally not treated as subject to taxation as UBI, since it is not regularly carried on.

## Sales of mailing lists

In contrast to sales of goods or services to supporters and others, many nonprofits raise money through the sale of their mailing lists. The value of such lists may be enhanced if the nonprofit also collects demographic information on its membership. Nonprofits may sell mailing lists only to other nonprofits, or to both nonprofit and for-profit entities. Typically, the sale of mailing lists and membership is taxable as UBI. In addition, states may impose restrictions on sales of mailing lists by nonprofit organizations. However, even if not required by law, to preserve member goodwill, many organizations give their members the opportunity to opt out by requesting that their information not be sold to other organizations.

# Internet Applications

Many nonprofit corporations have begun to take advantage of the Internet's wide range of business opportunities. The descriptions that follow address some of the legal implications of several such opportunities.

## On-line stores

Many nonprofits have established on-line stores or virtual storefronts, through which they sell merchandise and/or services from their web sites. For example, a museum that operates a physical gift shop might also operate an on-line store to allow visitors to its web site to purchase the same merchandise over the Internet. Or, a nonprofit that does *not* also operate a physical store might raise money and promote its visibility by selling books published by the organization over the Internet. In comparison to the overhead needed to maintain a physical store or catalogue operation, the low-overhead costs of maintaining a sales location on the web will enable many more nonprofits to sell goods and services in this fashion.

**UBI issues.**   Just as is the case for physical stores or catalogue sales, a nonprofit organization's revenue from the sale of goods or services over the web will generally be determined to be (nontaxable) related revenue or (taxable) unrelated business income, on an item-by-item basis. Directors of nonprofit corporations selling an extensive array of goods and services over the Internet should make sure that, just as for traditional store and catalogue sales, the nonprofit has an accounting system that tracks sales revenue and UBI status on an item-by-item basis.

**Sales tax issues.**   The state and local sales tax treatment of Internet sales is currently similar to that of catalog sales (described in the section "Sales in Stores..." above), such that sales taxes for Internet sales are generally not required to be collected and paid except in states in which the organization has some form of physical presence. Directors of nonprofit corporations that are selling goods and services over the web will need to stay informed as to how the sales tax debate is resolved to determine what, if any, sales taxes they may be responsible for collecting. While the standards in this area are still evolving, directors should be aware that making Internet sales to buyers located in other states or abroad may expose the corporation to potential tax liability and business regulation in such other jurisdictions. Moreover, if an organization is otherwise subject to sales tax liability (for example, in the jurisdictions in which it has physical locations), it cannot avoid paying such taxes for Internet sales to persons residing in such areas. A good number of states have participated in the Streamlined Sales Tax Project, which has been developing uniform standards and definitions for collection of sales tax, and has approved software from certain vendors to ease the collection burdens on sellers. Information on the model statutes that have been developed and the progress in getting the statutes adopted in various states is available at www.streamlinedsalestax.org.

**Whether Internet sales activity constitutes doing business in a state, requiring registration as a foreign corporation.**    Currently, the law is unclear as to whether reaching a state through the Internet—rather than through physical presence—will cause a nonprofit corporation to be doing business in that state. However, if a nonprofit corporation finds that it is generating significant sales activity in one or more states, it should obtain legal advice regarding whether registration is required in at least those states. Failure to register as a foreign corporation doing business in another state may prevent a corporation from availing itself of legal process against such state's residents, and could result in the imposition of other sanctions.

**Secure payment methods.**    In traditional store and catalogue settings, most individuals assume the security of credit card and other personal information provided in connection with a purchase. Security is still a significant issue in Internet sales transactions, given the possibilities of hacker theft of credit card numbers and other concerns regarding the transmission of one's personal information across the globally linked Internet. Accordingly, a nonprofit corporation engaging in Internet sales transaction should take care to verify that it has appropriate security measures in place to avoid liability from allowing unauthorized access to this information. Such security members should be frequently reviewed and improved as both security technology and hacker capabilities evolve.

### Charity auctions

On-line charity auctions are an increasingly popular means of fund-raising for nonprofits. Some nonprofit organizations administer the auctions themselves, while others rely on an outside provider. As noted above, charities that conduct traditional auctions generally do not pay UBIT on the income they receive from donors, because the auction is not regularly carried on and/or involves the sale of donated items. In contrast, however, many on-line charity auctions may not be held only once or a few times a year; because of the ease of setting up on-line auctions, some nonprofit organizations may hold auctions frequently, such as once a month, or even maintain a continuous auction, with a differing array a products available to be bid upon. Some such auctions, especially those held frequently, may be more likely to include purchased merchandise as well as donated merchandise. If both of these factors are present in on-line auctions conducted by a nonprofit, the revenues from such auctions may be taxable to the organization as UBI.

Even if an on-line auction is held only once a year, nonprofit organizations may encounter UBI issues if, due to unfamiliarity with the Internet environment, they rely on an outside provider to conduct their auctions. If the organization does not retain the primary responsibility for publicity of the auction and otherwise maintain certain controls to ensure that the auction is properly conducted as a fund-raising event for IRS purposes, the auction revenues may treated as UBI.[21]

## Virtual trade shows

Some trade associations have organized on-line virtual trade shows that are modeled on a traditional trade show format. The trade association may rent "display space" on its own site or may simply provide multiple links on its site to the web sites of various vendors, or "virtual exhibitors." Some trade associations sponsor year-round virtual trade shows, while others plan virtual trade shows to coincide with their organizations' regular annual shows. Directors of nonprofit corporations should be aware that although, as noted above, income from traditional trade show activities is generally not subject to tax as UBI, virtual trade shows raise a number of UBI issues. Although the IRS has not yet provided official guidance in this area, the UBI treatment of income from virtual trade shows is likely to depend on whether a trade organization can demonstrate that its on-line activities are substantially similar to those of a traditional trade show. For example, because a traditional trade show is a finite event, it is unlikely that income from a year-round virtual trade show would be excluded from UBI treatment.[22]

## Sale of e-mail addresses and other electronically-gathered information

Just as many nonprofits have found that there is a market for their member/subscriber mailing and other information, nonprofit organization have discovered that they may earn money from the sale of e-mail addresses, and/or other data on supporters that can be mined by other organizations. The sale of e-mail address and the sale and maintenance of other electronically-gathered information raises donor privacy issues. Although many such privacy issues are also present in the non-Internet context, individuals may have greater sensitivity about information that is gathered through Internet communications compared to more traditional means.

Local, state and federal legislators are all in the process of reviewing the need for legislation to protect individual-specific information gathered on-line. While federal law does not currently protect such information, the Federal Trade Commission (FTC) recommends that nonprofits that gather donor information using the Internet establish a policy regarding the privacy of donor information and post it on their web sites. The FTC has developed four "fair information practices," which would require nonprofits to:

(1) notify donors regarding what personal information they are gathering, how it is used, and with whom it will be shared;
(2) offer donors the option of directing that their information not be shared with third parties;
(3) provide donors with information regarding the security measures that protect their information; and
(4) allow donors to access their information, to review and correct it.[23]

Since the public is increasingly concerned with consumer and donor privacy issues, legislators are likely to respond by developing new laws and regulations in this area. (See further discussion of Internet privacy issues in the section "Protecting Electronic Records Information" below.) Directors of nonprofit corporations should consult with legal counsel on a regular basis to ensure that their practices involving donor information are in compliance with changing legal standards.

# Posting Information Returns and Exemption Applications on the Internet

## General Rule

Federal tax law requires tax-exempt organizations to provide copies of their exemption applications and three most recent information returns (Form 990s) to anyone requesting them in person or in writing.[24]

## Internet Application

Tax-exempt organizations can be relieved of the requirement to physically provide copies of their exemption applications and Form 990s if they post these documents on the organization's web site or another site collecting similar applications and returns.[25] The organization must provide the web address where the documents can be found to anyone who asks for it. Organizations electing this web-posting option should be careful to post a return identical to what was filed with the IRS (although confidential information may be excluded to the same extent as for 990s provided to the public by more conventional means). Having the return available on another site, such as www.guidestar.org—which posts all Forms 990 filed with the IRS—will also meet the legal requirement for disclosure, provided that it is a complete and accurate copy of what was filed with the IRS, with the exception of certain donor information on Schedule B of Form 990, which may be kept confidential. Guidestar, which gets copies of all Forms 990 from the IRS and posts them as a matter of course, redacts signatures from the documents to protect against misuse. As a technical matter, the redaction means that the Guidestar version is not a perfect copy of the return filed with the IRS. However, as it contains all the other information someone making a legitimate request could want to see, it should be rare for a nonprofit to encounter someone wanting a return who is not satisfied with what is available on Guidestar.

# Implications of a Nonprofit Corporation Serving as an Information Exchange

## Defamation and Other Torts

### General rule

Any organization may be held liable for defamation or invasion of privacy, based on statements about individuals made by the organization (such as in a publication) or persons associated with the organization (including a non-profit's volunteers).

### Internet applications

**Potential organizational liability from the provision of list serves and chat rooms.**    A nonprofit corporation may determine that its purposes are served by the provision of list serves (electronic mailing lists), chat rooms, and similar technological meeting places, available to organization members or other interested persons. Messages exchanged in such forums have the potential to reach a very large audience. Consequently, there is an increased potential for claims that the content of an individual message is defamatory, invades privacy, or constitutes impermissible political activities. Messages sent through these forums by employees and others who may be seen as agents for the corporation may be attributed to the organization for purposes of these tort claims.

A corporation offering list-servs, chat rooms and other such services may therefore wish to incorporate on-line disclaimers noting that the statements made in such contexts are solely those of the participants and are not endorsed or in any way attributable to the corporation.[26]

**Potential organizational liability from e-mail messages.**    Defamation, privacy and similar concerns are also present in e-mail use by an organization's employees and volunteers. The nonprofit corporation's board should therefore make sure that employees and others using the corporation's e-mail system are regularly reminded about the organization's policy of the appropriate use of e-mail, and to avoid making or distributing offensive or other derogatory remarks or material by e-mail.

## Liability Protection Available by Registration as an Internet Service Provider

The Digital Millennium Copyright Act permits organizations acting as "Internet service providers" to avoid liability for copyright infringement when users post material on a web site the organization maintains.[27] This law defines a "service provider" as "an entity offering the transmission, routing, or providing of connections for digital on-line communications, between or among points specified by a user, of material of the user's choosing, without modification to the content of the material as sent or received."[28] Operating a chat room or other interactive site may cause an organization to be treated as a service provider for purposes of this law even if it does not otherwise provide users with Internet access. To invoke the liability protection available under this law, the organization must register the name of an agent with the Federal Copyright Office (located within the Library of Congress), which is designated to accept complaints from those who believe their copyrights have been infringed on a web site maintained by an Internet service provider.

## Tax Consequences of Providing Internet Access to Others

Providing access to the Internet in exchange for a fee constitutes a trade or business, and unless that business is substantially related to the organization's tax-exempt purpose, the income generated will be subject to federal taxation as UBI. For example, providing Internet access for a fee substantially below cost to community centers in poor neighborhoods may be considered a charitable activity for a § 501(c)(3) organization, rather than an unrelated trade or business, if such activity is related to the organization's charitable purpose.[29] If providing Internet access is the organization's only function, it may qualify for tax-exempt status as an integral part of another exempt organization. Thus, a corporation may serve as an Internet service provider to members of a nonprofit university community and qualify as an integral part of the university, or perhaps as a § 501(c)(12) organization. (The latter category includes rural telephone cooperatives, electric cooperatives, and the like.)

Note: Trade associations should take care before offering Internet access to members. Trade associations violate the requirements for continuing federal income tax exemption if they provide "particular services" to members. The IRS has not yet ruled as to whether providing Internet access to individual account holders qualifies as a particular service. On the other hand, providing a list serve, chat room or web site for exchange of information among association members is unlikely to run afoul of the particular services restriction.[30]

# Protecting Electronic Records Information on Donors and Other Individuals

If a nonprofit organization maintains, in electronic form, medical records, student records, or other records that it is legally bound to keep private, it should verify that effective systems are in place to assure that unauthorized users cannot obtain access to those records through the organization's Internet connections. Because hackers continually become more proficient at finding ways to breach computer-based security systems, the board should require appropriate management personnel to periodically confirm that adequate security measures have been taken to prevent unauthorized access to confidential information of others or of the corporation that is stored in electronic form or transmitted over the Internet. Moreover, the organization should make sure that it keeps abreast of legal requirements relating to the electronic storage and transmission of different kinds of personal information relating to the organization's activities. For example, nonprofit health care providers must now comply with the detailed federal rules issued under the under the Health Insurance Portability and Accountability Act (HIPAA), regarding the disclosure of electronic and other medical records. The Children's Online Privacy Protection Act of 1998 ("COPPA") also provides special rules that apply to web sites that attract children.[31]

See the following checklist (page 128) to review the issues discussed in this chapter.

# Notes

1. See the "Findings of Fact" section of *ACLU v. Reno*, 929 F.Supp, 824, 830-838 (E.D. Pa. 1996), *aff'd*, 521 U.S. 844 (1997), for a helpful description of the creation of the Internet and the operation of the World Wide Web.

2. Approximately forty states and a relatively smaller number of cities and counties require registration of organizations that conduct charitable solicitations in such state or other jurisdiction. *See* Online Compendium, of Federal and State Regulations for U.S Nonprofit Organizations, *Current Controversies: Out of State Solicitation and Regulation*, EFFECT OF EXISTING LAWS AND REGULATIONS, *available at* <http://www.muridac.com/nporegulation>.

3. For a copy of the Unified Registration Statement, see <http://www.nonprofits.org/library/gov/urs>.

4. In March of 2001, the National Association of State Charity Officials (NASCO) approved a set of principles relating to regulation of charitable solicitations over the Internet: *see* <http://www.nasconet.org>. One of the stated premises of these principles (referred to as the "Charleston Principles" since the discussions from which the principles emerged began at the 1999 NASCO annual conference held in Charleston, South Carolina) is that "state charity officials should require registration of those over whom their state courts could constitutionally assert personal jurisdiction to enforce a registration requirement." General Principle I.D.

5. *See* I.R.C. § 170(f)(8).

6. *See* I.R.C. § 6113.

7. *See* Christina Nooney, *Tax Exempt Organizations and the Internet*, 27 EXEMPT ORGANIZA-TION TAX REVIEW 38, at 33-39 (2000).

8. *See* Cheryl Chasin, Susan Ruth, and Robert Harper, *Tax Exempt Organizations and World Wide Web Fundraising and Advertising on the Internet*, IRS EXEMPT ORGANIZATIONS TECHNICAL INSTRUCTION PROGRAM FOR FY 2000, at 139, for a good discussion of individual merchant affiliate programs. *See also* Alice Anderson and Robert Wexler, *Internet Issues for Tax-Exempt Organizations*, JOURNAL OF TAXATION, May 2000.

9. *See* IRS Announcement 2000-84.

10. *See* Anderson and Wexler, *supra* note 8; Nooney, *supra* note 7, at 38-39.

11. *See* I.R.C. § 513(i).

12. *See* Chasin, Ruth, and Harper, *supra* note 8, at 137; Donna Moore and Robert Harper, *Internet Service Providers Exemption Issues Under IRC § 501(c)(3) and § 501(c)(12)*, IRS EXEMPT ORGANIZATIONS TECHNICAL INSTRUCTION PROGRAM FOR FY 1999, 64.

13. In early 2000 the IRS requested comments regarding what constitutes qualified spon-sorship payments in the Internet context. *See Federal Register*, Notice of Proposed Rulemaking (REG-209601-92, March 1, 2000).

14. Prop. Reg. § 1.512-4(f), *Example 8*.

15. *See* Chasin, Ruth, and Harper, *supra* note 8, at 135.

16. See Anderson and Wexler, *supra* note 8, for a good discussion of issues to consider when developing a linkage policy. *See generally*, SUBCOMMITTEE ON INTERACTIVE SERVICES & COMMITTEE ON THE LAW OF COMMERCE IN CYBERSPACE, ABA SECTION OF BUSINESS LAW, WEB-LINKING AGREEMENTS: CONTRACTING STRATEGIES AND MODEL PROVISIONS (American Bar Association, 1997).

17. Letter dated Dec. 3, 2001, reprinted in *Tax Notes Today*, Dec. 19, 2001.

18. *See* Prop. Reg. 11 CFR § 117.2.

19. *See* IRS Announcement 2000-84.

20. A good survey of copyright and trademark issues for nonprofits can be found in MARIA MALARO, A LEGAL PRIMER ON MANAGING MUSEUM COLLECTIONS (Smithsonian Institute Press, 1998).

21. *See* Anderson and Wexler, *supra* note 8; Nooney *supra* note 7, at 37.

22. *See* Anderson and Wexler *supra* note 8; Chasin, Ruth, and Harper, *supra* note 8, at 135-37. *See* IRS Announcement 2000-84.

23. *See Privacy Online: Fair Information Practices in the Electronic Marketplace: A Federal Trade Commission Report to Congress*, May 22, 2000, *available at* <http://www.ftc.gov/privacy>.

24. *See* IRC § 6104(e).

25. *See* IRC § 6104(e)(3); Treas. Reg. § 301.5104(e)-2(b)(2).

26. Thoughtful commentary can be found in Elizabeth deGrazia Blumenfeld, *Privacy Please: Will the Internet Industry Act Protect Consumer Privacy Before the Government Steps In?*, 54 BUS. LAW. 349, 349–83 (1998).

27. Digital Millenium Copyright Act § 202(a), 17 U.S.C. § 512.

28. 17 U.S.C. § 512(k)(1)(A).

29. In a recent Technical Advice Memorandum, the IRS concluded that an Internet Service Provider that gave Internet access solely to low-income people and other § 501(c)(3) organiza-tions for fees set substantially below cost qualified as a § 501(c)(3) organization. TAM 200203069.

30. *See generally* Moore and Harper, *supra* note 12, at 55-66.

31. 15 U.S.C. 6501 et. seq. Details and current releases relating to COPPA can be found at <http://www.ftc.gov/privacy>.

# Suggested Questions for Directors Regarding Supervision of Internet Activities

(1) Does the corporation currently have, or is it considering creating, a web page, or does it engage in other activities using the Internet?

(2) If the corporation engages in fund-raising over the Internet, is it required to register under the charitable solicitation rules or foreign corporation laws of any other state, locality, or non-U.S. jurisdiction?

(3) Does the corporation receive donations from the Internet sites or activities of other entities? Has the corporation's board approved such activities? If other entities are collecting donations on the organization's behalf, are those other entities properly authorized to serve as agents for the organization?

(4) If the corporation has a web site, does its site contain any acknowledgements or advertisements for corporate sponsors? Does the board understand the difference? If it contains advertisements, is there a way those advertisements can be converted to acknowledgments to limit UBIT?

(5) If the corporation is making sales over the Internet, has it investigated any responsibility it has for collecting and paying over sales tax to those states where it has a physical presence or where its customers are located?

(6) If the corporation is making sales over the Internet, are the sales related to its exempt purpose? If not, are the sales regularly carried on? If so, how is the organization handling any UBIT liability?

(7) Has the board evaluated whether and in what manner it may wish to engage in lobbying activities over the Internet? If it chooses to use the Internet for lobbying, has the corporation—if it is a § 501(c)(3)—made an election under IRC § 501(h)? Has it developed policies informed by IRS definitions of lobbying that will allow for strong advocacy while limiting lobbying expenditures? If it chooses to do some lobbying over the Internet, does it have an accounting system in place to gather the data necessary to allocate common costs for things like web site maintenance and web site hosting?

(8) Is the board aware of the distinctions between activity that would constitute permissible public education on broad issues of public policy and democratic engagement, on the one hand, and impermissible involvement in political campaigns, on the other? If the organization intends to engage in activities that may fall into the first category, has the Board developed a web site policy that will help all staff and volunteers produce web site content that will not cross the line and become political campaign intervention?

(9) Has the organization reviewed the copies of its IRS returns that are available on www.guidestar.org to be sure they are accurate?

(10) If the organization uses the Internet to collect information about people, what privacy notices or protections is the organization required to place on its site?

# Checklist: Supervision of Internet Activities

*Note:* For purposes of simplicity in these checklists, we describe a corporation with a chair, who presides over the board of directors; a chief executive, who may be a staff person; an executive committee; a nominating committee; and an audit committee. (However, we recognize that in many smaller and other nonprofits, such committee functions may be performed by either the executive committee or the board as a whole.) We also assume a legal counsel—someone, paid or unpaid, having primary responsibility for the corporation's legal affairs. Many corporations, especially larger nonprofits, may have other committees established for specific purposes, such as reviewing staff performance, fixing compensation, monitoring compliance with legal requirements and periodic review of bylaws.

| Subject | To Be Reviewed By Whom | How Often | Comment |
|---|---|---|---|
| 1. Does the corporation raise money through contributions solicited or received over the Internet? | Chair, chief executive, legal counsel | At least quarterly, with annual reports to the full Board | There are multiple ways of fund raising over the Internet. Despite the relative ease of doing so from a technical and resource perspective, directors need to be aware of the legal implications of such activity. |
| 2. In what states and localities may the corporation be required to register under the charitable solicitation laws as a result of the corporation's Internet fund-raising activity? | Chair, chief executive, legal counsel | At least annually | Application of the charitable solicitation laws to Internet fund raising is not always clear, but standards can be expected to evolve rapidly. Smaller nonprofits lacking the funds to pay registration fees in multiple jurisdictions may take steps to limit the focus of their Internet fund raising to a few or even a single state. |
| 3. Do individuals or entities act as fundraisers or sources of contributions to the corporation? If so, do we understand the legal implications of such activity for the corporation and our donors? | Chair, chief executive, legal counsel | At least annually | If the corporation raises funds through web sites or the assistance of other organizations, the board should ensure that management staff and legal counsel have reviewed the arrangements for compliance with laws governing tax-exempt contributions. |
| 4. Are there acknowledgements or advertisements of for-profit companies on the corporation's web site? | Chair, chief executive, legal counsel | At least annually | The board may request management staff to recommend a policy for sponsor acknowledgments and third-party advertising on the corporation's web site. |

## Checklist: Supervision of Internet Activities *(Continued)*

| Subject | To Be Reviewed By Whom | How Often | Comment |
|---|---|---|---|
| 5. Does the corporation provide links to the web site of for-profit companies, nonprofit advocacy organizations or candidates for political office? Or, are we aware of any such organizations that have links to *our* web site on their site? What legal issues are raised by such links? | Chief executive, chief information officer (CIO) or lead technology staff person | At least annually | If a link on a tax-exempt corporation's web site is determined to constitute involvement in a political campaign or promotion of a candidate for political office, the corporation's tax-exempt status could be threatened. |
| 6. Does the organization engage in lobbying activity over the Internet? If so, does such activity meet the general "insubstantial" test, or if applicable, the standards for organizations that have made the election to have their lobby activity covered by § 501(h) of the Internal Revenue Code? | Chief executive, legal counsel, fund-raising staff | At least annually for report to the full board, with more frequent monitoring at the staff level | Internet lobbying activities may be very cost-effective but directors should be aware that the IRS' position on the appropriate ways to measure such activities is still developing. |
| 7. Are the corporation's copyrights, trade-marks and service marks properly protected on the corporation's web site and through e-mail activities of corporation employees? | Legal counsel, in consultation with lead technology staff person or chief information officer | At least annually | |
| 8. Are copyright restrictions and works by third parties complied with before such works are posted on the corporation's web site? | Legal counsel, in consultation with lead technology staff person or chief information officer | At least annually, and with educational reminders to staff | Staff should be educated regarding use of copyrighted works on the corporation's web site. |

*Continued*

## Checklist: Supervision of Internet Activities *(Continued)*

| Subject | To Be Reviewed By Whom | How Often | Comment |
|---|---|---|---|
| 9. Does the corporation sell goods or services over the Internet? If so; | Chief executive | | |
| a. Have UBI and sales tax issues been examined? | a. Legal counsel | a. Upon inception of any such activity; at least annually thereafter | |
| b. Does such activity require registration as a foreign corporation in any States? | b. Legal counsel | b. Upon inception of any such activity; at least annually thereafter | |
| c. Are the names, credit card numbers and other personal information of customers adequately protected from unauthorized disclosure, or hackers, and does the corporation otherwise comply with applicable privacy laws (and corporation privacy policies) regarding such information? | c. Chief executive, lead technology executive and/or technology consultant staff person | c. Ideally, at least quarterly | |
| 10. Does the corporation make its Form 990s available on its web site or the web site of a Form 990 compiler? | Chair, chief executive | At least annually | If the corporation relies on another organization to list the corporation's 990 on such organization's web site, the corporation should periodically check the accuracy of the posted information. |

## Checklist: Supervision of Internet Activities *(Continued)*

| Subject | To Be Reviewed By Whom | How Often | Comment |
|---|---|---|---|
| 11. Has the corporation taken appropriate steps to limit claims by third parties resulting from: | | At least annually | Defamation claims may be made by individuals or other entities based on comments made in such electronic settings. |
| a. chat rooms or list-servs provided by the corporation? | a. Technology legal counsel | | |
| b. employee e-mail activity? | b. Technology legal counsel | | |
| 12. If the corporation provides chat rooms or list serves, has it registered as an internet service provider? | Chief executive, technology counsel or consultant | When such activities begun; at least annually thereafter | |

# Volunteers

## *Contents*

CHAPTER **7**

# Volunteers

*Many nonprofit corporations find it useful or even essential to use the services of volunteers. The nonprofit director should understand not only how volunteers can be used to enhance the corporation's mission, but also the potential legal issues relating to the use of volunteers.*

The use of volunteers by nonprofit corporations is very prevalent. In some circumstances, use of volunteers is essential to implementation of the corporate purpose, especially when the nonprofit corporation simply does not have the resources to perform its services without volunteers. In many cases, use of volunteers is itself demonstrative of the corporation's mission. The board should periodically evaluate what part volunteers should play in the corporation. For example, is there a role or need for volunteers in implementing a new program or service? Are there services that volunteers might provide that would enhance the corporation's fulfillment of its mission and involve more of the nonprofit's community in the nonprofit's activities? If so, what are the legal implications of using volunteers?

## Volunteers Are Agents of the Corporation for Whose Acts the Corporation May Be Liable

Volunteers working on behalf of a nonprofit corporation are agents of the nonprofit corporation in the eyes of the law. That is, their acts or omissions and their care or negligence in performance of their activities as volunteers are, within limits, considered to be the acts or omissions of the nonprofit corporation. *As a general rule, the nonprofit corporation will not be exonerated from liability arising from the conduct of the agent simply because the organization is a nonprofit corporation or because the agent was uncompensated or a volunteer.*

Nonprofit corporations can be and are held responsible for the actions of their volunteers and are expected, within reason, to foresee and address the risks associated with the use of volunteers. The potential risks include situations in which a volunteer is used to represent the nonprofit corporation to the public or in providing services consistent with the organization's purposes—for example, a program in which the nonprofit corporation sends volunteers into homes to provide services, uses volunteers to work in a position of trust with vulnerable individuals such as minors or the developmentally disabled, or uses volunteers to drive or to perform other potentially dangerous activities.

# Minimizing the Liability of the Corporation Due to Acts of a Volunteer

Because of the potential for liability involved in the use of volunteers, the non-profit corporation should develop standards, guidelines and procedures for the use of volunteers rather than enlisting the assistance of volunteers on a random or sporadic basis. This does not mean that there must be a large number of staff devoted to development and administration of a volunteer program. Rather, the decision to use and the use of volunteers should include an evaluation of the requirements for each volunteer position and written standards for selection, training, and supervision of the organization's volunteers.

## Selection of volunteers: written standards

Nonprofit corporations should develop written standards for the selection of volunteers. Depending on the nature of the volunteer position, the standards for selection may include education, experience, training requirements, consideration of the volunteer's ability to commit time to the position, and the volunteer's suitability for the particular position, such as working with children. The non-profit corporation should then use these standards to verify a volunteer's suitability for the position. This can include requiring a written volunteer application form, personal interview, background check, driving record, reference check, or other method to verify that the volunteer is an appropriate individual for the position. If a criminal or other background check is determined to be necessary for a volunteer position, the nonprofit corporation should obtain a signed release from the applicant authorizing the nonprofit corporation to obtain the necessary information from the appropriate agencies. The board should consult with legal counsel in preparing the release form.

## Oversight of volunteer activities: policies and procedures

The nonprofit corporation should develop written materials for the training and supervision of volunteers. Such materials may include written procedures, policies or guidelines for a volunteer to use when acting on behalf of the nonprofit corporation. The nonprofit corporation should provide any volunteer with clear directions and sufficient training. Development of written policies and procedures is important because a nonprofit corporation may be directly liable for its own conduct if a volunteer injures a third party due to the corporation's inadequate training or supervision of the volunteer.

## Insurance

The board should make sure that the nonprofit corporation is covered by the corporation's insurance for the activities of its volunteers. For example, if a nonprofit corporation is engaged in the distribution of goods or services involving the volunteer's use of his or her own automobile, the corporation may be liable for injuries caused by the volunteer's negligent driving of that automobile, even though the nonprofit corporation does not own the automobile or pay the driver.

The nonprofit corporation's insurance policies should be reviewed and modified, if necessary, to ensure that they cover the potential liability of the nonprofit corporation due to the conduct of a volunteer. *Such coverage is not automatic*, and may be an issue under several types of coverage, such as the corporation's general liability insurance and directors and officers insurance. Some insurance policies specifically address the unique organizational aspects and activities of nonprofit corporations, including volunteer activities. It is good practice to review all policies with legal counsel or an insurance broker experienced in working with nonprofit insurance issues, to confirm that the activities of the organization and its agents are properly insured.

# Protection of the Volunteer from Individual Liability

Volunteers may also be sued individually for injuries they cause while acting in a volunteer capacity. The nonprofit corporation should consider what it should do to protect its volunteers in such situations.

## Statutes Protecting Volunteers

Most states have volunteer protection statutes limiting the liability of volunteers. Although the scope of the protection differs somewhat from state to state, most states provide at least some degree of immunity from civil liability for a volunteer if the volunteer acts within the scope of the volunteer's duties, in good faith, and the injury is not caused by the willful or wanton conduct of the volunteer.[1] There is also a federal Volunteer Protection Act, passed in 1997, which provides some liability protection for volunteers of a nonprofit organization or governmental agency. In general, under the federal statute, a volunteer will not be held liable for harm caused by the volunteer, if the volunteer was acting within the scope of his or her responsibilities, the volunteer was properly licensed or certified (if appropriate or required), the harm was not caused by the volunteer's willful or criminal conduct, gross negligence or reckless conduct, and the harm was not caused by the volunteer operating a vehicle for which the operator must have a license or that must be insured.[2] The federal statute preempts state law to the extent that it is inconsistent with the federal statute unless the state law provides additional protection from liability relating to volunteers. *The board of directors should make sure it understands the scope of available state and federal statutory protection for volunteers by consulting with legal counsel knowledgeable in the area.* To the extent (which is often substantial) that such statutes do not provide complete protection, the board should evaluate whether the corporation has adequate insurance coverage for volunteer activities. The board should also consider alerting volunteers to the potential need for personal insurance coverage for their own activities. (See further discussion in the section "Insurance for Volunteers" below.)

## Insurance for Volunteers

A volunteer should examine whether his or her individual insurance may cover any injury that the volunteer causes while acting as a volunteer. The board should make sure that, if possible, the corporation's volunteers are insured under its insurance policies, that is, the policy covers not only the corporation's liability for the acts of its volunteers, but also directly covers the volunteer. Special insurance riders or policies may be required to insure volunteers for a special occasion or fundraising event, such as a walkathon, run or other event. In such circumstances, an insurer may require that the corporation obtain a waiver and release of liability from the volunteers for the event.

## Indemnification of Volunteers

The board should examine whether it can, or should, include volunteers within any provision for indemnification for liability under the corporation's articles of incorporation or bylaws. Typically, indemnification provisions are contained in state nonprofit corporation acts. Such provisions generally *require* indemnification of directors in certain circumstances, but merely *permit* indemnification of agents—such as volunteers.[3] The board should review its articles of incorporation and bylaws to determine whether they address indemnification of volunteers. For instance, it is not unusual to find that the indemnification provisions of a nonprofit corporation's bylaws mandate that the corporation "shall" provide indemnification to the "fullest extent permitted by law". While the scope of such required indemnification may be limited to officers and directors, it may also specifically apply to the corporation's "agents"—a category most volunteers would presumably fit within. Before broadening the corporation's indemnification obligations to include volunteers, the board should assess the corporation's actual financial ability to indemnify volunteers and whether the corporation's obligation to indemnify its volunteers could be broader than its insurance coverage, potentially requiring the corporation to dip into its own assets to fulfill such indemnity obligations.

# Potential Claims by Volunteers against the Corporation

Use of volunteers may expose the nonprofit corporation to claims by the volunteer against the corporation. These can include a claim that the individual is an employee, not a volunteer, and therefore is entitled to compensation and benefits. This can also include a claim for compensation for injuries suffered while acting as a volunteer.

## Volunteer or Employee?

As discussed in Chapter 8, "Employees," nonprofit corporations are subject to most state and federal statutes that address employer responsibilities and liabilities. Consequently, it is important for a nonprofit corporation to be sure it is appropriately categorizing individuals as employees or volunteers. An individual's status as a volunteer rather than an employee may sometimes be difficult to establish. If an individual volunteers on a consistent basis for a nonprofit organization in a position that is similar to a paid position at the organization, under certain circumstances such person may be considered, or claim to be, an employee of the nonprofit corporation and therefore entitled to compensation and other benefits.

To avoid this possibility, the nonprofit corporation should periodically review the activities of its volunteers and the benefits they receive to evaluate whether some volunteers might be considered employees rather than volunteers under the law. For example, under the Fair Labor Standards Act, an individual is prohibited from volunteering to do the same work that he or she is paid to do by the same employer; that is, a nonprofit corporation cannot ask its paid staff to "volunteer" part of their time to the organization. Beyond this rule, the corporation should focus on such factors as whether the volunteer is doing the same work that some of the corporation's employees are being paid to do or that similar organizations often use paid staff to perform—and if so, if the volunteer is being paid or is receiving other financial or other benefits, such as meals, shelter, stipends, insurance, medical benefits, a savings or retirement plan or credit towards the volunteer's degree, or if the volunteer is volunteering solely for a civic, charitable or humanitarian reason. If the answers to these questions raise the possibility that a volunteer may be considered an employee (i.e., one who performs work for compensation), the board or chief executive should consult with legal counsel to review the volunteer's status.

## Employment Laws and the Volunteer

If volunteers are compensated for their efforts in a manner that makes them look more like employees, the nonprofit corporation may be subject to the minimum wage and overtime requirements of the Fair Labor Standards Act or a similar state law, federal or state discrimination statutes, and requirements regarding payment of employee benefits. For a discussion of issues that may arise with respect to employees of nonprofit corporations, see Chapter 8, "Employees."

Even though equal employment opportunity laws may not apply to volunteers, the board should consider whether to adhere to the principles discussed below in the selection, supervision and termination of its employees for its volunteers. Using a structured procedure for selection and screening of volunteers replaces a potentially arbitrary process with a fair and defensible method. Similarly, consistent application of performance and evaluation criteria for termination of volunteers will help prevent not only mistakes and hard feelings, but also potential discrimination complaints (whether or not valid).

## Obtaining a Waiver and Release of Liability from a Volunteer, and Workers' Compensation Insurance

Many nonprofit corporations may use volunteers for events or in situations that present a particular risk of harm to the volunteer, such as volunteering for a race or other outdoor event. Volunteers also may be injured by other volunteers or employees of the nonprofit corporation. Unlike an employee covered by workers' compensation, the volunteer, if injured, may be able to sue the nonprofit corporation for injuries that occur while acting as a volunteer. To address such risks, the nonprofit corporation should consider whether to include the volunteer in the corporation's workers' compensation insurance, if possible, or obtain a written waiver and release of liability from the volunteer before permitting him or her to participate in the nonprofit corporation's activities. One potential problem in seeking a waiver and release is practical, in that volunteers may not be willing to serve if required to sign a release.

Workers' compensation laws vary from state to state. In some states particular volunteers are covered by workers' compensation by statute; for example, in Colorado, volunteer firefighters for a municipal entity are automatically covered. Some workers' compensation laws may permit a nonprofit to elect to include volunteers in its existing workers' compensation insurance. One risk of including a volunteer in the workers' compensation insurance is the possibility that the volunteer would be considered an employee for other purposes. Again, this is an area in which the board should consult legal counsel in deciding how to address the organization's potential liability to its volunteers for injuries to the volunteer.

# Ownership of Materials Created by a Volunteer for the Nonprofit Corporation

To the extent that volunteers are creating written curricula, videotapes, audiotapes, printed publications, photographs, or other works for the nonprofit corporation, care should be taken to make sure that the nonprofit corporation is the owner of the work (with all rights to the work product) or that it obtains a license sufficient for its uses of the work. Therefore, *before* any works are produced, the nonprofit corporation should require any volunteer who produces work that would be protected under copyright laws to sign a statement that the work is "for hire" and owned by the nonprofit corporation or to provide a license or assignment to the organization. (See the section "Works for Hire: Whose Property Is It?" in Chapter 8, "Employees.")

See the following checklist (page 144) to review the issues discussed in this chapter.

## Notes

1. For example, in Colorado, the statute does not provide protection for the negligent act of a volunteer involving the operation of a motor vehicle. In Utah, the statute does not apply if the nonprofit organization fails to provide a financially secure source of recovery for individuals injured by the volunteer.

2. The federal statute does not apply to conduct that constitutes a crime of violence, an act of international terrorism, a hate crime, a sexual offense, or a violation of a federal or state civil rights law; or that occurred when the defendant was under the influence of drugs or alcohol.

3. *See* Model Act, § 8.56.

# Suggested Questions for Directors Regarding Volunteers

(1) Do I know which of the nonprofit corporation's programs use volunteers?

(2) How were they recruited?

(3) Do I understand what functions they perform?

(4) Do written guidelines, standards, or procedures exist for the nonprofit corporation's selection of volunteers?

(5) Is there a training program in place for the nonprofit corporation's volunteer programs?

(6) Do the corporation's insurance policies cover claims against the corporation based on acts of its volunteers?

(7) Do the corporation's insurance policies cover the volunteers individually?

(8) Do the corporation's insurance policies cover claims against the corporation by a volunteer?

(9) Do the corporation's articles of incorporation or bylaws require indemnification of volunteers?

　　a. If they do, should they?

　　b. If they don't, should they?

(10) Have the corporation's volunteer positions been reviewed to evaluate whether they may be employees instead of volunteers?

(11) Should the corporation require that its volunteers sign a waiver and release of liability for claims arising from the volunteer's activities for the corporation?

(12) Should the corporation obtain workers' compensation insurance for its volunteers?

# Checklist: Volunteers

*Note:*   For purposes of simplicity in these checklists, we describe a corporation with a chair, who presides over the board of directors; a chief executive, who may be a staff person; an executive committee; a nominating committee; and an audit committee. (However, we recognize that in many smaller and other nonprofits, such committee functions may be performed by either the executive committee or the board as a whole.) We also assume a legal counsel—someone, paid or unpaid, having primary responsibility for the corporation's legal affairs. Many corporations, especially larger nonprofits, may have other committees established for specific purposes, such as reviewing staff performance, fixing compensation, monitoring compliance with legal requirements and periodic review of bylaws.

| Subject | To Be Reviewed By Whom | How Often | Comment |
|---|---|---|---|
| 1. Does our corporation have a volunteer program? | Chief executive, full board | Annually, or at inception of new program | Volunteer programs should be formally approved by the board. |
| 2. Are its functions defined in the corporate resolutions? | Chief executive, full board | Annually, or at inception of new program | Volunteer programs should be formally approved by the board. |
| 3. Who administers the program at staff level? | Chief executive | As needed, but reviewed annually | |
| 4. Are volunteers properly screened when selected? | Chief executive, legal counsel | As needed, but reviewed annually | |
| 5. Is volunteer training adequate so that volunteers can competently perform their tasks? | Chief executive | As needed, but reviewed annually | |
| 6. Are the volunteers covered by the corporation's insurance program? | Chief executive, legal counsel | Annually | Directors should understand that the inclusion of volunteers is not automatic. |
| 7. Are they subject to indemnification under the corporation's resolutions and bylaws concerning indemnification? | Chief executive, legal counsel | Annually | Directors should understand that the inclusion of volunteers is not automatic. |
| 8. Do volunteers perform functions giving rise to significant risk such as driving automobiles on the corporation's business? | Chief executive, legal counsel | Annually | It may be prudent to examine volunteer's driving record, and personal auto insurance coverage. |

## Checklist: Volunteers *(Continued)*

| Subject | To Be Reviewed By Whom | How Often | Comment |
|---|---|---|---|
| 9. Are volunteers covered by the corporation's workers compensation insurance? Can they be? Should they be? | Chief executive, legal counsel | Annually | |
| 10. Do any volunteers receive compensation or benefits, such that they should be classified as an employee rather than a volunteer (and to whom the Fair Labor Standards Acts and other laws applicable to employees would apply)? | Legal counsel | Annually, or at inception of a new program | |

CHAPTER **8**

# Employees

## Contents

# Employees

*Most nonprofit corporations employ staff to assist in carrying out the mission and activities of the corporation. The nonprofit director should have a basic understanding of the legal risks relating to employees and responsibilities of the corporation to its employees.*

Although small nonprofit corporations may rely solely on volunteers to accomplish their missions, most nonprofit corporations employ paid staff to carry out at least some of these activities. The size of the staff can vary from a single part-time employee in a small, grassroots organization to a staff of a hundred or a thousand full-time employees. All nonprofit corporations generally must comply with federal and state laws regarding employees, although some legal requirements may vary depending on the number of employees. Nonprofit corporations often have the employment relationship with the chief executive defined by a formal contract. Directors should be aware of the terms of that contract and the law applicable to that employment relationship. The board of directors may also approve policies and employment terms applicable to other employees. In addition, because a significant number of the lawsuits generally brought against nonprofit directors and officers involve employment-related matters, it is important for directors to have a basic understanding of the range of legal requirements and potential liabilities that may arise in connection with employees. This chapter will outline some of the considerations and general legal requirements for nonprofit corporations who hire employees.

# Executive Employment Relationships

## Chief Executives and Other Management Employees

Nonprofit corporations commonly hire a chief executive, often called an executive director, who is responsible for day-to-day operations of the organization, including hiring and supervision of other staff. The chief executive reports directly to the board of directors.

## Executive Employment Agreements

Board members, or a committee of the board, typically will define, negotiate, and approve the chief executive's contract. Especially if the executive works directly with clients or the public, the board may want to conduct a background check before the initial hiring of an executive or approval of the contract. The executive's employment agreement should outline job responsibilities, compensation, and benefits (including any performance incentives) and contain termination provisions.

## Evaluation of Chief Executive

The board should establish a process for annual performance reviews of the chief executive. This process, which may be done by a committee of the board, should be designed to give the board sufficient information to evaluate the chief executive's contribution to the organization. For instance, the evaluation process might include interviews with clients or other constituencies served by the nonprofit corporation, interviews with other staff, and review of objective measures of the organization (e.g. budget, membership numbers, etc.)

# Employment Laws Applicable to Nonprofit Corporations

Generally, nonprofit corporations are subject to the same federal and state laws as other employers. These laws include statutes regarding equal employment opportunity, wage and hour issues, employee benefits, workers' compensation, and unemployment insurance. Nonprofit corporations are also subject to common law claims such as breach of contract or negligence. Because many of these laws apply to corporations with just one employee, even the smallest nonprofit corporations should have a staff member, counsel or other adviser who is responsible for and familiar with human resources issues, including all such laws applicable to the corporation. Likewise, legal counsel for the nonprofit corporation should review employment policies and practices for compliance with applicable law.

# Federal Equal Employment Opportunity Laws

Several *federal* statutes prohibit discrimination based upon a particular status. As set forth below, these statutes apply to nonprofit corporations that employ at least a specified minimum number of employees.

| Statute: | Prohibits discrimination based on: | Applies to corporations with at least: |
|---|---|---|
| Title VII of the Civil Rights Act of 1964 | Race, gender, national origin, religion[1] | 15 or more employees |
| Americans with Disabilities Act | Disability or perceived disability | 15 or more employees |
| Age Discrimination in Employment Act | Age (over 40) | 15 or more employees |
| Equal Pay Act | Discrimination with regard to compensation based on gender | No minimum number of employees |
| Immigration Reform and Control Act | National origin or citizenship | 4 or more employees |
| Pregnancy Discrimination Act | Pregnancy or childbirth | 15 or more employees |

Nonprofit corporations that are subject to these federal statutes may not discriminate in hiring, compensation, working conditions, promotion, discipline, termination or other employment practices. Boards of nonprofits that are not subject to some of the above laws (at least given current employee numbers) may nevertheless choose to adopt policies that conform to such laws. Even if not legally required, such policies will serve to prevent inadvertent violations when the number of employees increases, as well as discriminatory incidents that could result in public embarrassment, even if not legally actionable.

# Reasonable Accommodation for Disabilities

The Americans with Disabilities Act (ADA), mandates the giving of "equal opportunity" to persons with disabilities, by requiring an employer (whether nonprofit or for-profit) to provide "reasonable accommodation" to employees with disabilities.

"Reasonable accommodation" under the ADA may require

(a)  making existing facilities used by employees readily accessible to and usable by individuals with disabilities; and

(b)  job restructuring, part-time or modified work schedules, reassignment to a vacant position, acquisition or modification of equipment or devices, appropriate adjustment or modifications of examinations, training materials or policies, the provision of qualified readers or interpreters, and other similar accommodations for individuals with disabilities.[2]

Nonprofit corporations that also serve as public accommodations (schools, theaters, libraries, hospitals, etc.) likely will have additional responsibilities to provide equal access and reasonable accommodations to members of the public with disabilities.

## State and Local Equal Opportunity Laws

In addition to federal law, nonprofit corporations usually are subject to state or local equal employment opportunity laws that may impose the same or additional requirements. For example, some state laws parallel the federal requirements, but apply to employers of all sizes—*regardless of the number of employees*. Other state and local statutes and ordinances may prohibit discrimination based on a status, such as sexual orientation, not covered by federal law. However, as under federal law, state laws may provide certain exemptions for religious corporations with respect to laws prohibiting employment discrimination based on religion.

## Equal Opportunity Policies

To formalize commitment to equal employment opportunity and comply with relevant laws, nonprofit organizations should adopt a formal equal opportunity policy. This equal employment opportunity policy should be approved by the board of directors and comply with all relevant law. The policy should state the organization's commitment to equal employment opportunity, provide a procedure for reporting any alleged discrimination, and prohibit retaliation against anyone who makes a report or complaint. Once approved, the policy should be posted publicly and distributed to staff. The board should review such policy on an annual basis, and confirm that the policy conforms to current legal requirements.

# Anti-Harassment Policies

In addition to an equal employment opportunity policy, boards of directors of nonprofit corporations should adopt an anti-harassment policy for the corporation. Under certain circumstances, employers who have such a policy may be able to assert an affirmative defense to liability based upon the existence of a written policy and a victim's failure to make a complaint under it. This policy should contain a statement that harassment will not be permitted, a complaint procedure for victims or others to report harassment, and a prohibition of retaliation. The policy should be expressly applicable to both employees and volunteers.

# Family and Medical Leave

Under the federal Family and Medical Leave Act of 1993 (FMLA), nonprofit corporations with fifty or more employees are required to provide twelve weeks of unpaid leave for qualified employees upon the birth or adoption of a child, or if the employee or a family member has a serious health condition. The organization must maintain the employee's position and benefits during the leave. Some states have their own laws regarding family and medical leave that may place additional burdens on employers, including nonprofit organizations. *Nonprofit corporations that are subject to FMLA and/or state leave statutes should enact a family and medical leave policy that complies with all applicable statutes and regulations.* In addition, if the nonprofit corporation is subject to FMLA, strict notice and record keeping requirements apply.

# Wage and Hour Issues: Fair Labor Standards Act

Many nonprofit organizations are subject to the federal Fair Labor Standards Act (FLSA), which requires that employers pay at least the federal minimum wage and provide overtime pay (one and one-half the regular rate of pay) to non-exempt employees who work over forty hours in a single work week.

## Does the FLSA apply?

FLSA applies to hospitals, schools, and other organizations engaged in interstate or foreign commerce or in the production of goods for commerce, either directly or indirectly through one or more affiliates.[3]

Nonprofit organizations are *not* exempted automatically from coverage under the FLSA, even if they have no obvious commercial activities. Moreover, some kinds of organizations, such as those that operate hospitals, schools and similar institutions, are covered by the FLSA irrespective of whether they are "engaged in interstate commerce." Other nonprofits are subject to the FLSA if they meet two tests: first, they have two or more employees engaged in commerce or in the production of goods for commerce, or employees handling, selling, or otherwise working on materials that have been moved in or produced for commerce by any person"; and second, they have an annual gross volume of sales of $500,000 or more.

Whether a nonprofit corporation is "engaged in commerce" or "the production of goods for commerce" as defined by FLSA will depend on the activities of it and its affiliates. When a nonprofit engages in a commercial activity of any kind it is considered a business purpose, which makes it subject to the FLSA, just as a for-profit commercial entity would be. Neither tax-exempt status nor charitable purposes render an otherwise commercial activity exempt from coverage. For example, fraternal orders and country clubs are considered to be operated for a business purpose, and thereby subject to the FLSA, despite their nonprofit status. On the other hand, religious and other nonprofit corporations may escape FLSA coverage if they solely engage in nonprofit activities, or only use volunteers for their commercial activities.

With regard to the requirement that the commercial activities be "interstate," this definition has been applied broadly to a wide variety of activities, including the use of supplies produced in another state.

Because courts and the Department of Labor are likely to strain to make FLSA apply and because it is a prudent business practice to pay minimum wage and overtime to non-exempt employees, *many nonprofit organizations may find it wise to comply with FLSA, even if a plausible argument can be made that it does not apply.* A nonprofit board should make sure that the organization has received legal advice before concluding that it need not comply with the provisions of the FLSA, if it otherwise meets the coverage description set forth above.

### Exempt employees under the FLSA

Even if a nonprofit corporation is subject to the FLSA, not all of its employees are covered by the act. FLSA exemptions apply to certain executive, administrative, and professional employees who are compensated on a salary basis and whose job functions meet the tests set forth in the FLSA. Special care should be given to classifying an employee as "exempt" or "non-exempt," since a disgruntled former employee may challenge his or her classification after the fact, demanding overtime and penalties from the nonprofit corporation.

## State Wage and Hour Laws

In addition to federal law (and even if the nonprofit is not subject to FLSA), most states have wage and hour laws that apply to nonprofit organizations. These laws may impose additional burdens such as a state minimum wage, requiring over-time pay for all hours over twelve worked in a single workday, payment for unused vacation pay upon termination, compensation for on-call or sleep time (also covered by FLSA), and payment of expenses related to uniforms.

# Employee Handbooks and Personnel Policies

Nonprofit boards of directors often approve employee handbooks. Commonly, employee handbooks are a collection of policies ranging from attendance, to benefits, to compensation, to workplace violence. An employee handbook that does not contain conspicuous disclaimer language may be considered a contract that alters the otherwise "at-will" nature of employment.[4] For example, language in a handbook regarding progressive discipline, termination procedures (e.g. defining "for cause"), or even broad promises of "fair treatment" may change this status. An employee who is terminated might use the handbook as the basis for a breach of contract claim, arguing that the organization is bound to use progressive discipline procedures outlined in the employee handbook. To avoid these results, consideration should be given to introductory language that states the purpose of the handbook. A prominent disclaimer that states that the handbook does not alter the "at-will" nature of employment should also be included. The board of directors should make sure that legal counsel familiar with employment-law issues reviews the handbook or policies before they are approved and distributed to staff.

## Grievance Procedures

Some nonprofit corporations have grievance procedures (often contained in the employee handbook) in which officials in the organization (such as the chief executive) or the board may hear and rule upon employee grievances with management. These grievances most typically involve adverse actions taken against an employee such as discipline, denial of promotion or termination. Boards should decide whether or not to have such policies—since the existence of a grievance procedure or other appeal process, like a progressive discipline policy in an employee handbook, may be deemed to alter the "at-will" status of employees. If the board decides to have a grievance procedure that includes review of an employment action by the board, board members should make sure they understand their role in the grievance process and whether the board's decision is binding or merely advisory.

## Workplace Violence

As part of an employee handbook or as a separate stand-alone policy, it is recommended that a nonprofit corporation have an anti-violence policy that prohibits violence and weapons on the premises or any place where activities of the corporation may be conducted. Such a policy will also assist the organization to comply with Occupational Health and Safety Administration (OSHA) rules requiring a safe workplace.

# Employee Benefits

Nonprofit boards of directors often approve employee benefit plans to be offered to the organization's employees. Such plans include retirement and deferred compensation plans, welfare benefit plans (health, disability, life insurance, etc.), and various fringe benefit arrangements. Directors should make sure they are informed regarding the duties and liability exposure created by such plans. Some key issues relating to employee benefit plans are discussed below.

## Reasonable Compensation

The value of employee benefit plans must be considered part of an employee's overall compensation in determining whether an employee is receiving reasonable compensation for services. If the value of a key employee's total compensation package is less than what similar organizations provide, the corporation may be in danger of losing the employee. On the other hand, an overly generous benefits package may, when combined with the employee's salary, raise private benefit/inurement concerns for tax-exempt organizations (see the discussion in the section "Limitations on Private Benefit and Private Inurement" in Chapter 4, "Taxation"). With respect to § 501(c)(3) and § 501(c)(4) tax-exempt organizations, this is especially important in avoiding the excise tax on excess benefit transactions that can be imposed both on recipients and responsible organization managers under the IRS's intermediate sanctions powers (discussed in the section "Intermediate Sanctions: Excise Tax on Public Charities' Excess Benefit Transactions" in Chapter 4, "Taxation").

## ERISA Requirements

Most types of employee benefit plans are subject to the requirements of the Employee Retirement Income Security Act of 1974, as amended (ERISA), unless the plan is one adopted by a church or governmental plan exempt from ERISA and, in the case of a church plan, the organization has not elected to be governed by ERISA. ERISA imposes a number of reporting and disclosure requirements, creates certain minimum rights for plan participants, and imposes numerous fiduciary responsibilities. The employer organization, and under certain circumstances one or more of its employees, officers, or board members, is typically viewed as a fiduciary with respect to the plan. In addition, for certain employee benefits that are intended to receive favorable tax treatment, there are a number of technical requirements under the Code that must be satisfied, including rules intended to prevent discrimination in favor of highly compensated employees.

## Plan Documents

Most types of employee benefit plans must be maintained pursuant to written plan documents. Such documents should be carefully reviewed by the human resources manager or an outside benefits expert, to ensure that they reflect the actual practices for operating the employee benefit plans and that they satisfy the technical requirements of ERISA and the Code.

## Special Rules for Nonprofits

Employee benefits offered by tax-exempt organizations are subject to some special rules, particularly with respect to retirement and deferred compensation plans.

### Tax deferral arrangements

Unlike taxable organizations, tax-exempt organizations are somewhat more limited in the amount of tax-deferred compensation that can be offered to the organization's executives or other key employees. Although the restrictions on tax-deferred compensation arrangements were significantly loosened beginning in 2002, tax-exempt organizations are still subject to certain maximum amounts (generally, $11,000 in 2002, increasing to $15,000 in 2006) of deferred compensation that can be provided in any year to an employee, pursuant a non-qualified plan that is an "eligible deferred compensation plan" within the meaning of Code § 457(b). Such limits are now in addition to—and are no longer offset against—any amounts that such employee has elected to defer under the organization's 401(k) or 403(b) plan. If a tax-exempt organization desires to provide any additional deferred compensation beyond the new § 457(b) limits, such compensation must be subject to a "substantial risk of forfeiture" as determined under Code § 457(f).

Directors of tax-exempt organizations should make sure that their organization has taken advantage of recent liberalizations in the tax-deferred compensation rules. Such changes may make it easier for tax-exempt organizations to attract and retain qualified executives, by lessening the difference between the kind of deferred compensation arrangements that can be offered by tax-exempt corporations compared to those provided by for-profit organizations.

### Section 403(b) and Section 401(k) plans

Tax-sheltered annuity or mutual fund custodial account arrangements described in § 403(b) may only be offered by tax-exempt organizations described in § 501(c)(3). Other types of nonprofit organizations cannot contribute to § 403(b) plans. Previously, nonprofit corporations were not permitted to maintain § 401(k) plans; however, nonprofits are now permitted to offer such plans to their employees.

# Other Laws Relating to Nonprofit Corporation Employees

## Tax Withholding and Payroll Taxes

Nonprofit corporations are also required to comply with state and federal laws regarding tax withholding and payment of payroll taxes. Directors, especially director/officers, may be personally liable for any unpaid taxes or penalties if they are found to be responsible for the unpaid taxes.[5] In comparison, volunteer nonprofit directors who do not participate in day-to-day or financial operations, and who have no responsibility for the payment of payroll taxes and no knowledge of the failure to pay payroll taxes, would generally not be liable for unpaid payroll taxes and any accompanying penalty.

## Workers' Compensation and Unemployment Insurance

Nonprofit corporations with employees are subject to state laws regarding workers' compensation and unemployment insurance. These laws vary from state to state, but typically, a nonprofit organization, like any other employer, is responsible for obtaining insurance for on-the-job injuries (workers' compensation) or the effects of terminating employees (unemployment). In some states, nonprofit corporations may elect to self-insure for unemployment compensation claims; in such cases, the nonprofit does not make standard state unemployment tax payments, but pays its share of actual unemployment claims. Further, many states specifically exempt churches from unemployment insurance obligations. Board approval of workers' compensation insurance policies is recommended if the policies would be material to the corporation, unless the board has delegated such approval to the corporation's chief executive or other managerial personnel.

## Immigration Laws

The Immigration Reform and Control Act of 1986 (IRCA) prohibits the employment of unauthorized aliens (i.e., non-citizens who are not authorized by the Immigration and Naturalization Service to work in this country). IRCA applies to nonprofit corporations and places administrative burdens on nonprofit corporations to verify that all employees are authorized to work in the United States. IRCA also has non-discrimination provisions that prohibit discrimination on the basis of national origin or citizenship.

## Work for Hire: Whose Property Is It?

To the extent that employees, volunteers, or third parties are creating curricula, videotapes, audio tapes, printed publications, photographs, or other works for the nonprofit corporation, care should be taken to make sure that the nonprofit corporation is the owner (with all rights to the work product) or that it obtains a license sufficient for its uses of the work. Original works of authorship authored by an employee are deemed to be authored and owned by the employer if the work was prepared by the employee within the scope of his or her employment. On the other hand, work done by an independent party, or an employee working outside the scope of his or her employment, is deemed to be authored and owned by the original author unless the parties expressly agree, in a signed writing executed *prior* to the work's creation, that the work shall be considered a work made for hire.

## Confidential Information

The nonprofit corporation should also exercise care to protect its confidential and proprietary information. Employees, volunteers, and others may have access to trade secrets or confidential information such as donor or member lists, personnel information, medical records, patient or client information or other data or materials that must be kept confidential. The nonprofit corporation should adopt a confidentiality policy and should take reasonable precautions (such as passwords, limited distribution, stamping materials "CONFIDENTIAL") to protect against unauthorized dissemination of the organization's confidential information.

# Liability to Others for Acts of Employees

## Negligent Hiring and Supervision Claims

Negligent hiring and negligent supervision are typically raised by clients or members of the public who allege they have been injured by an employee (such as a child who is allegedly sexually abused by a daycare worker) and claim that the corporation failed to properly screen the employee before hiring, or to supervise him or her once hired. To avoid such claims, and as a prudent business practice, the corporation should screen candidates for employment, especially if they work with children or other vulnerable populations. Likewise, systems should be in place to monitor and supervise employees. (Similar issues apply to volunteers who work independently with the public or vulnerable groups; see the discussion in the section "Volunteers Are Agents of the Corporation for Whose Acts the Corporation May Be Liable" in Chapter 7, "Volunteers.")

# Liability to Employees

## Wrongful Discharge in Violation of Public Policy

Employees may bring a wrongful discharge claim if they believe they were terminated because they refused to participate in an illegal act on behalf of the corporation or because they asserted rights under a statute, such as filing a workers' compensation claim.

## Right to Privacy: Disclosure and E-mail Review

Most states recognize a common law right of privacy of some kind. There are generally four types of privacy rights that may be asserted by employees: intrusion upon physical solitude, public disclosure of private facts, false light in the public eye, and appropriation of name or likeness. An employee could bring an action against the nonprofit corporation if the organization did an egregious act that violated the employee's right to non-disclosure of private facts, such as disclosing publicly that an employee had AIDS.

Privacy concerns are magnified with employer's monitoring of electronic mail and Internet usage. Generally, employers are permitted to conduct such monitoring, provided that employees are notified in advance that the e-mail and Internet systems are subject to monitoring at any time without prior notice. Such statements often are contained in a written e-mail and/or Internet policy that may be a freestanding policy or part of an employee handbook.

## Lifestyle Discrimination

Many states prohibit discrimination against employees who use tobacco products outside of the workplace. Other states have broader language that prohibits discrimination for lawful activities carried on by employees outside the workplace.

# Collective Bargaining

Nonprofit corporations of a certain size or in certain industries may face issues involving unions or unionization activities. A discussion of these issues is outside the scope of this *Guidebook*.

See the following checklist (page 164) to review the issues discussed in this chapter.

# Notes

1.  In some cases, there may be exceptions for religious corporations to laws prohibiting discrimination on the basis of religion, where the religious organization employs individuals of a particular religion to perform work connected with the carrying out of the religious corporation's activities. *See* 42 U.S.C. § 2000e-1 (exemption to Title VII prohibition on discrimination on the basis of religion).

2.  42 U.S.C. § 12111(a).

3.  29 U.S.C. § 203(s)(1).

4.  In most states, employment is presumed to be "at-will," meaning that either side may terminate the relationship at any time for any reason, or no reason at all.

5.  *See* I.R.C. § 6672(e).

# Suggested Questions for Directors Regarding Employees

(1)  How many employees does the corporation have?

(2)  Which employees report directly to the board?

(3)  Are there written employment contracts with these employees?

(4)  How are performance reviews conducted for the chief executive?

(5)  Does the corporation have an equal opportunity policy?

(6)  Does the corporation have an anti-harassment policy?

(7)  What kind of family and medical leave policy exists?

(8)  Does the corporation pay minimum wage and overtime pay to non-exempt employees?

(9)  Who classifies employees as exempt or non-exempt?

(10)  Does the organization have an employee handbook?

(11)  Does the employee handbook contain a disclaimer?

(12)  Does the organization have a grievance procedure in which employment actions may be reviewed by the board? If so, what is the board's role?

(13)  Does the corporation comply with applicable laws regarding workers' compensation, unemployment insurance, and tax withholding?

(14)  Does the corporation comply with relevant requirements of the Immigration and Naturalization Service?

(15)  Does the corporation have "work for hire" agreements with third parties (or employees acting outside their scope of employment) who produce copyrighted works?

(16)  Does the corporation take adequate precautions to protect trade secrets and confidential information?

(17)  If employees work with children or other vulnerable people, does the corporation do adequate pre-employment screening and background checks?

# Checklist: Employees

*Note:*    For purposes of simplicity in these checklists, we describe a corporation with a chair, who presides over the board of directors; a chief executive, who may be a staff person; an executive committee; a nominating committee; and an audit committee. (However, we recognize that in many smaller and other nonprofits, such committee functions may be performed by either the executive committee or the board as a whole.) We also assume a legal counsel—someone, paid or unpaid, having primary responsibility for the corporation's legal affairs. Many corporations, especially larger nonprofits, may have other committees established for specific purposes, such as reviewing staff performance, fixing compensation, monitoring compliance with legal requirements and periodic review of bylaws.

| Subject | To Be Reviewed By Whom | How Often | Comment |
|---|---|---|---|
| 1. What employment arrangements are in place with chief executive? | Chair, chief executive, personnel committee or full board | Annually or when chief executive or terms of employment change | Key terms of employment agreements with chief executives should be approved by the full board. |
| 2. How is the performance of the chief executive evaluated? | Chair, personnel committee | Annually | The chief executive's performance should be evaluated annually by the board. |
| 3. Does the corporation have an equal opportunity policy? | Chief executive, legal counsel, board | Annually | The board should approve an equal opportunity policy. |
| 4. Does the corporation have an anti-harassment policy? | Chief executive, legal counsel, board | Upon adoption, then reviewed annually to keep updated | The board should approve an anti-harassment policy. |
| 5. What kind of family and medical leave is provided to employees? | Chief executive, legal counsel | Upon adoption, then reviewed annually to keep updated | Family and medical leave policies should be in writing and comply with applicable law. |
| 6. How are employees classified as exempt/non-exempt? | Chief executive, legal counsel | As job descriptions and positions are created | Compliance with the Fair Labor Standards Act should be monitored by legal counsel. |
| 7. Does the organization have an up-to-date employee handbook with appropriate disclaimers? | Chief executive, legal counsel, full board or personnel committee | Upon adoption, then reviewed annually to keep updated | Boards often review and approve employee handbooks since they often contain mission statements and broad policies. Special care should be taken to have appropriate disclaimers and that policies comply with applicable laws. |
| 8. Does the board "hear" appeals or employee grievances? | Chief executive, full board or committee of board per policy | As grievances are filed | Most nonprofits will not have such a process. If they do, the Board should be familiar with the process and its role. |

## Checklist: Employees *(Continued)*

| Subject | To Be Reviewed By Whom | How Often | Comment |
|---|---|---|---|
| 9. Does the corporation have systems to comply with applicable laws regarding tax withholding, immigration, workers' compensation, and unemployment insurance? | Chief executive, legal counsel | Annually | Legal counsel and the officers of the Board should make sure contracts and systems are in place to insure compliance. |
| 10. Does the corporation own rights protecting original materials under the Copyright Act? | Chief executive, legal counsel | As works are created or commissioned | "Work for hire" agreements should be entered into with independent contractors and volunteers. |
| 11. Does the corporation protect its confidential information? | Chief executive, board | Upon adoption, then reviewed annually | A confidentiality policy should be adopted and other precautions taken to protect secrecy of confidential information. |
| 12. Does the corporation adequately screen employees before hiring? | Chief executive | As employees are hired | Thorough background and reference checks should be conducted on all employees who work with children or other vulnerable populations. |

# Duties of Directors under Special Circumstances

## *Contents*

CHAPTER **9**

# Duties of Directors under Special Circumstances

*This chapter discusses the duties of a director for the following special circumstances: (1) disposition of unique property; (2) mergers, sales, or other change of control events; and (3) insolvency or bankruptcy.*

## Disposition of Unique Property

### Disposition of Unique Property Issues May Arise in a Variety of Circumstances

Some nonprofits, particularly museums (but also a wide variety of other entities), may find that legal restraints, public perceptions, and functional necessities require the sale or other disposal of property that cannot be placed on the market in a conventional manner. Thus, an art museum may decide that a given painting lacks sufficient quality to merit a regular place in its galleries, or its original attribution to a great artist is proved to be erroneous. A social service institution may find that an original settlement house, no longer practical as a center for its services, is nonetheless regarded as a symbol of the community's commitment to service to the underprivileged. A church may occupy a building that is an architectural masterpiece but the congregation that built it and supported it has moved away from the neighborhood.

We offer no one-size-fits-all advice here, but provide some examples. In the case of art museums, the problem is both eased and made more difficult because a ready market exists for works of art, even those that a museum considers unworthy of its walls. On the other hand, the possibility, real or apparent, of an officer or trustee of such a museum exploiting a deaccessioning decision to acquire, for personal use or resale, an arguably disposable object is too obvious to be disregarded. As an example of the kind of policies and procedures that can be adopted to avoid such problems, this chapter contains a copy of the deaccession policy of one institution, the Art Institute of Chicago. (See Exhibit in this chapter.)

## Board Considerations in the Sale of Unique Property

A nonprofit board finding itself with the need to dispose of unique assets should seek the aid of other organizations with expertise related to the property at issue, including nonprofit organizations that have an interest in protecting the particular kind of property at issue. For example, a nonprofit evaluating disposition of a landmark piece of architecture could seek advice from a nonprofit association dedicated to such functions. Similarly, in the case of vacant land, a local conservation group would likely be delighted to work with the board to help identify options that serve both the corporation's and the community's interests. Further, if the property constitutes a significant portion of the corporation's assets, the corporation should determine whether it has an obligation under state law to either notify or receive approval for the sale from the state attorney general.[1]

Because such dispositions are by their nature unique, the best advice for board members is to proceed with care—and consider the best way to balance any competing community interests—before making a final decision.

# Mergers, Sales, and Other Change of Control Events

When faced with a prospective change of control, a nonprofit corporation director should understand what actions may be required to be taken to satisfy the director's fiduciary duties to the corporation with respect to such event. Further, the director should ask management staff or legal counsel to determine if the state attorney general or other regulatory authorities have notice rights or approval powers over the change of control decision. In addition to regulators, community interest groups may seek to change or influence the board's decision; thus, the directors will need to evaluate to what degree and in what manner the board will provide information to or seek input from such interest groups.

## Change of Control of Nonprofit Corporations

In the course of a nonprofit corporation's existence, there may come a time when its board is faced with a traumatic decision: Will the corporation's mission be better served if the corporation merges with another entity, sells all or some of its assets, converts to for-profit status, changes its membership or undergoes some other event that will result in change of control over the corporation's opera-tions? The processes that a nonprofit board uses to make a change of control decision must be sufficient to satisfy the directors' fiduciary duty obligations to the corporation and its mission, as well as other applicable legal requirements.

# How the Duties of Care and Loyalty Apply to Change of Control Decisions

## In general

As discussed in Chapter 2, "Duties and Rights of Nonprofit Corporation Directors," directors of nonprofits are considered fiduciaries with duties of care and loyalty to the corporation. When a change of control is contemplated, the processes used by the directors to evaluate the potential change—including deci-sions among various alternatives—is likely to be subject to scrutiny. Persons and groups outside the board may have reason to evaluate whether the board's deci-sion process was handled in a manner that satisfied the directors' duties. Nonprofit directors should be aware that they may be judged in part by standards that have developed in the for-profit world, in case law challenging the propriety of board actions in change of control situations.[2] Although some issues arising in nonprofit change of control circumstances do not arise in the for-profit world (and vice-versa), a number of basic guidelines drawn from the for-profit arena are equally applicable to non-profit boards. Such guidelines generally focus on what actions are necessary or sufficient to show that the directors have fulfilled their fiduciary duties of care and loyalty in connection with a change of control event.

## Satisfying the duty of care

**How and when the duty of care applies.**   The director duty of care requires that the process by which a change of control decision is made should mirror the significance of the decision. (For further discussion of a director's duty of care, see the section "The Duty of Care" in Chapter 2, "Duties and Rights of Nonprofit Corporation Directors.") Sometimes, the decision process is initi-ated by an external prompt—for instance, another nonprofit with a similar mis-sion proposes a merger to maximize joint corporate resources and community support, or a nonprofit or for-profit entity approaches the corporation about purchasing some or all of the nonprofit's assets and operations. More often, the corporation's own management or board initiates an evaluation process to determine the corporation's options in light of declining revenues, an inability to garner community support for new projects, loss of a stable source of volun-teers, or other factors that make it difficult to fulfill the corporation's mission.[3] Occasionally, the need for change is not recognized until the corporation is in or near the brink of insolvency; unless such situation was brought about pre-cipitously by unexpected events, the late discovery of such a problem may indicate a failure by the board to properly oversee the corporation's operations. (See discussion in the section "Insolvency or Bankruptcy" below for other board considerations in the event of insolvency.) In most cases, however, the board is aware for some time of the factors leading up to a potential need for change.

**Duty to be informed.**    The primary means for satisfying the director's duty of care in any situation is to be adequately informed before making a decision. The recommended information gathering and evaluation process that meets the board's duty of care in a change of control context has two main components: first, identifying the nature and quality of information that should be obtained to make an informed decision, and second, ensuring that independent consultants and/or committees composed of disinterested directors take the lead in evaluating aspects of change of control decisions in which some members of the board have an interest or potential interest.

**Key issues to be addressed.**    While each change of control decision is unique, certain issues are typically present. Directors should make sure that they have thorough and reliable information on these and other material issues:

(1) What are the factors requiring or motivating the board to consider a change of control of the corporation?
(2) What are the alternatives to change of control generally?
(3) What are the pros, cons and alternatives for any considered form of change of control?
(4) Should an auction or a bidding process be used to maximize the value to be paid for the corporation's assets (if applicable), or to broaden the search for parties who may be interested in engaging in a change of control transaction with the corporation? Alternatively, will the mission of the corporation be better served by a transfer of the assets to another nonprofit organization?
(5) What is the fair market value of the corporation's assets and activities?
(6) What non-monetary criteria should be considered by the directors when making a change of control decision?
(7) What experts and other resources are available to assist the board in analyzing the relevant issues pertaining to the change of control decision?
(8) If the assets of the corporation are to be sold to another (nonprofit or for-profit) entity, what will happen to the proceeds?
(9) What governmental authorities must receive notice or give their approval for a change of control transaction?
(10) When and how will beneficiary groups and other parties be informed of a proposed change of control? Should the change of control evaluation process include a mechanism for obtaining input from any such groups?

**Board evaluation process.**    The time available for the board to evaluate a proposed change of control is dictated by the circumstances at hand. In some cases, directors have some luxury of time; in other cases, financial or other circumstances require fairly quick action. In either case, however, the board should be aware that the *process* they use to make their decision—as well as the ultimate decision itself—may be subject to a high degree of scrutiny, before or after the change is completed. Once the board has identified the key issues to be addressed, it is faced with the decision of how to address them. The use of independent legal and financial advisors is highly recommended; in some cases, failure to obtain objective and expert opinions on certain key issues (such as the value of the corporation's assets or whether the terms of the proposed transactions are fair to the corporation) may be regarded as a breach of the directors' duty of care.[4]

**Independent board committees.**   For most change of control decisions, certain members of the board have a personal interest or stake in the decision. In particular, board members who are also employees of the corporation and who may lose their positions, or gain new positions with a merged or acquiring entity, have conflicts of interest that make it difficult for them to objectively evaluate change of control decisions. Board chairs may also be too self-identified with the corporation to be able to be truly objective. Because of such conflicts, both for-profit and nonprofit corporations commonly appoint a committee consisting solely of independent (i.e., non-management) directors to evaluate a change of control decision and make a recommendation to the board. The independent committee may engage its own independent experts (i.e., ones not regularly employed by the corporation), including attorneys, accountants, and other consultants, to assist it in evaluating the proposed transaction.

## Duty of loyalty issues

The duty of loyalty requires each nonprofit director to act in the best interests of the corporation, and to not make decisions that further the director's own interests at the corporation's expense. If a change of control decision presents a conflict of interest for one or more directors—such as a director who is also the organization president, and who may lose or keep her job depending on who acquires the corporation's assets—the entire board must take steps to make sure that such conflict of interest does not affect the decision of the board on what is in the corporation's best interest.

First, directors who have a conflict or potential conflict of interest related to a proposed change of control (or relating to one of several alternatives) should disclose the conflict, and follow the board's usual procedures for handling conflicts of interest. Second, the directors should evaluate whether the nature of any conflicts suggest that a special committee of independent directors should be used to evaluate a change of control proposal.

"Insider" directors who are involved in the negotiation of change of control transactions need to be aware of both actual and perceived conflicts of interest. Such directors should make sure to document that decisions made and actions taken by them in the course of such negotiations were in the best interests of the company. In addition, such directors should assure that other directors are aware of any conflicts of interest and have taken the necessary steps (such as obtaining the advice of independent consultants) to allow the board to make decisions based on objective criteria.

## Role of State Attorney General

Nonprofit corporations contemplating a change of control may be required to give the state attorney general notice of the proposed change. In some states, the attorney general must approve the proposed change before it occurs. Such notice and approval requirements may be set forth in the state nonprofit code or other statute, and may apply to all public benefit corporations, or only to those in specific industries (for example, health care).[5] Such statutes may apply even if the proposed acquiring or successor entity is another nonprofit, or only when a for-profit corporation is proposed to assume control of the nonprofit's operations. Even in states in which no statute specifically requires a nonprofit to give notice to or obtain approval from the attorney general in connection with a change of control transaction, the attorney general may assert rights to notice or approve the transaction based on the doctrine of *cy pres*. A state attorney general is generally considered a necessary or appropriate representative of the public interest with the power to review and/or approve a transaction that may change the charitable purpose of a nonprofit, public benefit corporation.[6] Directors of nonprofit corporations that are considering a change of control transaction should obtain the advice of counsel as to the whether and how the state attorney general may become involved in the change of control decision process.[7]

## Other Regulatory Approvals

Depending on the nature of the nonprofit organization, regulatory authorities other than the state attorney general may be required to receive notice of or approve the change of control, or some aspect of the change. As part of evaluating a change of control proposal, the board should ensure that legal counsel have identified what governmental approvals are required to implement the change, and at what stage. For instance, where only notice is required, should such notice be given a certain number of days before or after the change is to be effective? If approval is required before the change is effective, how long will the approval process take? The directors should factor in regulatory approval periods when determining the date that a change of control will occur. The board should also be informed as to whether the approval process would be routine or involve intensive review and potential requests for changes to the structure of the transaction.

## Other Interest Groups Affected by a Change of Control

A nonprofit corporation's beneficiaries, donors, and employees, as well as other members of the community, may all have an interest in—or an opinion on—a nonprofit's proposed change of control transaction. From a legal perspective, such groups generally lack any legal right to receive advance notice, evaluate, or comment on a nonprofit change of control (unlike the state attorney general, who may have such rights in his or her role as the representative of the public interest and/or a charity's beneficiaries).[8] Nonetheless, beneficiaries and other groups who learn about a proposed change of control may believe they have a right to participate in, or even to challenge, a nonprofit's proposed change of control. Such groups may also animate the interests of local politicians or governmental bodies in the proposed change.[9] As part of the board's change of control planning and evaluation process, the directors should consider the likely reaction of key constituencies to the proposed change, then decide whether any specific actions should be taken to inform such constituencies or give them opportunities to formally express their views and concerns. In some cases, professional public relations consultants may be able to assist the directors in effectively addressing community concerns.

## Summary

It is unlikely that directors of a nonprofit corporation will enter into a change of control decision lightly. However, directors should be aware of the high level of legal and public scrutiny that may be applied both to their ultimate decision, and the process by which they arrived at such decision. In addition, directors should know that there is legal precedent (often drawn from the for-profit content) regarding what actions and procedures are and are not considered sufficient means for directors to fulfill their fiduciary duties when making a change of control decision. Change of control decisions present a challenge to nonprofit directors to exercise their decision-making authority consistently with their fiduciary duties. In addition, the directors must be able to justify and explain their decision to numerous interested constituencies.

# Insolvency and Bankruptcy

## The "Zone of Insolvency"

A nonprofit organization can become insolvent, just as a profit-making entity can. Nevertheless, a nonprofit entity and its directors may face different issues in dealing with insolvency.

These basic issues are common to both profit-making and nonprofit entities:

(1) Insolvency can mean either an excess of debts over assets, or it can mean an inability to pay debts as they come due, even though the debtor may appear solvent on a balance sheet.

(2) Whenever an organization enters such a "zone of insolvency," the organization's officers and directors suddenly have a new constituency to whom they owe duties—namely, the creditors.[10]

(3) Both for-profit and nonprofit entities (including nonprofit entities with unconventional structures)[11] are eligible to file for bankruptcy protection.

Two significant differences applicable to insolvent nonprofit organizations, as compared to for-profit entities, are first, nonprofit entities cannot be forced into involuntary bankruptcy by their creditors,[12] and second, estates and trusts may not file for bankruptcy.[13]

## What Is Bankruptcy?

### In general

Bankruptcy is a method of discharging (forgiving) debts either through the liquidation of assets or the reorganization of the debtor's financial affairs. Bankruptcy is a uniform federal law (the Bankruptcy Code)[14] administered by a corps of United States bankruptcy judges who serve as units of federal district courts.[15]

### Differences between Chapter 7 and Chapter 11 bankruptcies

There are two types of bankruptcy applicable to private nonprofit entities—Chapter 7 and Chapter 11. In Chapter 7 a trustee appointed by the court liquidates the assets of the debtor. The debtor's operations cease and debtor's management is removed from control. After the assets are converted to cash, the trustee distributes the money to creditors on a pro-rata basis according to priorities established in the Bankruptcy Code. In Chapter 11, the debtor's management ordinarily remains in control and possession of the assets (called "debtor-in-possession"). Nevertheless, in cases of fraud, dishonesty, incompetence or gross mismanagement, the bankruptcy court may appoint a Chapter 11 trustee to manage the affairs of the debtor during the reorganization process.[16] The debtor can reorganize and continue its normal operations pursuant to a plan approved by a majority of creditors and the court, or the debtor can conduct an orderly liquidation and distribute the proceeds, much as in Chapter 7.

In a liquidating bankruptcy, whether in Chapter 7 or Chapter 11, the debtor ceases to exist after the case is over and does not receive a discharge. In a Chapter 11 reorganization, the debtor continues its existence, and its debts are discharged whether or not paid in full.

# What Laws Prevail during Bankruptcy?

The activities of many nonprofit organizations are regulated by federal or state law. For example, charitable institutions are regulated by state law, labor unions are regulated by federal law, and health care facilities are regulated by both federal and state law.

During a bankruptcy proceeding, do those regulatory laws continue to apply? The answer is affirmative, provided the two sets of laws do not conflict. When a conflict arises, the bankruptcy court's first obligation is to harmonize the two laws and allow them to operate concurrently.[17] In the last analysis, however, federal bankruptcy law will prevail.[18]

# Role of State Attorney General

In most states, the attorney general regulates and has considerable power to deal with charitable institutions. If such an institution becomes a debtor under the jurisdiction of the bankruptcy court, the question often arises as to whether the attorney general continues to have a role, and whether the attorney general may exercise his or her powers outside the bankruptcy court. The attorney general may participate in the bankruptcy case as a party in interest and may be able to engage in enforcement action outside the bankruptcy court, if that action falls within the state's police powers, which are not stayed by the Bankruptcy Code. However, the attorney general will be subject to the bankruptcy court's jurisdiction in areas traditionally governed by bankruptcy law.

# Chapter 11 Reorganization of Nonprofit Entities: Special Problems

It is now well established that a nonprofit entity may avail itself of Chapter 11 to reorganize and continue its operations and functions.[19] Nevertheless, some aspects of the Chapter 11 reorganization sections of the Bankruptcy Code present special problems in the cases of nonprofit organizations.

## Good faith test

The Bankruptcy Code requires that a plan of reorganization be proposed "in good faith."[20] This term has several applications, but the most common is in deciding whether the debtor is doing all it can to maximize the return to creditors and whether the reorganization is serving the rehabilitative purposes of Chapter 11. For a nonprofit corporation with members, the good-faith test may evaluate whether such members should be required to make an extraordinary contribution to the reorganization.

The answer depends on the facts and circumstances. If the members served by the nonprofit organization are relatively affluent and benefit from the organization's existence, then good faith may require them to dig into their pockets more deeply if they want the debtor to be permitted to reorganize. On the other hand, in a bankruptcy case involving a nonprofit labor union, the Chapter 11 plan was confirmed without requiring a dues increase because the debtor demonstrated that its members worked for relatively low wages and had recently voted down a proposed dues increase.[21] In a similar case, the residents served by a hospital district and who elected the district directors were not required to pay increased taxes to fund the district's chapter 9 plan of adjustment.[22]

### Best interests of creditors

Chapter 11 requires that the distributions to creditors under a plan equal or exceed what creditors would receive in Chapter 7 liquidation.[23] For a nonprofit entity, this can be a subtle issue, because it often is unclear what the liquidation of its assets would realize. The assets may serve a single purpose with little profit-making potential, such as a church or inner-city hospital, or the organization may have an income stream based on pledges or assessments that probably would not be honored or enforceable if the entity ceased to perform its functions or if its operations were sold to a for-profit organization.

Another issue that is likely to arise in nonprofit cases is whether assets contributed to the nonprofit for a specific use or purpose would be included in the assets available to creditors under Chapter 7. Assets that the debtor holds as trustee for the benefit of another are not included in the bankruptcy estate.[24] Whether assets of a nonprofit entity are held in trust for the benefit of others would depend on the facts of each case.

The bottom line is that any nonprofit entity seeking to reorganize would need to present some kind of evidence, such as expert testimony, as to the value (or lack thereof) of its assets in a liquidation. Then any plan would have to provide for distributions to creditors that at least equal that value.

### The absolute priority rule

The Bankruptcy Code requires that, absent consent to the contrary, in a plan of reorganization certain creditors must be paid before others and creditors generally must be paid before the owners ("interest holders") receive anything under the plan. This is referred to as the "absolute priority rule." In its purest form it means that, unless creditors of a Chapter 11 debtor are paid in full (or consent to less), the interest holders of the debtor must surrender all their interests in the debtor.[25] In for-profit organizations, the equity holders are either shareholders or partners. However, except for mutual benefit corporations, no one (including members) "owns" a nonprofit entity. In fact, in at least two cases, the courts have held that the absolute priority rule simply does not apply in the Chapter 11 reorganization of a nonprofit debtor.[26]

It is possible, however, that in any given situation a court might find that there is a class of persons who do in effect own and directly benefit from (in a financial sense) the continuation of the debtor's operations. In such a case, the court may require such persons to make a contribution to the plan (i.e., contribute "new value") as a prerequisite of confirmation of the plan. Note the close relationship between the absolute priority rule and the good faith test in this context.

### Directors' and officers' insurance

When their organization files for bankruptcy, directors and officers often want to know whether their Directors' and Officers' insurance policies will be available to protect them from liability, or whether, because the organization paid the premiums, such policies become assets of the bankruptcy estate. The general rule is that, although the policies themselves are owned by the debtor and therefore are part of its bankruptcy estate, the *proceeds* of such policies must be used for the purposes intended, i.e. to pay any liability assessed against the directors and officers.[27]

### Preferential transfers

The Bankruptcy Code discourages payments to preferred creditors on the eve of bankruptcy. Thus, payments on account of existing debt made ninety days before a bankruptcy filing are considered "preferential transfers," and the debtor in possession or trustee may require the transferees to refund the payments received to the bankruptcy estate. If the recipient of the payments was an insider of the debtor (e.g., officer or director) the preference period is one year prior to bankruptcy. There are defenses to preference claims, including the fact that the payment was made in the ordinary course of business (e.g., payment of a monthly utility bill) or that the transferee gave new value to the debtor after receiving the payment.

## Summary

Bankruptcy, including Chapter 11 reorganization, is a viable option for an insolvent nonprofit corporation. Nevertheless, nonprofit bankruptcies raise special issues of which the directors should be aware before authorizing the commencement of a bankruptcy case.

## Notes

1. The Model Act (§ 12.02(g)) requires that twenty-day prior notice be given to the state attorney general before disposition of "all or substantially all" of the property of a public benefit or religious corporation.

2. *See* Colin T. Moran, *Why Revlon Applies to Nonprofit Corporations*, 53 BUS. LAW. 373 (1998). *See also* Revlon, Inc. v. MacAndrews & Forbes Holding, Inc., 506 A.2d 173 (Del. 1986). Under *Revlon* and other cases, courts have found that once a board has determined that a change

of control of the corporation is inevitable, the board has a duty to effect the change that best maximizes the price to be received by the company's shareholders. However, the *Revlon* maximization principle does not apply in all change of control circumstances; *see* Paramount Communications, Inc. v. Time Incorporated, 571 A.2d 1140 (Del. 1990). In nonprofit change of control transactions, the state attorney general or others may argue that the changing corporation should be sold to the highest bidder, thus maximizing the proceeds available to be transferred to a charitable foundation or to be used for other charitable purposes. However, other considerations—such as whether to sell to a nonprofit or a for-profit—may also be valid factors for the board to evaluate, depending on the circumstances.

3.   In 1999, the United Jewish Appeal merged with the Council of Jewish Federations and the United Israel Appeal, to form the United Jewish Communities. A major impetus cited for the new combined fund-raising organization was changing donation patterns, in which donors desired to contribute to specific projects rather than making general gifts. *See* "Donors Alter Patterns of Philanthropy," *Chicago Tribune* (November 27, 1999), at 1-25.

4.   *See* Model Act, § 11.02, "Limitations on Merger by Public Benefit or Religious Corporations," and Official Comment thereto.

5.   See Richard Westfall, Richard H. Forman and Richard Djokic, *Attorney General Review of Asset Transfers by Nonprofit Hospitals*, THE COLORADO LAWYER 37 (February 1999), discussing the Colorado statute.

6.   The Model Act requires nonprofit public benefit or religious corporation to give at least twenty days advance notice of a proposed merger to the state attorney general. *See* Model Act, 11.02(b).

7.   For a useful summary of state laws governing the change of control of nonprofit hospitals and other health care providers, see Marian R. Fremont-Smith and Jonathan A. Lever, *Analysis & Perspective: State Regulation of Health Care Conversations and Conversion Foundations*, BNA's HEALTH LAW REPORTER 715 (5/11/00).

8.   *See* State of Tennessee, ex rel Adventist Health Care System/Sunbelt Health Care Corporation v. Nashville Memorial Hospital, 914 S.W. 2d 903, 910 (Tenn. App. 1995), holding that because the state attorney general had reviewed and approved a proposed sale of a nonprofit hospital to a for-profit corporation, other parties had no standing to challenge the sale, stating that "[t]he decision of the … Attorney General in those matters in which he is the legislatively designated representative of the public interest must bind everyone who might claim to represent that interest." However, in other states, unsuccessful bidders for the assets of a nonprofit have been allowed to file suit challenging a nonprofit board's change of control decision. *See* Leo T. Crowley, *Hospital Case: Significant Governance Questions*, 223 N.Y.L.J., February 10, 2000, at 3, discussing case before the state Supreme Court, County of New York, involving opposition by the state attorney general to a nonprofit corporation's petition to sell its specialty hospital building, and in which two hospitals that had previously sought business combinations with the proposed selling corporation were allowed to intervene.

*See also* Cook v. The Lloyd Nolan Foundation, CV-99-592 (Ala. 2001) (holding that neither members of the community nor the local district attorney had standing under the state Nonprofit Corporation Law to challenge actions of a nonprofit corporation that planned to sell its hospital).

9.   *See Losing Patience: Sell the Local Hospital? The Very Idea Splits a Usually Placid Town*, WALL STREET JOURNAL (March 18, 1997): A1. This article, about the furor caused by the proposed sale of a local hospital in Boca Raton, Florida, notes that "[t]he directors of the community hospital here had no premonition of the rage about to descend upon their collective heads" when the community learned of the proposed sale.

10.   The directors of an insolvent corporation may owe fiduciary duties to the creditors of the corporation when the corporation enters "the zone of insolvency." *See* Weaver v. Kellog, 216 B.R. 563, 583 (S.D. Tex. 1997). That means that the directors must at that point act to protect the interests of the creditors in making business decisions, especially with respect to avoiding dissipation of the assets of the corporation. One advantage of filing bankruptcy once insolvency arises is that it may offer the directors a means of adhering to their duties to creditors, because the bankruptcy court will require it.

11.   *In re* The Miracle Church of God in Christ, 119 B.R. 308 (Bankr. M.D. Fla. 1990) [Religious association]; *In re* Fund for a Conservative Majority, 100 B.R. 307 (Bankr. E.D. Va. 1989) [Political action committee]; *In re* Joliet-Will County Community Action Agency, 847 F.2d 430 (7th Cir. 1988) [Community service organization].

12.   Title 11 U.S.C. § 303(a). However, secured creditors or tax-exempt bond insurers may have sufficient leverage to force a distressed nonprofit to take necessary steps to resolve its financial difficulties. *See* K. Pallarito, *Bond Insurers Put the Squeeze on Strapped Hospitals*, MODERN HEALTHCARE (March 15, 1999).

13.   Estates and trusts are not eligible to file for bankruptcy by process of elimination, because they are not included within the definition of "persons" who may file for bankruptcy. *In re* Goerg, 844 F.2d 1562 (11th Cir. 1988); *In re* Hunt, 160 B.R. 131 (9th Cir. BAP 1993).

14.   The Bankruptcy Code is contained in Title 11, United States Code.

15.   28 U.S.C. § 151.

16.   11 U.S.C. § 1104(a)(1).

17.   *In re* General Teamsters, Local 890, 225 B.R. 719, 738 (Bankr. N.D. Cal. 1998)

18.   *See In re* County of Orange, 191 B.R. 1005, 1017 (Bankr. C.D. Cal. 1996) [state law vs. bankruptcy law]; *see also* 28 U.S.C. § 157(d), which requires that a case be withdrawn from a bankruptcy judge and be heard by a federal district judge when "the proceeding requires consideration of both [bankruptcy law] and other laws of the United States regulating organizations or activities affecting interstate commerce." This provision undoubtedly was included by Congress to avoid bankruptcy courts exercising a bias in favor of the bankruptcy laws with which they deal on a regular basis as opposed to other federal laws with which they may be less familiar.

19.   Wabash Valley Power Association, 72 F.3d 1305 (7th Cir. 1995) [nonprofit electric cooperative]; *General Teamsters*, 225 B.R. 719 [local labor union].

20.   11 U.S.C. § 1129(a)(3).

21.   *General Teamsters*, 225 B.R. 729-31.

22.   *In re* Corcoran Hospital District, 233 B.R. 449 (Bankr. E.D. Cal. 1999).

23.   11 U.S.C. § 1129(a)(7).

24.   11 U.S.C. § 541(d).

25.   11 U.S.C. § 1129(b)(2)(B)(ii).

26.   *Wabash Valley*, 72 F.3d at 1312-1319; *General Teamsters*, 225 B.R. at 736-7.

27.   *See In re* First Cent. Financial Corp., 238 B.R. 9 (Bankr. E.D.N.Y. 1999).

# Suggested Questions for Directors Regarding Duties of Directors under Special Circumstances

## Disposition of Unique Property

(1) Why is a unique corporate asset being considered for sale?

(2) Could any directors, officers or other corporate insiders personally benefit in any way from the sale?

(3) What other organizations, such as specialized nonprofits, appraiser agencies or other groups, could assist the corporation in maximizing the benefits of a sale, while minimizing concerns of the community or other interested groups?

(4) What information does the board need to properly evaluate a proposed change of control?

## Mergers, Sales, or Other Change of Control Events

(1) What board members, officers, or other corporate insiders may be personally affected by a change in control?

(2) What processes should the board put in place to address conflict of interest issues during the consideration of a potential change of control, as well as during any negotiation with third parties? Should a committee of independent board members be appointed to make recommendations to the board regarding a proposed change of control, or to negotiate key deal terms?

(3) Will approval of the state attorney general or other regulators be required before a change of control may be effected?

(4) How will community groups, employees, and constituencies of the corporation likely react to news of a change of control proposal or event? Should such concerns be addressed as part of the board's evaluation and negotiation process? Should public relations professionals be used to help communicate information about a change of control?

## Insolvency or Bankruptcy

(1) Is our organization in a "zone of insolvency"? Are we able to pay our debts as they come due? Can we foresee a day in the near future when that will not be true?

(2) Is our organization eligible to file for bankruptcy, or is it an estate or trust?

(3) If the corporation is or becomes insolvent, do we want to reorganize and continue, or liquidate and "close up shop"?

(4) Are there members or others affiliated with our organization who derive economic benefit from its activities who might be considered its "owners"? If yes, should they be asked to contribution to a reorganization effort? Can we legally require them to do so?

(5) What is the fair value of our corporate assets? What would they realize in a forced liquidation?

## EXHIBIT

# SAMPLE DEACCESSION POLICY
THE ART INSTITUTE OF CHICAGO *

The deaccessioning of works of art from the collections of The Art Institute of Chicago is an exceptional event done with the greatest care. Only works of art that are free of any legal restrictions against deaccessioning may be deaccessioned.

The following procedures are normal for deaccessions and mandatory for any object worth $5,000 or more.

1. Deaccessions are made for any of the following reasons:

    a. The object is intrinsically poor in quality;
    b. A better and comparable example is in the collection;
    c. The object is an exact duplicate, deemed unnecessary to retain;
    d. The object is in such poor state that proper repairs are unfeasible or will render the object essentially false.
    e. Other reasons as circumstances arise.

2. The Curator concerned recommends to the Director an object for deaccessioning and if approved, the procedure may be initiated. The Director may also initiate the deaccession procedure. Upon the joint approval of the Curator and the Director, a written recommendation to deaccession shall be made to the appropriate Curatorial Advisory Committee. A majority vote of a quorum of the Committee will be required for recommendation to the Trustees.
3. The objects to be deaccessioned shall receive an outside appraisal before any further action is taken.
4. For objects which are appraised at $5,000 or more, the written opinion of at least one outside expert supporting the deaccession recommendation shall be obtained, — which describes the object exactly, lists its source and its accession number, and the reasons for the opinion to be recorded in the Committee's minutes if the Committee votes to deaccession.
5. If the Committee votes to deaccession an object, the Curator will make reasonable efforts to get in touch with donors, their heirs, or their executors, to inform them of the proposed deaccession, but such action shall not in any way be construed as a request for permission to deaccession.
6. After Committee approval to deaccession, the objects shall be presented to the Trustees for final approval, with any pertinent observations by the Director or Curator. A list of the objects shall be provided to the Trustees a week before they are to vote. The decision of the Board of Trustees shall be reflected in their meeting minutes.

*Exhibit 1 is reprinted with the permission of The Art Institute of Chicago.

7. The objects approved for deaccessioning are to be handled by one of the means herein listed, in the order of listing:

   a. If, in the opinion of the staff or an outside advisor, the object is of sufficient interest, it shall first be offered at the Trustees' discretion, as a gift, as an object in trade, or sold to another museum or suitable institution.
   b. If method (a) is not exercised, the object shall be sent to public auction with a suitable reserve on it (based on an outside appraisal) and shall be designated either as "Sold by order of the Board of Trustees of The Art Institute of Chicago" or as "Sold by the order of the Board of a Midwestern Museum." No Trustee, Advisory Committee member, appraiser, staff member, or agents of theirs, shall buy property of The Art Institute of Chicago at such an auction.
   c. If neither method (a) nor (b) is exercised then, upon the recommendation of the Director and with the approval of the Board of Trustees or the Executive Committee, one or more dealers, known to the museum staff, may be invited to bid, either on individual objects or on entire lots, and the highest bidder shall be the buyer, subject to a reserve set by The Art Institute of Chicago.
   d. Whenever appropriate, funds from such sales shall be for the purchase of works of art in the department concerned. The original donor's name is always retained on the credit line.
   e. At the discretion of the staff, before sales, all paper labels, where appropriate, shall be removed; numbers and notations on the objects themselves shall remain if to remove them would cause damage to the object.
   f. Normally, no object approved for deaccession is to be used in direct trade with a dealer for another object; rather, if after procedure (b) has failed, upon the recommendation of the Director and with the approval of the Board of Trustees, a dealer may buy an object at its auction reserve price, and the proceeds received may then be applied to the purchase of an object, approved by the Committee for acquisition, from this same dealer.

8. If The Art Institute of Chicago should find that it is in the possession of an object which can be demonstrated to have been stolen or illegally exported from its country of origin (and/or the country where it was last legally owned); the Art Institute will, if legally free to do so, take reasonable steps to cooperate in the return of the object to that country or the rightful owner. The deaccession procedures set forth herein, with the exception of paragraph 7, shall be utilized to review the possible deaccession and return of the object under this paragraph.

   In conformity with AAM and AAMD policies, and in conformity with existing practice at The Art Institute of Chicago, the funds received from all sales of works of art are to be used exclusively for the purchase of additional works of art for the permanent collections, with the newly purchased works credited to the original donors of the deaccessioned works.

CHAPTER **10**

# Director Liability Risks and Protections

## Contents

CHAPTER **10**

# Director Liability Risks and Protections

*The failure (or alleged failure) of directors of non-profit corporations to fulfill their duties may expose them to liability to third parties, or to the corporation. Directors should therefore be aware of protections that may be available against such liability.*

In recent years, litigation against directors of many varieties of nonprofits has increased in frequency. The demise of the charitable immunity exemption[1] that was previously available to many kinds of nonprofit corporations has increased the frequency of suits against directors and officers of public benefit and religious corporations.[2] (Mutual benefit corporations and their directors have never enjoyed the protection of the charitable exemption.) Although many small nonprofit corporation boards face little or no practical liability risk, all directors need to understand the actions that may be taken to protect them against liability related to their service on a nonprofit corporation's board.

A nonprofit corporation director should understand what the corporation's basic documents provide as to indemnification and insurance, and know if there are any statutory exemptions or other legal provisions that may limit the director's liability.

## The Director's Exposure to Liability

A director's possible liability in litigation does not arise simply because the corporation may be liable for a matter. It arises because the director is charged with some breach of duty or other harm done by the director to the corporation or to a specific party. A director should understand that the corporation itself may be the party asserting a claim.

A director's liability does not automatically arise from corporate liability. For directors to be endangered by litigation, they must hold a duty to, or have directly harmed, some party entitled—or allegedly entitled—to sue the director. Suits against directors are typically brought in one of three ways:

(1) An outside party may attempt to sue a member of the board directly, in a suit alleging some injury done *by* the corporation, but claiming the director to be a principal or implied co-conspirator in connection with the injury.

(2) An aggrieved party may assert some right of the corporation against the director, suing to remedy claimed harm done to the corporation; lawsuits of this type are referred to as "derivative actions."[3] In effect, someone is suing the director on behalf of the corporation, generally because of the

director's breach of the duty of care or the duty of loyalty. (See the discussion of director duties in Chapter 2, "Duties and Rights of Nonprofit Corporation Directors.")

(3) The director may be held *personally* liable under various federal and state laws dealing with issues such as environmental claims, tax delinquencies (for example, failure to pay sales taxes, payroll taxes, or make proper withholding), and antitrust claims.[4]

Although a director's exposure to potential liability will vary according to the size of the entity, the nature and degree of exposure will be determined more by the type of nonprofit corporation than by its size. Generally, liability exposure is based on allegations of negligence or failure to oversee.

# Avoidance of Liability Risks

Some litigation risk may be avoided. As discussed in Chapter 9, "Duties of Directors under Special Circumstances," the board should identify areas in which the corporation is vulnerable to litigation or potential legal liability, and then make sure that appropriate procedures and reporting mechanisms are put in place to avoid or minimize such risks. In some cases, the directors may wish to employ advisers and consultants to aid in decisions that are of a kind likely to be scrutinized by regulators or others. Use of outside advisers may help the board demonstrate that it satisfied its duty of care when it made a particular decision. Similarly, in situations in which duty of loyalty issues are present, the use of an outside opinion, even to verify what seems obvious, may be prudent, and offer legal protections not otherwise available. For example, under the IRS's excess benefit rules, transactions with insiders that are approved by the board or a disinterested committee may be afforded a presumption of reasonableness if the transaction is ever challenged as involving an excess benefit (see discussion of excess benefits liability in Chapter 4, "Taxation.")

# Director Indemnification

The director should seek a program of corporate indemnification to the maximum extent permitted by applicable corporation law. Such a program of indemnification should be sought even if the corporation's liquid net worth may make such protection limited in value.

Although the value of indemnification depends on both the legal and financial ability of the corporation to pay, the legal right of the director to be indemnified in connection with a lawsuit or other proceeding depends on the type of loss the director has incurred. In some instances the corporation is required to indemnify a director, while in other cases the corporation is permitted to indemnify, if the board chooses to do so. A corporation may also advance certain litigation expenses to the director in certain circumstances.

## Discretionary Indemnification

Initially, it should be noted that even if the board of directors wants to indemnify another director, such indemnification must be consistent with state law and the corporation's articles and bylaws. Mere goodwill of the board is not sufficient to authorize indemnification.

Most, if not all, states provide for indemnification rights of nonprofit officers and directors by statute.[5] The Model Act gives the corporation discretion to indemnify the director if the director has acted in good faith and with the reasonable belief that his or her actions were in the best interests of the corporation.[6] Such indemnification may include sums due under a settlement agreement. Indemnification for proceedings by the corporation against the director (whether direct or derivative) is limited under the Model Act to the reasonable expenses incurred by the director in connection with the proceeding.[7] Such discretionary indemnification may be made mandatory by appropriate provisions in the corporation's articles of incorporation or bylaws.

## Mandatory Indemnification

Under the Model Act as well as most state laws, directors have the *right* to indemnification from the corporation under certain circumstances. Although individual state statutes may differ from the Model Act, the issues treated by the Model Act are ones that the director must face in any event. Under the Model Act[8], a corporation is required to indemnify a director for reasonable expenses if the director is "wholly successful" in his or her defense of any proceeding[9] of which the director is a party as a result of being a director of the corporation. Note, however, that such mandatory indemnification is contingent on a director being deemed wholly successful in defense of the matter for which indemnification is sought. Such success seems clear when there is a verdict or final ruling in the director's favor (including dismissal with prejudice) in a lawsuit, arbitration, or other legal proceeding. However, depending on the facts and the applicable state, a settlement of a proceeding may or may not trigger a director's mandatory indemnification rights under the Model Act.[10]

The director should endeavor to have corporate indemnification to the fullest extent permitted by applicable law. This means that the corporate obligation should be set forth in the articles of incorporation or bylaws, in language as broad as the applicable statute permits. A director may also wish to have a separate contract with the corporation providing for indemnification. In the Model Act, corporations are permitted to contract to provide indemnification rights, by contract and/or insurance, that are greater than those otherwise allowed by law.

However, the director must recognize that the corporation's uninsured obligation to indemnify may be of little value, if the corporation's net worth is insufficient to cover the director's expense or the director's exposure.

## Advancement of Expenses

A director should know what specific measures have been adopted by the corporation to provide for advancement of legal expenses. A director will want the corporation to have taken actions that will maximize the corporation's ability to advance expenses of directors who are made parties to proceedings because of their director status. In some states, the ability to advance expenses is provided for under state law;[11] in other states, advancement of expenses may be permitted (or required) only if set forth in a corporation's articles or bylaws.[12]

The director should not underestimate the importance of a procedure permitting the corporation to advance expenses, since having a right of indemnification does not mean that the director can require the corporation to immediately assume the costs of litigation or other proceeding while the matter is being pursued. Rather, indemnification rights are generally triggered only at the end of a litigation or similar proceeding, and result in reimbursement for expenses already incurred. The right of indemnification is therefore of limited help to the director without an advance for expenses. Thus, directors should know whether the corporate documents require the corporation to advance expenses to the maximum extent permitted by the state's indemnification laws.

The Model Act[13] sets forth conditions upon which such advances may be made. Most states have similar conditions, although certain specifics may vary. Under the Model Act, a nonprofit corporation may advance expenses to a director if:

(1) the director furnishes a written affirmation of the director's good faith belief that the standard of conduct permitting indemnification has been met;

(2) the director furnishes a written undertaking to repay any sums advanced if it is ultimately determined that the director did not meet the applicable standard; and

(3) a determination is made that the facts known to whomever makes the determination would not preclude indemnity. (Under the Model Act, such determination must be made by a disinterested body, which may be the board, a board committee, independent legal counsel, or disinterested members of a mutual benefit corporation; however, not all state laws require such determination before advances may be made.[14])

## Third-Party Indemnification

In addition, indemnification for directors may be sought from any third party who may agree to indemnify the corporation on a related matter. For instance, the owners of a group of assets sold to the corporation may agree to indemnify the corporation—and if specified, its officers and directors—against any liability relating to periods prior to the corporation's purchase. The director should learn whether such third-party indemnification runs directly to a director, or runs only to the corporation. The director should further ascertain at what point this protection becomes available.

## Attorney General Notice

Under the Model Act, and in some states, indemnification of a director of a public benefit corporation may not occur until at least twenty days after the corporation has given written notice of the proposed indemnification to the state attorney general.[15]

# Protection of Directors through Insurance

A nonprofit corporation should obtain insurance to protect its directors and officers. A directors and officers insurance policy (D&O insurance) *may*, subject to the applicable corporation act, provide coverage that is broader than any indemnification permitted by the Model Act or by relevant state law. Under the Model Act,[16] a corporation can protect a director by insurance, even if the insurance coverage extends protection to situations in which the corporation is otherwise prohibited by applicable law from providing indemnification. For instance, a number of state statutes prohibit indemnification against settlements and judgments in derivative actions (i.e., lawsuits asserting the corporation's rights against the director) if a director is found liable, unless the court determines that special circumstances entitle the director to indemnity despite that judgment.[17] However, most nonprofit corporation statutes *permit* the corporation to procure insurance for the director for such events even though the corporation could not directly indemnify from its own funds.

## Why Purchase D&O Insurance?

A director should expect the corporation to provide D&O insurance (or properly-funded self-insurance) protecting him or her from liability. If such insurance is not provided, the director should examine the risks of serving without it.

Even if a nonprofit corporation has expansive indemnification provisions in its articles of incorporation or bylaws,[18] these assurances must be considered in light of the financial strength of the corporation offering them. To the extent that qualified board members may be deterred from participating because of inadequate financial reserves to pay such claims, D&O insurance may be the most viable method of providing both the perception and reality of adequate protection for board members-current and prospective. On the other hand, nonprofit corporations with good financial resources may determine that it is more cost-effective to self-insure against director and officer litigation expenses by maintaining a self-insured fund. Such a fund gives the corporation more control over the cost of director and officer protection. It also allows the corporation to more closely tailor such protection to the needs of the corporation, its officers and directors. Nonprofit corporations should not ask directors to serve without insurance coverage if adequate insurance is available to the corporation at reasonable cost.[19]

## Review D&O Policy to Determine Who and What Is Covered

At least annually, the corporation's management or staff should review what individuals and entities are covered by its D&O policy. Where a corporation has (or has recently acquired) affiliates or subsidiaries, the extension of the insurance coverage to these entities should be verified. If the policy provides coverage to directors and officers specified by name, rather than position, the policy may need to be updated whenever new officers or directors are selected. The D&O policy should also be examined to determine if it covers the activities of non-director members of committees, or other persons (such as volunteers) who may be subject to liability due to their activities on behalf of the corporation.

# Dual Roles of a Director May Affect D&O Coverge

Many typical D&O policies do not cover the activities of a director or officer when she or he is acting in other capacities. For example, when a board member who is an attorney is acting in the capacity of counsel, whether paid or volunteer, his or her conduct is probably not included in the corporation's D&O protection. Such dual roles can give rise to difficult questions concerning coverage. For example, legal malpractice insurers may specifically exclude claims that arise if the attorney was acting as an officer or director of an organization. The typical D&O policy may have a similar provision excluding work performed as a lawyer unless the attorney is specifically named in the policy. Thus, there may be a gray area in which neither coverage may apply, especially if the attorney or his or her law firm is also legal counsel to the corporation.[20] Similar problems can arise in other dual roles. These problems may be addressed by obtaining special riders or endorsements on policies; however, the need for clarification should be recognized by those individuals wearing multiple corporate hats.

# The Nature of "Claims-Made" Policies

Most D&O policies are written on a "claims-made" basis; thus, a director should understand the limits of this type of coverage.

The claims-made type of policy contrasts with an "occurrence" policy. Occurrence policies cover all claims arising out of incidents occurring during the policy period, regardless of whether the insurance policy is still in effect at the time the claim is made. Most insurance policies with which a director will be individually familiar—e.g., automobile liability, fire and extended coverage—are occurrence policies. Thus, it is important to understand the nature and limits of claims-made coverage.

Policy coverage on a claims-made basis means that a claim is covered by insurance only if the policy is in effect at the time that the claim is made, regardless of when the event causing the claim occurred. For instance, suppose that a corporation had coverage for the past ten years, but because of a changeover in clerical staff the policy lapsed for a month before being renewed. The corporation would not be covered for any claim made during the one month of noncoverage, even though the claim related to corporate action during the prior period in which the corporation's policy had been in effect. Furthermore, some D&O policies will limit the coverage of prior events to those arising in a specified number of years prior to the inception of the policy with that particular carrier. As can be seen, claims-made coverage may offer a very limited protection. The director should further understand that if the corporation discontinues a D&O policy after she or he ceases to be a director, the director may be uninsured even as to acts occurring during the director's term of office, if the claim is made after the policy is discontinued.

In addition to the requirement that the D&O policy be in effect as of the date a claim is made, D&O policies have other requirements that must be adhered to in order to ensure that coverage is available. For instance, D&O policies typically require the corporation to advise the insurer promptly of facts that could trigger claims, and delicate issues arise as to what constitutes adequate notice of a claim. When making a D&O claim, the corporation should make sure that the form of notice conforms to the policy requirements.

## Policy Coverage

D&O policies are typically divided into two parts. The first part covers reimbursement of individual directors and officers for losses for which they are not indemnified by the corporation. The second part provides reimbursement to the corporation for amounts that it has paid, or is required to expend, in indemnifying its directors and officers.[21] In other words, it provides the funds that enable the corporation to discharge its obligation to indemnify.

The type of coverage, retentions, exclusions and other aspects of the policies are sufficiently complex as to require study by the corporation's insurance committee, an insurance consultant, and possibly by legal counsel experienced in this area. The issues should also be reviewed whenever insurance carriers are changed.

## What Losses Are Covered?

The D&O policy should be analyzed to determine whether the duty to defend and the cost of defense are covered. The corporation should provide the director with a memorandum on this subject as well as the losses covered or not covered. Usually, for example, there is no duty to provide attorneys to defend a lawsuit; nor do typical D&O policies provide for the payment of legal expenses, except after a final determination of liability under the policy.[22] Thus, technically, a D&O policy is an *indemnity* policy, as distinguished from a *liability* policy.

Under an indemnity policy, such as the typical D&O policy, the insurer is not required to make any payments until the insured has suffered an actual loss (as defined in the policy). In comparison, a liability policy, such as the typical automobile insurance policy, requires the insurer to make certain payments even though the insured has not yet incurred a loss or paid any out-of-pocket money.[23] It is because of the nature of a D&O policy that the advances for expenses mentioned above are so crucial for the director's protection.

A director will also want to know:

- the limits of coverage of the D&O policy (i.e., the highest amount of money the insurer will pay for each loss);

- the retention level imposed on the insureds, more commonly known as the deductible (i.e., how much of the loss must be borne by the director before the insurer will begin to provide payment for the loss); and
- the amount of co-insurance, if any (i.e., the percentage that the insured continues to be responsible for paying, even when deductibles have been satisfied and the insurance is providing coverage for a loss).

## Policy Exclusions

Virtually all D&O policies have substantial exclusions that must be fully understood.

In addition to the scope of coverage, directors should understand their D&O policy's exclusions. The excluded risks are not just limited to the exclusions section alone but occur throughout the policy. For example, the term "loss" may be defined to exclude fines or penalties imposed by law for matters uninsurable under applicable law, such as punitive damages. Other definitions and terms also set forth exclusions.[24]

The standard exclusions often involve some types of risks that could produce sizable claims against directors and officers. Often excluded are the following liabilities: losses covered by other insurance; sickness or death resulting from pollution; ERISA claims; fair employment claims; libel or slander actions; and liabilities arising from intentional conduct, including fraud, dishonesty, and criminal conduct. Most policies also will not cover fines, penalties, or punitive damages.

Just because an area of risk is excluded from a standard D&O policy, however, does not mean that coverage for such risk cannot be obtained. Many exclusions may be deleted by negotiation and payment of a separate premium. A few specialized exposures (such as ERISA claims) may be covered by specific policies. While a request for additional coverage may constitute the "red-flagging" of a problem, the disclosure of potential claims is required in the application in any event. Thus, it is in the interests of the corporation and its officers and directors to identify whether the corporation's activities result in a significant risk of liability for a type of claim excluded by its D&O policy. The corporation can then determine whether such exclusion can be eliminated, or if coverage for such claims can be obtained by other means.

## The Application

All applications for D&O insurance should be carefully prepared and reviewed for accuracy.

The application for D&O insurance and the statements made in it are part of the insurance contract and may be relied upon by the insurer when an issue is raised as to the policy's coverage. Because of the peculiar importance of D&O insurance, all directors should be sure that not only the policy itself, but also the application for it, have been reviewed with particular care since a misstatement in the application (even if the director is unaware of it) may result in a denial of coverage.

# Statutory Protections for Directors

Many state statutes limit the liability of directors of certain kinds of nonprofit corporations.

## Elimination of Liability to Third Parties

As a partial response to the increased exposure of directors, and the possible unavailability of insurance, more than one-half of the states have amended their nonprofit corporation statutes to limit a director's liability except in special situations such as those involving gross negligence or willful malfeasance.[25] An example of such a provision is found in § 8.30(d) of the Model Act, which provides that a director who has discharged his duties in good faith and consistently with the Act's other provisions will not be liable to the corporation, any member, or any other person for any action taken or not taken as a director. In some states, such liability-elimination provisions apply only to directors of public benefit corporations or corporations exempt from taxation under § 501(c) of the Internal Revenue Code,[26] or to directors who serve without compensation.[27] In addition, under some statutes, such liability-elimination only applies if the corporation has satisfied certain requirements, such as including a liability-elimination provision in its articles of incorporation or obtaining a certain level of insurance coverage.[28] Directors should make sure that all actions needed to make this protection available have been taken.

## Elimination of Liability for Monetary Damages to the Corporation or Its Members

Some states also allow nonprofit corporations to eliminate or limit the personal liability of a director to the corporation or its members for monetary damages resulting from the breach of the director's duty of care owed the corporation or its members.[29] Such statutes usually require such liability-elimination to be set forth in the corporation's articles of incorporation. In addition, such statutes generally do not permit elimination of liability for breach of the director's duty of loyalty, acts or omissions not in good faith or involving intentional misconduct or a knowing violation of law, any transaction in which the director derived an improper personal economic benefit, loans to the director by the corporation, or unlawful distributions approved by the director.

## Limitations of Liability Protection Statutes

The director should be aware of several fundamental weaknesses in statutes pur-porting to eliminate the liability of directors. First, many plaintiffs will pre-dictably assert in the initial complaint that the act or omission involved falls within the exception to the applicable statute, i.e., that the director *was* grossly negligent or willful, or that the matter involved breach of the director's duty of loyalty. Therefore, the director may still have to defend himself or herself in a court proceeding. Hence, once again, the need for advances of expenses (see dis-cussion in the section "Advancement of Expenses" above). Second, whether or not such state statutes protect against director liability for claims arising under federal law is unclear. (Although the federal Volunteer Protection Act of 1997 may provide a similar level of protection, at least to uncompensated directors, it is subject to the same fundamental weaknesses identified herein.[30]) Third, immunity from liability is not automatic under such statutes; the director must *prove* that he or she met the due care, good faith and other statutory require-ments for elimination of liability. Therefore, even directors who are eligible to rely on such liability-elimination statutes should still request the corporation to maximize director indemnification rights available under state law and supple-ment such statutory protections with a D&O policy if possible.[31]

## Protection against Certain Kinds of Claims

Other statutes limit the liability of corporations, or of volunteers other than directors, for certain types of claims. For instance, in New Jersey, nonprofit corporations are not liable for negligently causing injury to a beneficiary of the corporation.[32] To the extent such statutes effectively block claims to which the corporation (and potentially its directors and officers) are subject, they provide an added level of protection against such litigation risks.

# Conflicting Interests: The Director and Legal Counsel

In general, the board of directors is the highest authority of the corporation, and, in matters concerning the entire board, the corporation and the board are roughly identical in their legal exposure. But in some instances, the members of the board and the corporation may have conflicting interests. If the corporation and members of the board are both defendants in a proceeding, the corporation may wish (or be forced for its own protection) to assert cross claims against all or some of its directors. Further, individual directors may, through their own acts or omissions, find that they have different potential liability compared to other members of the board.

With respect to the role of legal counsel in claims made both against the corporation and some or all of the directors, the director should recognize the following:

(1) The legal positions of the board of directors and that of the corporation are not *necessarily* identical; in some situations the board or a portion thereof needs to seek counsel of its own, since the corporate general counsel may be obligated to pursue or assert claims against the directors in order to avoid liability of the corporation.

(2) An individual director may need independent counsel if such director finds that his or her situation differs markedly from that of other members of the board.

# Summary

Directors and prospective directors will benefit from a thorough understanding of the protections against liability afforded them under state law, the corporation's articles of incorporation and bylaws, and the corporation's D&O policy or self-insurance fund. Directors may wish to require that senior management, board officers, or a committee conduct an annual review of the scope and limitations of such protections and evaluate whether it is feasible to take any actions to enhance such protections. The persons who conduct such review should report their conclusions to the full board.

See the following checklist (page 204) to review the issues discussed in this chapter.

# Notes

1. In the past, many states held that charities were immune from lawsuits arising from injuries caused by employees or agents. This immunity has virtually disappeared through legislation and judicial decision. *See* President of Georgetown College v. Hughes, 130 F.2d 810 (D.C. Cir. 1942). *See also* Sanner v. Trustees of Sheppard and Enoch Pratt Hospital, 278 F. Supp. 138 (D. Md. 1968), *aff'd* 398 F.2d 226 (4th Cir. Md. 1968).

2. Individuals working in the nonprofit sector have faced an increase in personal liability. Since the 1980s, there has been a marked increase in the number of suits filed against individuals acting for nonprofit organizations. *See Developments in the Law—Nonprofit Corporations*, HARV. L. REV. 1578 (1992).

3. Derivative suits may be brought in some states by a corporation's members. *See, e.g.,* S.C. CODE ANN. § 33-31-304 (1999). In all states the Attorney General may bring a derivative suit against a director. *See, e.g.,* S.C. CODE ANN. § 33-31-304(b).

4. *See* W. VA. CODE § 11-15-17 (2000) (tax delinquencies); CONN. GEN. STAT. § 42-110b (antitrust liability).

5. While a number of nonprofit indemnification statutes follow the indemnification provision of the Model Act or the Model Business Corporation Act, others have less standard provisions. *See* Brenda Kimmery, *COMMENT: Tort Liability of Nonprofit Corporations and their Volunteers, Directors and Officers: Focus on Oklahoma,* 33 TULSA L.J. 683, 691 (Winter, 1997). *See also* John F. Olson & Josiah O. Hatch, III, *Director and Officer Liability: Indemnification and Insurance,* § 11.03[2] (West Group; 2000 Update).

6. Model Act, § 8.51.

7. Model Act, § 8.51(e).

8. Model Act, § 8.52.

9. The Model Act, at § 8.50(7) defines "proceeding" broadly, to encompass trials, hearings and investigations; some state statutes may have different and more limited definitions. *See* GA. CODE ANN. § 14-3-140(25); N.C. GEN. STAT. § 55-1-40(18); ARK. STAT. ANN. § 4-33-850(7).

10. See Olson and Hatch, *Director and Officer Liability, supra,* note 5, at § 5.03[4][a]. Settlement amounts paid in connection with derivative suits may not be considered liabilities payable under the indemnification provision of the Model Business Corporation Act. See Official Comment 5, MODEL BUS. CORP ACT, § 8.50.

11. *See* COLO. REV. STAT. § 7-129-104 (1999).

12. *See* N.J. STAT. ANN. § 15A:3-4 (2000).

13. Model Act, § 8.53.

14. ARIZ. REV. STAT. § 10-3853.

15. *See* Model Act, § 8.55(d). *See also* ARK. STAT. ANN. § 4-33-855.

16. Model Act, § 8.57.

17. *See* MISS. CODE ANN. § 79-11-281.

18. *See* Frederick, *Indemnification & Liability of Corporate Directors and Officers,* J. MO. B. (July-August 1987) regarding the provision of additional indemnity pursuant to MO. REV. STAT. § 351.355(7) (1986). Since the Missouri statute requires shareholder approval for additional indemnity provisions that are contained in a corporation's bylaws or in a separate agreement, many practitioners have advised that, in the case of nonprofit corporations, any additional indemnity provision must be included in the entity's articles of incorporation in order to comply with the statute.

19. In the past, some homeowners' policies contained coverage for specific nonprofit civic activities of the insured. These provisions have largely been eliminated. Moreover, although some corporate general liability and individual personal liability policies will cover an individual's service as a director, such coverage is rarely complete.

20. *See* D. Stern, *Avoiding Legal Malpractice Claims,* J. MO. B., 263 (June 1988).

21. Knepper & Bailey, *Liability of Corporate Officers and Directors,* § 23-2 (6th ed., 1998).

22. Zaborac v. American Casualty Co., 663 F. Supp. 330 (C.D. Ill. 1987). *But see* Okada v. MGIC Indemnity Corporation, 823 F. 2d 276 (9th Cir. 1987), which held to the contrary. There is considerable dispute among courts as to when legal fees would be payable. Some courts require legal fees to be paid as they are billed and payable. Pepsico, Inc. v. Continental Casualty Corp., 640 F. Supp. 656 (S.D. N.Y. 1986).

23. In addition, an insured can be liable for legal defense costs as well as for damages on the claim itself when they exceed policy limits. A large deductible can subject a corporate insured to paying a significant portion of the initial defense costs. See Dan L. Goldwasser, Practicing Law Institute, *Directors' and Officers' Liability Insurance 1988* : 66-7, at 457. Thus, many nonprofit corporations may be underinsured.

24. Knepper & Bailey, *Liability of Corporate Officers and Directors, supra,* note 21.

25. *See* IND. CODE ANN. § 23-1-35-1; TENN. CODE ANN. § 48-58-601; CAL. CORP CODE § 5239.

26. *See* CAL. CORP CODE § 5239.

27. *See* § 108.70(a) of the Illinois General Not For Profit Corporation Act of 1986, as amended (in addition, the elimination of liability provision only applies to directors and officers of tax-exempt corporations).

28.   See *State Liability Laws for Charitable Organizations and Volunteers* 6 (Nonprofit Risk Management Center <http://www.nonprofitrisk.org>, 2001). This publication provides an excellent summary of state laws and leading court cases limiting or eliminating the liability of nonprofit corporations, directors and/or volunteers.

29.   See Model Act, Alternate Section 2.02(b)(5). *See also* TENN. CODE ANN. § 48-2-102.

30.   See Volunteer Protection Act of 1997, 42 D.C. Cir. §§ 14501-14505; *see also* Lisa A. Runquist and Judy F. Zybach, "Volunteer Protection Act of 1997: An Imperfect Solution," *published in Nonprofit Governance and Management* (Victor Futter, ed.; American Bar Association 2002)

31.   For a discussion of state laws providing for limited liability of nonprofit organizations' directors and officers, *see* Olson & Hatch, *Director and Officer Liability*, *supra*, note 5, at § 11.03. For a critical view of one such statute, *see* Harrison & Marhoun, *Protection for Unpaid Directors and Officers of Illinois Not-For-Profits: Fact or Fiction?* 79 ILL. BAR J. 172 (April 1991), and a critique of the latter article, 79 ILL. BAR J. 267 (June 1991).

32.   See N.J. STAT. ANN. § 2A: 53A-7; *referenced in State Liability Laws for Charitable Organizations and Volunteers*, *supra*, note 28, at 8, 70-71.

# Suggested Questions for Directors Regarding Director Liability

(1) What exposure do I have to claims or litigation that may be brought against me? Who could potentially assert such claims and for what reasons?

(2) Have the directors of the corporation, past or present, been subject to litigation or threats of it? Why, and with what result?

(3) Do I know of a similar corporation in which the directors have been sued?

(4) What provisions do the corporation's articles and bylaws have with regard to the director's risk, indemnification, and insurance?

(5) Of those provisions, which ones are mandatory ones upon which I can insist, and that require some approval or ratification? By whom? According to what standard?

(6) Do the mandatory provisions include the advance of expenses?

(7) Do I know what our corporation's D&O policy provides? What is not covered by it?

(8) What is the earliest date for which a matter would be covered even if a claim comes within the policy period?

(9) Who has read or examined the corporation's D&O policy, and how recently?

(10) Have I been provided with a memorandum describing our D&O coverage, available indemnification, and statutory protections available?

(11) Have I been informed as to the interrelationship of the corporation's D&O coverage and other policies insuring me, such as professional malpractice or umbrella liability policies? Are there gaps in my protection?

(12) If I cease to be a director, for how long a period, if any, will the corporation's D&O policy cover me?

(13) If I have D&O coverage supplied in connection with another corporation, does it cover me as a director of this nonprofit corporation?

(14) Do applicable statutes limit my liability or exonerate me? Has the corporation taken all steps necessary to make those limitations or exonerations effective?

# Checklist: Director Liability

*Note:*   For purposes of simplicity in these checklists, we describe a corporation with a chair, who presides over the board of directors; a chief executive, who may be a staff person; an executive committee; a nominating committee; and an audit committee. (However, we recognize that in many smaller and other nonprofits, such committee functions may be performed by either the executive committee or the board as a whole.) We also assume a legal counsel—someone, paid or unpaid, having primary responsibility for the corporation's legal affairs. Many corporations, especially larger nonprofits, may have other committees established for specific purposes, such as reviewing staff performance, fixing compensation, monitoring compliance with legal requirements and periodic review of bylaws.

| Subject | To Be Reviewed By Whom | How Often | Comment |
|---|---|---|---|
| 1. Do we have D&O insurance? What events does it cover? | Legal counsel, chief executive or board chair; prospective Board members; risk manager/risk management committee (if any) | Perform evaluation and update all directors, at least annually | Review and evaluation of the adequacy of D&O coverage may also be merited at each change in corporate activities or structure, as well as at each change of insurer or alteration in policy coverage. |
| a. What event dates are covered by D&O insurance? | Legal counsel, chief executive or board chair; risk manager/risk management committee (if any) | At least annually | This is not just an analysis of dates of policy itself, but analysis of how far it covers prior events. |
| b. Is the policy providing coverage on a "claims made" basis? | Legal counsel, chief executive or board chair; risk manager/risk management committee (if any) | At least annually | The board should understand what event constitutes a claim, and the nature of a claims-made policy. A memorandum to the directors should cover this issue. |
| c. What events are not covered? Are special riders or policies available to cover specific excluded risks? | Legal counsel, chief executive or board chair; risk manager/risk management committee (if any) | At least annually | The board should understand what event constitutes an insurable event, and what events are not covered. A memorandum to the directors should cover this issue. |
| d. What are the deductibles? What co-insurance is required? | Legal counsel, chief executive or board chair; risk manager/risk management committee (if any) | At least annually | A memorandum to the directors should cover this issue. |

## Checklist: Director Liability *(Continued)*

| Subject | To Be Reviewed By Whom | How Often | Comment |
|---|---|---|---|
| 2. Does our D&O policy exclude coverage when an otherwise insured person is covered by another liability policy—e.g., an attorney's malpractice policy? | Legal counsel, chief executive or board chair; risk manager/risk management committee (if any) | At least annually | Directors having dual coverage should inform audit committee and counsel. |
| 3. Have we reviewed how possible gaps in coverage can be plugged? | Legal counsel, chief executive, or board chair; risk manager/risk management committee (if any) | At least annually | Larger corporations may use professional risk consultants in this task. |

CHAPTER **11**

# The Legal Environment of the Nonprofit Corporation

## Contents

CHAPTER **11**

# The Legal Environment of the Nonprofit Corporation

*Directors need to understand the corporation's legal environment, in order to ensure the corporation acts within the bounds of the law and maximizes its performance for its constituency of service.*

## The Board's Responsibility

### Understanding the Corporation's Legal Environment

To fully understand the scope of his or her duties, the director should have a clear picture of the corporation's legal environment, that is, the substantive law governing all the things the corporation is organized to do. *The directors must understand that this environment of laws and regulations surrounds the corporation at all times*, regardless of whether the corporation employs a lawyer, whether or not it is involved in a lawsuit, or whether some license or permit is required for the corporation's operations. Parts of this same legal landscape surround each of us individually; for the most part, we adjust to it unconsciously, without any need for professional help or guidance. The corporate director, however, must be more conscious of the corporation's legal environment, since it affects what the corporation can or cannot do.

For an analogy, think of driving a car. It is sitting in the garage; someone enters it to drive it. The law defines who that driver may be, on what side of the street the driver will drive, when the car must stop, when and where it cannot turn, and how fast it may go. The law imposes conditions of insurance, and requires pollution-free status. In some states, the law governs how many people may be in the car, or whether or not the driver must be wearing a seat belt, and other matters.

And yet, of course, no one of us gives any of this a moment's thought. Driving a car is such a normal part of our lives that we take for granted the commands of the law in doing so. If we were to drive a car from here to Mexico City, we might have different thoughts. We might find it necessary to inquire somewhere of the Mexican requirements for a permit to drive, how fast we may drive, and what should we do if we had an accident, etc. And then, if we went further and decided we wanted to take a passenger for hire to Mexico, we might see some complex legal problems emerge.

# Role of Legal Counsel

Helping the corporation to navigate safely through its legal environment is a responsibility primarily of counsel for the corporation—whether a volunteer or paid—but that responsibility is most effectively assigned when the board of directors understands how the corporation faces the legal landscape surrounding it. On the one hand, we do not counsel the board of directors to try to resolve legal problems themselves on a do-it-yourself basis, but on the other hand, we counsel against the other extreme: assuming that the problem is entirely one to be assigned to counsel, and if counsel is not available, it is a problem that somehow ceases to exist. Counsel (whether internal or external, paid or volunteer) is a means to be used. It is the job of the board to use such means appropriately and effectively.

# What We Mean by Law

In determining a corporation's legal environment, a director should first understand what the "law" is. This question is answered in three parts:

## Predictable Acts by Authorities

The law is a question of how people holding power over the corporation—legislators, regulators, officials of various kinds, judges and the like—will behave in certain situations. A distinguished jurist once said that he thought of the law as the "predictable behavior of judges,"[1] and we adopt basically this definition. A large part of the legal environment of the corporation is the predictable behavior of power: power held by legislatures, by the administrators, by the judges, etc.

## Private Acts (Contracts) That Bind the Corporation

Corporations through their own voluntary actions are frequently making law: by contracts, agreements, leases, etc. These private actions, which are part of the daily business of the corporation, create a set of legal restraints that are as effective within their limited sphere as any statute or regulation. Yet, no business could survive if every contract, every purchase of goods, etc., required the services of a lawyer. Here, the prudent board attempting to control its legal environment will separate those contracts which require the assistance of counsel from those which can be handled by corporation's staff as part of the corporation's day-to-day business.

## Litigation

The determination of law applicable to the corporation must include an understanding of the impact of litigation involving the corporation either as a plaintiff or defendant. This *Guidebook* does not elaborate on this particular aspect of legal activity because in most situations if the corporation is entering the courtroom voluntarily, or forced into it involuntarily, the corporation must employ counsel.

# Analysis of the Corporation's Legal Environment

## Identifying Potential Areas of Legal Exposure

To understand the corporation's legal environment, directors should make the following inquiries:

(a) Does the corporation's activity require that it have relatively long-term contracts or agreements with other entities or persons?

(b) Are any activities of the corporation similar to those of other corporations that have faced litigation in connection with such activities— whether brought by a government entity or by some private entity or individual?

(c) Do any of the activities of the corporation require the concurrent expenditure of money or provision of effort by another party—such as a joint venture partner?

(d) Do any of the corporation's activities require a license or permit? Is there a government body that can require reports or make inspections?

From a list such as that set forth above, the directors can note those issues where the expectations of the corporation (or the party contracting with the corporation) may not be met and where a failure to meet expectations would seriously impact the corporation. These are the areas in which the board should probably consult counsel. The board's recognition of the corporation's potential legal exposures will help the directors determine what actions may be taken in advance to minimize the likelihood that the corporation would suffer any damage in connection with any particular relationship or activity.

# Annual Review

A general review of the corporation's legal environment should be conducted once a year. This review serves in part to promote consciousness-raising, to help make the board aware of its potential problems and legal vulnerabilities, even though no immediate solution may be needed. *This Guidebook does not assume that the answer to all of the demands of the corporation's legal environment is, automatically, the employment of a lawyer.* However, once the board has performed a review of its legal vulnerabilities and needs, it will be in an appropriate position to determine when counsel is and is not, appropriate.

# The Corporation's Contractual Environment

### When to involve counsel in the contracting process

The section "Private Acts (Contracts) That Bind the Corporation" above refers to the private law-making function of the corporation, that is, the drafting and execution of contracts and agreements. The board should set forth certain standards as to when counsel should be employed, such as the following:

- The moneys to be committed by the corporation, or to the corporation, are a significant fraction of the corporation's budget.
- The contract involves more than two parties.
- The proposed contract involves the employment of a key person;
- The agreement is material to the corporation's activities.
- The performance to be promised (by either party) requires clear definition to avoid potential misunderstandings (such as for certain consulting or management services).
- The terms of the contract extend beyond one year.
- The activity touches on controversial issues such as fair employment, public health disputes, etc.
- The activity exposes the corporation to substantial risks, even if indemnification and insurance are available.

# The Litigation Environment

Litigation differs from other aspects of the legal landscape in its potential expense, the necessity of the use of legal counsel, and its unpredictable outcome.

### Insurance and indemnification to limit litigation risk

The possibility that the corporation may be exposed to litigation is a risk of loss against which the board should shield the organization by insurance or indemnification if it is feasible.

Any exposure to litigation generally means an exposure to costs of significant size. Litigation requires the use of paid counsel, with substantial uncertainty as to cost. Even if a lawsuit against the corporation is frivolous, and the corporation may be awarded its attorneys' fees by a court or its costs are covered by insurance, by the time all expenses, including diversions of staff time and lost opportunities have been totaled up, the corporation will still have been adversely affected. If the corporation finds that other corporations having similar activities have been exposed to litigation, the director should examine why this has been so, and what differences, if any, exist between his or her corporation and the other corporations.

If litigation on behalf of the corporation seems essential to protect the corporation or to fulfill its mission, it must be budgeted as best can be done. However, in a lawsuit of anything more than routine nature, such budgeting is extremely difficult; this is an occasion on which the board may benefit from receiving counsel *regarding* counsel, from attorney board members or trusted attorney volunteers. A board contemplating engaging an attorney for a litigation matter should recognize the following:

- No lawyer can totally control, and hence no lawyer can guarantee, the time that a lawsuit may consume. Tactics of the opponent, unforeseen developments, and congestion in the courts all add to the unmanageable character of litigation.
- Although some lawyers may undertake to handle a lawsuit for a fixed maximum fee, in doing so the lawyer may be either including a substantial contingency allowance in that quotation, or counting on readjusting the fee in some manner if the litigation proceeds in an unexpected fashion.
- No corporation should enter the court room on its own behalf on the assumption that it can withdraw at will; it may be subject to a counterclaim that holds it in the courthouse, or to substantial penalties imposed by the court.

# The Corporation's Political/Legal Environment

## Restrictions on Involvement in Political Arena

Nonprofit corporations that are tax-exempt under § 501(c)(3) of the Code are prohibited from using the organization's resources on behalf of a candidate in a political campaign. (See the discussion in the section "The Absolute Prohibition on Political Campaign Activities" in Chapter 4, "Taxation.") Such tax-exempt corporations may, however, engage in lobbying in connection with an issue of concern to the organization, provided that such lobbying activities are limited to an "insubstantial" amount (generally five percent of its total activities, or other amount if the corporation elects to rely on the safe harbor under Code § 501(h)) (See the discussion in the section "Limitations on Lobbying" in Chapter 4, "Taxation.") Nonprofits that engage in lobbying must also comply with federal, state, and local lobbying regulations, such as the federal Lobbying Disclosure Act.[2] Despite such restrictions and limitations on tax-exempt corporation's involvement in the political arena, directors of § 501(c)(3) corporations and other nonprofits should still be aware of the legal/political environment in which their organization operates.

## How Nonprofits Are Affected by the Legal/Political Environment

As discussed earlier in this chapter, all nonprofits are affected by laws and regulations relating to one or more of the organization's activities. In some cases, nonprofits look to governmental sources for grants or other revenues. In all cases, the activities of nonprofits—including hiring employees and providing services to the public—are subject to various legal requirements and restrictions. Changes in the political environment relating to a nonprofit corporation's activities can have a significant effect on the nonprofit's ability to fulfill it mission, or even to survive. For example, an arts organization that sees its public funding diminish, or another organization suddenly faced with burdensome governmental record-keeping requirements, may need to reassess a significant portion of its operations. Similarly, any changes in the Code that affect the deductibility of certain kinds of gifts—whether artwork, appreciated stock or other assets—may have substantial consequences for nonprofit organizations.

## Keeping the Board and Others Aware of the Impact of Proposed Legal Changes

Since many nonprofits operate on slim profit margins, directors of nonprofit corporations should stay informed regarding what impact proposed legislative and regulatory changes could have on the organization. Nonprofit boards may request that their staff or outside advisors periodically review pending legislative activity relating to the nonprofit's operations, as well as identify opportunities for the organization to receive assistance from governmental bodies in connection with the organization's mission. Some organizations may wish to adopt a lobbying plan, to ensure that their voices are appropriately heard on issues of importance to the organization or its beneficiaries. On significant topical issues, the organization may effectively pool its resources with similar nonprofits or other groups with like concerns. Even without adopting a formal lobbying plan, a nonprofit may benefit from surveying its board members and any significant donors, to identify those with connections to legislators who are active in areas of interest to the organization, or who may otherwise be willing to listen to the organization's concerns. Nonprofits should be aware that although they must at all times adhere to the legal restrictions on lobbying activity, lobbying may occasionally, or even frequently, be an important means by which they assure their continued ability to fulfill their mission.

# The Choice of Counsel

## Differences among Kinds of Nonprofit Corporations

The situation of certain nonprofit corporations should be distinguished from others with regard to employment of counsel. Large mutual benefit corporations and substantial public benefit entities will, and should, solve their needs for legal services much as a business corporation would: by the employment of professionals, either as salaried attorneys or as outside counsel. The considerations that lead to their choice of counsel remain very much those that would guide the director of a business corporation.

In comparison, the directors of small public benefit corporations and religious corporations frequently have special problems and opportunities in the choice of counsel. First of all, most such corporations have lawyers serving as directors. Such persons clearly offer certain benefits to the corporation, but also present certain problems, discussed below. However, many such corporations have given little attention to planning or managing their legal exposures and often let them reach crisis proportions before taking action.

## Budgeting for Predictable and Recurrent Legal Needs

### Legal budget considerations
The first step of the board in this area is budgetary: Given the corporation's legal environment and needs, how much of the corporation's funds should the corporation set aside for predictable and recurrent needs for counsel? This estimate should be a part of an appropriate reserve for emergencies or other unbudgeted items.

Wise boards may choose to ignore available uncompensated legal services of volunteers or board members when preparing the corporation's legal budget. Such a source of services, discussed later in this chapter, may on occasion be both available and appropriate; however, the corporation should not *budget* on the assumption that legal problems of serious dimensions can be so handled. If a volunteer lawyer is available and appropriate, the saving of money should be treated as an unexpected financial benefit, not as a budgetary offset.

## When needs exceed capacity

If a realistic legal services budget—again, for only the predictable and recurrent legal needs—is apparently beyond the means of the corporation, it should examine, just as it would with any other excess of expected expenses over receipts, whether the corporation's resources are too small for its functional survival. The board should recognize that the risks it is unwilling to lessen or minimize here will always go somewhere: They will be borne in the disappointment of donors who see a program jeopardized or encumbered, or by staff who find devoted efforts going for naught, or by beneficiaries who may not be served. As with every other item of expense, the board must prudently provide for it, just as it must budget the corporation's income.

## Making decisions within the legal budget

Given a budgetary floor, the chief executive or other appropriate officer should recommend to the board whether to:

- retain counsel on a regular basis, as a predictably necessary part of corporate existence; or
- retain counsel to deal with particular problems as they occur.

The above distinctions are inevitably one of degree: Is the predictable frequency of problems such that the services of a designated lawyer or firm that deals with all of them would be more efficient? Or is the frequency so slight or the diversity of events so great that a separate choice should be made for each case?

If a single lawyer or firm handles the bulk of the corporation's work, there are significant economies in the time necessary to initiate each engagement. If the predictable volume of work indicates continuing exposure to problems, a general retainer may be advisable.

# Selection of Counsel

In selecting counsel, the corporation should enter into a professional engagement, regardless of whether counsel is compensated or volunteer.

Certain generalizations can be offered about the choice of counsel, regardless of whether the lawyer is paid or unpaid.

## Professional engagements

The relationship between the corporation and the lawyer serving as counsel (whether for a fee or on a volunteer basis) must be a professional engagement. It should be entered into formally, with the lawyer and the corporation each specifying (preferably in writing) what they expect the engagement to entail.

### Identifying the kind of legal counsel required

Lawyers are not one-size-fits-all products, each one of whom is capable of doing everything or being the best person available. The services needed for the particular corporation may be unique and somewhat specialized. A large professional or trade association, for example, needs regular antitrust counsel—lawyers with some experience in this area, whose work keeps them abreast of recent developments in the field that may affect the corporation. In comparison, this specialized expertise would be of little use to the board of an art museum.

On the other hand, there are a large variety of professional skills needed by a nonprofit corporation that vary little between the largest trade association and the smallest community enterprise. All these corporations need competent tax advice; all of them, from time to time, will need skill in drafting employment contracts, reviewing leases, arranging a bank loan, and the like. In analyzing needs, the corporation should separate its routine, legal "housekeeping" needs from its specialized needs.

With that said—and other things being equal—it is desirable to get most legal services from a single-source supplier. This will probably save money, and it enables a lawyer to have an overview of the total activities of the corporation; as a peripheral or fringe benefit of that corporation, he or she may offer an insight into some overlooked aspect of the corporation's activities. The corporation may decide that some legal housekeeping can be done by volunteer lawyers and other problems referred to paid counsel.

### "Peacemaker" functions of counsel

There is another role that paid counsel in the proper circumstances can perform, and which may be of enormous importance. We refer to a function of an internal "peacemaker" within the corporation. Often this means simply that the lawyer conveys and certifies unwelcome truths, where other concessions to that reality may be fraught with political tensions within the board. It may be also that the lawyer, as an informed outsider, can suggest alternatives in the midst of a polarized controversy, or establish the objectivity of some of the controverted issues.

## Understanding the Respective Rights and Obligations of the Corporation *vis à vis* Its Legal Counsel

### Significance of client–lawyer relationship

The law regards the relationship of a lawyer and a client in a unique and peculiar way, *and does so regardless of whether the lawyer is paid or unpaid.* However, the mere fact that a person who serves on a board of directors is a lawyer does not make the corporation involved that lawyer's client. If a client relationship does exist, certain consequences follow for both the lawyer and the corporation.

## Authority of lawyer to bind client

The corporation must recognize that, in general, a lawyer who can describe a corporation as a client has the apparent authority to bind that client to certain kinds of commitments in certain situations. This is particularly true in the courtroom. The limits of the lawyer's apparent authority are, to some degree, discernible from common sense. Nonetheless, it is always well in engaging an attorney (again, whether volunteer or paid) to define the scope of that engagement so that any generally implied authority of an attorney can be limited to specific actions. Wherever feasible, the employment of an attorney should be defined and documented in a written letter of engagement. Such contracts of engagement are, in many states, required by the rules governing the profession. Such a document can further clarify the business aspects of the arrangements such as fees, payments, advancing cash expenditures, etc.

## Standards of loyalty

When the lawyer is engaged, the client is entitled to expect certain minimum standards of loyalty. To some degree, these parallel the obligations a corporation may expect from anyone acting on its behalf, e.g., a real estate broker or an executive search firm. One expects such agents to keep confidences and not to use the information obtained from the organization for the agent's advantage outside the scope of the engagement.

## Confidentiality for certain client-lawyer communications

The relationship with a lawyer differs, however, in that the client can confide in the lawyer as to matters related to the professional engagement and the communications to the lawyer generally may not be disclosed by the lawyer (without a serious breach of his or her obligations). A court might not require the lawyer to make that disclosure, even under a subpoena. Hence, consultations with lawyers concerning complicated and frequently delicate matters are given protections that are not available in consultations with, for example, an accountant or personnel consultant. In dealing with controversial or sensitive matters, this distinction may be of great importance to the corporation. In certain circumstances, however, such confidentiality protection can be lost, such as when the client (through an officer, employee, or other agent) discloses the sensitive information to a third party in addition to the lawyer. Therefore, the board should caution its members and representatives of the corporation against disclosure of such matters to persons other than the corporation's counsel.

## Potential lawyer conflicts of interest

A cost of client confidentiality is imposed on the corporation's lawyer. The receipt of confidences from client, whose interests may be opposed to that of another party, may prevent the lawyer from accepting certain engagements with such other parties, unless the client agrees to waive the conflict.

## Use of Volunteer Lawyers

Volunteer lawyers, whether or not members of the board, may present certain opportunities to the corporation, but they should be used with caution, and with a clear understanding of their role.

Public benefit and religious corporations frequently have lawyers as board members; they may also have outside volunteer lawyers willing to serve the organization. In some areas of the country, there may be volunteer organizations of lawyers serving such corporations. The availability of such resources should not be overlooked, but should be approached with caution.

It should be realized that the lawyer-volunteer could expose him or herself to a substantial risk in undertaking a legal engagement of any significant depth while serving on a corporate board. The following issues need to be considered:

- The fact that the lawyer is unpaid is insignificant in terms of professional malpractice liability of the individual involved and in terms of what the corporation is entitled to expect.[3]
- A lawyer acting in an area outside her or his regular experience and expertise may expose her or himself to risks of professional liability.

## Responsibility for Monitoring the Corporation's Tax Environment

If a corporation seeks to solve most of its legal problems through the use of board members or other volunteers, at least one such volunteer should undertake to maintain regular familiarity with the tax laws affecting the corporation. A public benefit corporation should know, for example, the limits of its activities imposed by § 501(c)(3) of the Code and the distinctions between influencing legislation, where some flexibility is permitted, and engaging in political campaigns, which is absolutely prohibited. The administration of such an inquiry is time-consuming, and in fact is rarely made. Because of a director's familiarity with the ongoing activities of the corporation, this is a valuable service that may be provided by a qualified lawyer-director alone or in periodic contact with specialized tax counsel.

## Special Problems of the Board Member As Counsel

A director who also serves as counsel for the corporation may weaken the corporation's representation in certain circumstances.

Although it is hardly uncommon for a lawyer who is a member of a corporation's board to serve also as counsel for the corporation, the practice is frequently criticized, for the following reasons:

- The lawyer's independence and objectivity in advising the corporation is at least somewhat impaired.
- A confusion of roles may affect the lawyer's ability to assert, on behalf of the corporation, its right to confidential treatment of certain communications.
- The lawyer's ability to negotiate on behalf of the corporation, as a professional facing another professional, is sometimes impaired by the ambiguity of roles.

A further problem arises with a board member acting as lawyer. Effective representation of any entity—whether a hospital, school or dance troupe—requires the full and informed confidence of the persons controlling that entity. In other words, a lawyer serving on a nonprofit board should know if his or her designation as counsel had the active consent of all the fellow directors. Some board members who would prefer using outside counsel may be uncomfortable challenging a fellow director who offers his or her legal services. A board member serving as counsel may be put in a difficult position if called upon to give advice regarding a matter that touches on some controversial policy or field of activity about which the board is divided. In addition, when an attorney board member also acts as corporation counsel, it is difficult to distinguish which "hat" the director is wearing at any given time. What would otherwise be considered protectible attorney-client communication may become subject to discovery if characterized as discussion among board members.

Frequently, outside counsel handling a problem area is able to bring to the board an objectivity concerning a decision to be made, since the lawyer stands aside from the substantive controversy involved. This is, to a certain degree, a traditional function of lawyers serving organizations and it is a role that may be difficult for an inside lawyer to perform.

At the same time, it may be unrealistic to suggest that a small public benefit entity should avoid the use of volunteer legal services and always seek outside paid counsel. To the extent possible, however, an attorney sitting on the non-profit corporation's board should not act as the corporation's counsel. An attorney board member who does choose to act as counsel should consider and discuss with the other board members the potential hazards of serving in such dual roles.

## Who Is the Client?

A lawyer representing a corporation owes her or his professional obligations to the corporation and not to the board as a whole, or to any individual director or officer.

In controversies involving corporate actions, a claimant may assert that both the corporation and one or more directors are accountable, or the corporation may wish to assert that certain directors bear the real responsibility for the controversial events. A director should understand *that in such circumstances the corporation's lawyer does not and cannot represent both the corporation and the affected directors.* Among other things, this means that the corporation's lawyer cannot receive confidences from a director that are kept from the corporation.[4]

When a situation arises that involves an actual or potential dichotomy of interest between the corporate entity and one or more directors, the affected directors should seek independent legal counsel, and the corporation's lawyer should so advise the directors.[5]

See the following checklist (page 225) to review the issues discussed in this chapter.

## Notes

1. Oliver W. Holmes, 10 HARV. L. REV. 557 (1896).
2. 2 U.S.C. 1610. For a good summary of the requirements of the Lobbying Disclosure Act, see R. Boisture, *What Charities Need to Know to Comply with the Lobbying Disclosure Act of 1995*, the Independent Sector web site, *available at* <http://www.govrel@indepsec.org>.
3. The Model Rules of Professional Conduct, promulgated by the American Bar Association, are the basis of the professional regulation of lawyers in the vast majority of states. Rule 1.1 of the Model Rules states that "[a] lawyer shall provide competent representation to a client. Competent representation requires the legal knowledge, skill, thoroughness and preparation *reasonably necessary for the representation.*" (emphasis supplied)
4. American Bar Association Model Rules of Professional Conduct, Rule 1.13 states, in part:

> A lawyer employed or retained by an organization represents the organization . . . In dealing with an organization's directors . . . a lawyer shall explain the identity of the client when it is apparent that the organization's interests are adverse to those of the [directors] with whom the lawyer is dealing.

5. *See* Michael W. Peregrin and James R. Schwartz, *When Does the Board Need its Own Counsel?* TRUSTEE, April 2001, at 23.

# Suggested Questions for Directors Regarding the Corporation's Legal Environment and Selection of Counsel

## Legal Environment

(1) Do we depend on the help of another group, individual, or entity to carry out a major part of our corporate mission? Does such a party need us in a similar way?

(2) If we are in a position of dependency as described above, are the relationships clearly defined? How?

(3) Is the other party involved expending money in reliance on our activity with them? Are we devoting funds to the activity?

(4) Does the size of the undertaking or its contemplated duration suggest that the relationship be defined by a formal agreement? Do we have one?

(5) Do any such undertakings seem to be failing to achieve their purposes? Will we, or our partner in the undertaking, lose substantial funds in the event of failure?

(6) Have we ever been sued? Why? With what result?

(7) Do I know of a corporation similar to ours that was sued? Why? With what result?

(8) Is there any government agency (other than the IRS) that controls or regulates our activities? What limits does this agency place upon us?

(9) Do we engage in public controversies during which we make statements attacking or criticizing some other person or entity?

(10) Do we regularly review the corporation's legal exposures?

## Selection of Counsel

(1) Do we include legal fees as part of our regular budget? If we do, how is the amount determined?

(2) Do other corporations with activities similar to ours find it necessary to retain counsel? Why? Or, if they do not, why not?

(3) Is there a lawyer, paid or unpaid, to whom we generally look for legal advice?

(4) Have we analyzed that individual's particular skills in relation to our problems?

(5) What legal skills do we need that are unique, specialized or unusual?

(6) Is our corporation presently a plaintiff or defendant in litigation? Why? What are the prospects of a termination thereof?

(7) If a volunteer lawyer is presently acting as legal counsel, do I feel she or he is qualified to serve our needs?

(8) [If I am a lawyer:] Am I asked to give legal advice to the board of directors? Do the board and I understand when my discussion of a problem is or is not a legal opinion?

(9) [If I am a lawyer:] If I am asked to serve as counsel to the corporation for some matter, am I protected under my professional malpractice policy?

# Checklist: The Legal Environment of the Nonprofit Corporation

*Note:*   For purposes of simplicity in these checklists, we describe a corporation with a chair, who presides over the board of directors; a chief executive, who may be a staff person; an executive committee; a nominating committee; and an audit committee. (However, we recognize that in many smaller and other nonprofits, such committee functions may be performed by either the executive committee or the board as a whole.) We also assume a legal counsel—someone, paid or unpaid, having primary responsibility for the corporation's legal affairs. Many corporations, especially larger nonprofits, may have other committees established for specific purposes, such as reviewing staff performance, fixing compensation, monitoring compliance with legal requirements and periodic review of bylaws.

| Subject | To Be Reviewed By Whom | How Often | Comment |
|---|---|---|---|
| 1. The Corporation's Legal Environment | | | |
| a. Do we know in what areas our organization may be vulnerable to legal liability? | Chair, chief executive | Annually | |
| b. How does the Board monitor the Corporation's compliance with applicable laws? | Chair, chief executive | Annually | |
| c. What actions should the Corporation take to minimize known legal risks? | Chair, chief executive | Annually | |
| 2. The Selection of Counsel | | | |
| a. Do we need regular counsel? | Chair, chief executive | Annually | An analysis of how the board solves recognized legal problems should be made. |
| b. Can we use volunteer legal counsel? | Chair, chief executive | Annually | Review must examine fitness of particular volunteer counsel's ability to meet corporation's specific needs. |

# Director Orientation and Revitalization

## Contents

CHAPTER **12**

# Director Orientation and Revitalization

*The corporation should institute formal actions and procedures to assure that all directors have received (and continue to receive) key documents regarding the corporation. New directors should be given specific orientation as to the corporation's history, structure, and activities, and be encouraged to share their unique perspectives with the board. Current board members should periodically be given the opportunity to engage in strategic planning, self-evaluation, and other analysis that show how well both the corporation and the board are fulfilling their missions.*

## New Director Orientation and Materials

### New Director Orientation

The corporation's board and management should organize specific events or meetings to welcome the new director. They should also make sure the director is provided with sufficient information to become an effective member of the board without a prolonged breaking-in period.

Effective use of a new board member requires that she or he learn as much as possible about the organization, its mission, history and hopes, as quickly as possible. Leaving the new arrival to find this knowledge on his or her own, over a series of meetings, is a slow and inefficient process, and one in which the promise of many a board member can be lost to a corporation.

Set forth below is an outline of the type of reading material the corporation should provide to the new board member, in the form of directors' manuals. Such information should be supplemented by site tours and specific meetings with senior staff and officers (outside of board meeting reporting sessions). Such meetings are very effective for new board members and may be scheduled prior to a new member's first meeting. However, it may also be useful to schedule some meetings *after* the new member has attended a few meetings and become acquainted with the range of corporate matters within the board's purview.

### Directors' Manuals

A threshold obligation of a director is to know and understand the purpose, function and goals of the nonprofit corporation the director is serving. An invaluable tool in acclimating new directors of nonprofit corporations—as well as assisting all directors in satisfying their duties—is a manual or manuals containing important documents relating to the governance and operation of the corporation and other information that will keep the director apprised of the current state of the corporation. These may be simple loose-leaf binders, with a table of contents and a tab for each item. Use of such a binder makes updating the manual easy.

The board may wish to have two manuals: one containing material that a director should have with him or her at every board meeting, and a bulkier volume for the director's home or office. If a two-manual system is chosen, then the board-meeting manual would include the items listed below:

### Basic documents (first manual)

The basic director's manual should contain, at a minimum, the following documents:

(1)  a calendar of dates and events compiled for the year, listing board, committee, and other significant meetings, activities and deadlines, which can be updated periodically;

(2)  a copy of the corporation's articles of incorporation or charter, and any amendments to same;

(3)  a copy of the current bylaws of the corporation;

(4)  a copy of the corporate mission statement;

(5)  a copy of a corporate organization chart, showing any affiliated organizations, and/or any departments and divisions of the corporation;

(6)  a listing of names, addresses and phone numbers of the directors and officers of the corporation;

(7)  a list of the corporation's committees, including the name of each committee chair and all committee members; and

(8)  a list of staff members of the corporation, including positions, addresses and phone numbers.

### Additional material (second manual)

The following material, probably too bulky to be taken regularly to board meetings, is recommended for a director's personal use:

(1)  minutes of board and committee meetings, that can be retained in the manual for a year and then disposed of or filed elsewhere;

(2)  financial statements of the corporation for the prior fiscal year and the operating and capital budgets for the current year;

(3)  biographical data on directors and staff;

(4)  a summary of D&O insurance, bylaw indemnification provisions, and statutory limitations on director liability;

(5)  current news releases by or about the corporation;

(6)  annual reports for the past two or three years;

(7) conflict of interest policies; and

(8) current long-range or strategic plan.

# New Director Review of Information about the Corporation and Its Board

Another aspect of new director orientation (or evaluation of an invitation to become a director) requires the new or prospective director to review material on the corporation's operations and resources, as well as the operations of the board. At a minimum, the new or prospective director should review carefully the material recommended above for inclusion in the director's manuals, as well as the following materials:

## Past board and committee minutes

The new or prospective director should review the minutes of the meetings of the board and its main committees for the last three years or so. Such a review is an excellent way to become knowledgeable regarding the recent history of the corporation, the issues faced by the board, and the board's methods for addressing such issues.

## Past financial statements and reports

A new or prospective director should also review the financial statements of the corporation for at least the last few years, noting particularly if there are any restrictions that have been placed on gifts to the corporation. For tax-exempt corporations, the director should consider reviewing the corporation's annual informational returns filed with the IRS on Form 990. For corporations that acquired tax-exempt status fairly recently, a review of the corporation's Form 1023 (Application for Recognition of Exemption) may also be useful. If the corporation has issued tax-exempt bonds, the official statement related to any recent bond financing also should be reviewed; the first appendix to the official statement can provide a useful overview of the corporation and its management.

## Current directors and management personnel

Ideally, before a new director joins the board, he or she should have met the chief executive and other principal officers. The new board members should also have met the board chair and at least a few other board members—including both senior and junior members, so that the new member will not feel surrounded by strangers at his or her first meeting.

## Compliance with law and internal control

As noted throughout this *Guidebook*, the use of assets of a nonprofit corporation is subject to certain limitations. For example, corporate assets must be used for the purpose for which they are given (generally, as stated in the corporation's articles of incorporation and bylaws). The assets of tax-exempt corporations cannot be used to inure to the benefit of private individuals. (For a more in-depth discussion of limitations on tax-exempt corporations, see Chapter 4, "Taxation.") A prospective director should become familiar with the role of the corporation's accountants and legal advisors in regard to matters of internal control and legal compliance. He or she should learn the corporation's policies and procedures regarding conflict of interest. If the corporation does not have a public accountant or regular corporate counsel, the individual should determine what steps the corporation has taken to make sure it is in compliance with any applicable limitations. In addition, some nonprofit corporations are subject to being accredited or licensed by outside agencies. Review of accrediting or survey reports, if available, can be most helpful in determining problem areas needing attention. (For additional suggestions for becoming familiar with the corporation's legal environment, see Chapter 11, "The Legal Environment of the Nonprofit Corporation.")

### Corporation's outlook

The new or prospective board member may find it helpful to have an in-depth discussion with the chief executive and board chair about the corporation's current plans, current prospects, critical issues being or expected to be confronted, and long-range objectives.

### Board culture

If possible, a prospective director should ask to attend a board meeting in advance of accepting a board position. Although new members are generally expected to fit in to the existing board structure and culture, they may also be able to offer new perspectives and suggestions that will help the board operate more effectively. (Nonetheless, a prospective board member may need to think twice before agreeing to serve on a board that operates in a fashion he or she believes ineffective.)

# Board Revitalization: Retreats, Strategic Planning, and Self-Evaluation

## Board Retreats

Many of the most successful nonprofit organizations have periodic board (or board/management) retreats. Retreats are used to give the board members an opportunity to take stock of the corporation and renew their individual commitment to helping the corporation satisfy its mission. A retreat may take the form of an extended board meeting, or may have a different format. The agenda may focus on larger issues of mission and the future, or on particular problems facing the corporation. Retreats often include sessions designed to enhance the relationships among board members, and thereby facilitate open discussions both then and at future board meetings. Often retreats are scheduled at locations away from the corporation's offices, where the board members will also have the opportunity to socialize and build personal rapport. Such retreats are ineffective unless all, or a very high proportion, of the board can attend. Therefore, retreats should be scheduled long in advance, and annually if possible—or at least on a regular schedule, such as every two or three years.[1]

## Reviewing the Board Decision-Making Process

All directors should be aware of board discussion and decision-making style. If a director believes such style is not conducive to effective decision-making, the director should discuss the issue with the board chair or other directors, preferably apart from the boardroom. For example, are all board members given the opportunity to participate in discussions? Is adequate time allotted for questions? Do a few board members—or the board chair—tend to dominate discussions? Does the board chair give his or her opinion before other board members have had a chance to speak? Has the corporation had difficulty retaining chief executives? If so, could board function or board members' style be a source of the difficulty?

## Evaluating Whether the Board Needs to Be Restructured

Over the course of time, the board of a nonprofit corporation may require structural adjustments to enable the corporation to continue to meet its mission. For instance, the size of the board may need to be adjusted upward or downward. The resources of a large board may be more effectively channeled by using multiple committees that act in smaller groups and report back to the board. In some cases, fresh faces may be needed to help the board move away from entrenched attitudes and assumptions, and to meet changing realities affecting the corporation and its mission.

### Periodic review of board structure

The board should periodically provide for a process whereby the need for board structural changes can be assessed. Such process may occur every three to five years at board retreats, be initiated by the board chair or chief executive, be handled by a special committee, or consist of a report by outside advisers (in some areas, consultants or scholars in the area of non-profit management may be available to conduct a review on a no-fee or low-cost basis). Because such reviews can be sensitive—particularly if members of the existing board feel threatened, or vulnerable to criticism for past decisions—it is recommended that such a structural review be institutionalized so that it occurs automatically every few years.

## Self-evaluations of individual board members

Nonprofit corporations may benefit from board members engaging in annual or other periodic evaluations of each member's performance individually as well as the board's performance as a whole. Such evaluations, or assessments, can be accomplished by use of forms developed internally or adapted from samples developed by others, including other nonprofits, local trade associations or writers in the area of nonprofit governance. (See discussion of information resources for nonprofit corporations in the section "Other Sources of Information, Inspiration, and Guidance" below, and selected titles and web sites in Appendix C.)

Individual board members may be evaluated by the board chair and the corporation's chief executive, or a committee of a small number of board members or former board members. (Board members on the committee should be evaluated by a similar group.) After such evaluations, the board or committee chair should discuss the results of the evaluation with each board member. Such discussion should serve as an opportunity both to acknowledge the individual director's contributions as well as to suggest ways in which the director's effectiveness could be improved.

## Evaluations of the board

All board members should also complete periodic evaluations of the effectiveness of the board and the resources provided to it. Such an evaluation should include questions regarding each individual director's views on the strengths and weaknesses of the board and its committees, and provide an opportunity for directors to make suggestions for ways to improve board effectiveness. Such an evaluation should cover all aspects of board and committee functions, including new board member orientation, selection of future board candidates, adequacy of information provided before board meetings, conduct of board and committee meetings, effectiveness of board retreats, and opinions on future board needs.

# Information Gathering for Strategic Planning and Mission Measurement

Whether in the form of retreats or otherwise, many of the most successful nonprofit corporations require the board and staff members to engage in regular (often annual) strategic planning sessions. In order to make the most of such brainstorming and self-evaluation opportunities, the board should ask itself and its staff what information is available to determine whether the corporation has been successful in meeting its mission. For instance, are members/donors/ visitors/users surveyed regarding their experiences, perceptions and needs? Is such data available from or on comparable organizations? What other information is available quantifying the experience of the individuals who are the intended beneficiaries of the nonprofit corporation? What information *could* become available if the corporation sought to obtain it? Could volunteers be used to help gather such information? Have grant-makers required the corporation to compile information that could also be useful to review within the organization?

In general, nonprofit organizations, both big and small, tend to be much less sophisticated in terms of the information they routinely gather about their markets (both actual and potential) and market perceptions, when compared to for-profit organizations. Partly, this is a reflection of the unique nature of nonprofit corporations. A nonprofit corporation generally cannot measure success or failure of its mission in simple monetary terms. Often, the primary mission of the nonprofit cannot be measured in amounts of X and Y calculated by an accounting firm. But this does not mean that nonprofits should not seek to count what can be counted, rather than relying on intuition or traditional assumptions. Through the use of the Internet, computer programs, interns, and volunteers, even small nonprofits with limited resources can access a wide range of information. Such data can confirm correlations between factors that an organization assumes to be relevant, or reveal correlations between factors that are not intuitively obvious.

Without obtaining and analyzing available information on how well the organization is achieving its mission (and where improvement may be needed), it is very difficult for the board of a nonprofit organization to properly evaluate whether it is using its resources to their maximum potential. The organization runs the risk of becoming fixed in outdated perceptions—"this is the way things have always been"—without any mechanism to test the accuracy of such perceptions. Although most nonprofits will not have the luxury of a full-time research department, nonprofit board members should regularly ask what information could and should be obtained in order to assist the board in evaluating whether the organization has been successful in meeting its mission. Such information can also provide board members with the tools they need to recognize when it is time to redefine the corporation's mission or make other charges to reflect new realities.

# The Challenge of Quantifying What Constitutes Success for a Nonprofit Corporation

Quantification of the success or failure of a corporation is a considerably more challenging exercise in the nonprofit world compared to the for-profit business environment. While the board of directors of a for-profit must consider a large number of non-numerical phenomena related to the operation of the corporation—legalities, risks of lawsuits, employee morale, quirks of consumer preferences, etc., at the end of the day one factor reigns supreme: the "bottom line." In the long run, no conceivable success in personnel management, marketing skills, or product development, will excuse the failure of a for-profit corporation to produce a profit, or at least break even. In the nonprofit world, in comparison, it is possible to achieve an outstanding success in some mission and yet become financially insolvent.

Thus, the key challenge for any nonprofit board is both to fulfill the corporate mission and to see to it that the nonprofit survives to maximize the public benefits resulting from fulfilling its mission. A further burden on the nonprofit management is to achieve those goals with maximum efficiency. The process of assuring efficient survival will require the consideration of various numbers, including many things other than revenue dollars—such as the number of persons entering an art museum during a given month, or the increase in symphony orchestra memberships by certain minority groups and young professionals.

The subtleties of the "quantification challenge" in evaluating the success of a nonprofit corporation may be illustrated as follows: It is clear that the board of directors of an art museum must know what dollars are needed to keep the doors open and where that money can be found; it should also be able to know how many people come to the museum and when, who gives money and when, and how much a "needed" art work will cost. All these matters are capable of being reduced to numbers. But, as an institution seeking to change a visitor's behavior and perceptions, what else does it and can it know and measure? How can it compare, numerically, one painting versus another or a visitor's different experiences after viewing those paintings—or a specific collection?

No ready answers rise to the surface, but let us examine what could be determined and counted. Probably one can learn, at relatively small cost:

- how many people come to the museum;
- on what days;
- at what hours;
- how many of those are dues-paying members;
- how many attend a given exhibit;
- how many buy books describing the exhibit;
- how many of the above are adults, children, men or women; and
- how many live within certain zip-code areas.

In addition, for each of those questions, the organization can determine the correlation (or the lack thereof) of one classification with another. For example, do more women come on Tuesday morning than at any other time or any other day? The answers may be insignificant or mysterious, but they may, as one tracks them down, lead to other, more significant questions. All of the above data can be obtained without asking for any specific personal identification of those whose behavior is being measured, and none of it involves hidden cameras or other invasions of privacy.

But the board of a nonprofit institution, such as our hypothetical art museum, should not stop there. If it can cross the barrier that inhibits personal identification, it will want to know:

- how many of our sample live in which suburb or city area;
- how old are they;
- what is their race or ethnic identification; and
- did they come with others, and if so, who.

These last described questions can be asked on a voluntary basis (with the increased margin of error, as many of the subjects will refuse the information, or worse, give deliberately misleading answers).

At this point our illustrative board has obtained a mass of information that can be assembled at relatively low cost—and some of it is already assembled by most museums. But at some point, it may want to go further. It will want to know:

- how would a visitor (of one of the classifications listed above) describe the motivations which brought him or her to the institution;
- were those aims satisfied;
- what other museums (of art or other purpose) does the visitor patronize; and
- what particular object or painting drew the visitor's most prolonged attention.

Once the nonprofit staff has compiled all the above answers and presented them to our board in numerical form, the board may be able to trace the correlations between trait X and trait Y, and ask if those correlations suggest management changes in the museum's programs. But such information may also lead to further questions, such as, "What is the correlation we wish to obtain? Why are we here?" These are the kind of ultimate questions that will continue to challenge the board of directors of a nonprofit corporation throughout its existence. In exercising the rights and duties described in this *Guidebook*, successive generations of a single nonprofit board will undoubtedly find different answers to such questions.

# Other Sources of Information, Inspiration, and Guidance

Although this *Guidebook* has attempted to provide directors of nonprofit corporations with an overview of nonprofit corporation board service, there are a host of topics that we have not had space to address in depth or even at all. Board members seeking additional information on topics discussed in this *Guidebook*, or topics not addressed herein, may take advantage of other resources available to nonprofit corporations in their community or available through the Internet. For example, the California Management Assistance Partnership, a network of thirteen independent nonprofit support organizations located across California, maintains the "Nonprofit Genie" web site (www.genie.org), with information about the training, technical assistance, grant, and other information available through each of the organizations in its network. Similarly, the nonprofit Donor's Forum of Chicago, an association of grant-makers, presents educational programs and maintains an extensive library of materials on nonprofit governance, financing and operational issues.[2] Many other communities have similar nonprofit resource organizations. College and public libraries, as well as commercial bookstores, are other resources for such materials. In Appendix C, we have provided a non-exhaustive sampling of publications and Web sites that may be of interest to nonprofit corporation directors and their advisers.

See the following checklist (page 240) to review the issues discussed in this chapter.

## Notes

1. *See* Barry S. Bader, *Planning Successful Board Retreats* (National Center for Nonprofit Boards, Nonprofit Governance Series, No. 10, 1992).
2. *See* <http://www.donorsforum.org>.

# Suggested Questions for Directors Regarding Director Orientation and Revitalization

(1) Do we have a regular manual containing the basic documents of the corporation?

(2) What documents does it contain?

(3) How do I keep it up to date?

(4) What files do I keep concerning my service as a director?

(5) Does the board have an orientation program for new directors? Does the board leadership encourage new members to participate in meetings? Are the board leadership and the more experienced board members receptive to statements from (new or continuing) members questioning aspects of board culture or procedures?

(6) Do I know of practices of other corporations concerning director orientation and training that our corporation could adopt?

(7) Does the board have meetings or retreats reviewing the corporation's overall policies, mission, or specific problems?

(8) Does the board have a strategic-planning process? How have past strategic plans been evaluated and updated?

(9) Does the board ask its directors to engage in annual or other periodic self-evaluations or evaluations of the board as a whole?

(10) How does the board evaluate whether the corporation is fulfilling its mission? Is there information available from or about similar corporations or grant-making agencies that could help us measure the corporation's effectiveness in meeting its mission?

# Checklist: Director Orientation and Revitalization

*Note:* For purposes of simplicity in these checklists, we describe a corporation with a chair, who presides over the board of directors; a chief executive, who may be a staff person; an executive committee; a nominating committee; and an audit committee. (However, we recognize that in many smaller and other nonprofits, such committee functions may be performed by either the executive committee or the board as a whole.) We also assume a legal counsel—someone, paid or unpaid, having primary responsibility for the corporation's legal affairs. Many corporations, especially larger nonprofits, may have other committees established for specific purposes, such as reviewing staff performance, fixing compensation, monitoring compliance with legal requirements and periodic review of bylaws.

| Subject | To Be Reviewed By Whom | How Often | Comment |
|---|---|---|---|
| 1. Director's manual | Chair, chief executive | At least annually, and in preparation for each meeting at which directors are elected | A specific committee to undertake this task is recommended. |
| 2. Orientation | Chair, chief executive, nominating committee | At least annually, and in preparation for each meeting at which directors are elected | A successful orientation meeting will take extensive time in planning and arranging for both board and staff participation. |
| 3. Board retreats | Chair, chief executive | Annually or at least every other year | The board may wish the retreats to be planned by staff, with input from the chief executive and a committee of junior and senior board members. |
| 4. Self-evaluations and assessments | Chair, chief executive | Annually or at least every other year | Results of individual director evaluations should be discussed with that director; results of overall board assessments should be presented to and reviewed by the entire board. |
| 5. Strategic planning | Chair, chief executive | Annually | Some nonprofit corporations of sufficient size have strategic planning committees who meet periodically through the year to assess the implementation of the corporation's current strategic plan, and report to the board on areas of shortcomings and recommendation for changes to future plans. |

# Appendices

## Contents

# Appendix A
## Sample Conflicts of Interest Policy

The following is a sample conflicts of interest policy recommended by the Internal Revenue Service to be adopted by tax-exempt health care organizations to demonstrate that the organization operates exclusively for charitable purposes, rather than to benefit private interests.

Because many concepts developed by the IRS in connection with tax-exempt health care organizations tend to evolve towards a general application to other tax-exempt organizations, all tax-exempt corporations should consider adopting a conflicts of interest policy similar to the sample policy below. Note, however, that before adopting such a policy, the board should make sure that it contains any provisions necessary to comply with applicable state law relating to conflicts of interest.

## SAMPLE CONFLICTS OF INTEREST POLICY
### (For Tax-Exempt Health Care Organizations)*

### Article I

*Purpose*

The purpose of the conflicts of interest policy is to protect the Corporation's interest when it is contemplating entering into a transaction or arrangement that might benefit the private interest of an officer or director of the Corporation. This policy is intended to supplement but not replace any applicable state laws governing conflicts of interest applicable to nonprofit and charitable corporations.

---

*Lawrence M. Brauer and Charles F. Kaiser, *Tax-Exempt Health Care Organizations Community Board on Conflicts of Interest Policy, available at* <http://ftp.fedworld.gov/pub/irs-utl/topic-c.pdf>.

# Article II

## *Definitions*

1. Interested Person

   Any director, principal officer, or member of a committee with board-delegated powers who has a direct or indirect financial interest, as defined below, is an interested person. If a person is an interested person with respect to any entity in the health care system of which the Corporation is a part, he or she is an interested person with respect to all entities in the health care system.

2. Financial Interest

   A person has a financial interest if the person has, directly or indirectly, through business, investment or family—

   a. an ownership or investment interest in any entity with which the Corporation has a transaction or arrangement, or
   b. a compensation arrangement with the Corporation or with any entity or individual with which the Corporation has a transaction or arrangement, or
   c. a potential ownership or investment interest in, or compensation arrangement with, any entity or individual with which the Corporation is negotiating a transaction or arrangement.

   Compensation includes direct and indirect remuneration as well as gifts or favors that are substantial in nature.

# Article III

## *Procedures*

1. Duty to Disclose

   In connection with any actual or possible conflicts of interest, an interested person must disclose the existence and nature of his or her financial interest to the directors and members of committees with board-delegated powers considering the proposed transaction or arrangement.

2. Determining Whether a Conflict of Interest Exists

   After disclosure of the financial interest, the interested person shall leave the board or committee meeting while the financial interest is discussed and voted upon. The remaining board or committee members shall decide if a conflict of interest exists.

3. Procedures for Addressing the Conflict of Interest

  a. The chairperson of the board or committee shall, if appropriate, appoint a disinterested person or committee to investigate alternatives to the proposed transaction or arrangement.

  b. After exercising due diligence, the board or committee shall determine whether the Corporation can obtain a more advantageous transaction or arrangement with reasonable efforts from a person or entity that would not give rise to a conflict of interest.

  c. If a more advantageous transaction or arrangement is not reasonably attainable under circumstances that would not give rise to a conflict of interest, the board or committee shall determine by a majority vote of the disinterested directors whether the transaction or arrangement is in the Corporation's best interest and for its own benefit and whether the transaction is fair and reasonable to the Corporation and shall make its decision as to whether to enter into the transaction or arrangement in conformity with such determination.

4. Violations of the Conflicts of Interest Policy

  a. If the board or committee has reasonable cause to believe that a member has failed to disclose actual or possible conflicts of interest, it shall inform the member of the basis for such belief and afford the member an opportunity to explain the alleged failure to disclose.

  b. If, after hearing the response of the member and making such further investigation as may be warranted in the circumstances, the board or committee determines that the member has in fact failed to disclose an actual or possible conflict of interest, it shall take appropriate disciplinary and corrective action.

# Article IV

### *Records of proceedings*

The minutes of the board and all committee with board-delegated powers shall contain—

  a. the names of the persons who disclosed or otherwise were found to have a financial interest in connection with an actual or possible conflict of interest, the nature of the financial interest, any action taken to determine whether a conflict of interest was present, and the board's or committee's decision as to whether a conflict of interest in fact existed.

  b. the names of the persons who were present for discussions and votes relating to the transaction or arrangement, the content of the discussion, including any alternatives to the proposed transaction or arrangement, and a record of any votes taken in connection therewith.

# Article V

## Compensation committees

a. A voting member of any committee whose jurisdiction includes compensation matters and who receives compensation, directly or indirectly, from the Corporation for services is precluded from voting on matters pertaining to that member's compensation.

b. Physicians who receive compensation, directly or indirectly, from the Corporation, whether as employees or independent contractors, are precluded from membership on any committee whose jurisdiction includes compensation matters.

# Article VI

## Annual statements

Each director, principal officer and member of a committee with board-delegated powers shall annually sign a statement which affirms that such person—

a. has received a copy of the conflicts of interest policy,
b. has read and understands the policy,
c. has agreed to comply with the policy, and
d. understands that the Corporation is a charitable organization and that in order to maintain its federal tax exemption it must engage primarily in activities which accomplish one or more of its tax-exempt purposes.

# Article VII

## Periodic reviews

To ensure that the Corporation operates in a manner consistent with its charitable purposes and that it does not engage in activities that could jeopardize its status as an organization exempt from federal income tax, periodic reviews shall be conducted. The periodic reviews shall, at a minimum, include the following subjects:

a. Whether compensation arrangements and benefits are reasonable and are the result of arm's-length bargaining.
b. Whether acquisitions of physician practices and other provider services result in inurement or impermissible private benefit.
c. Whether partnership and joint venture arrangements and arrangements with management service organizations and physician hospital organiza-

tions conform to written policies, are properly recorded, reflect reasonable payments for goods and services, further the Corporation's charitable purposes and do not result in inurement or impermissible private benefit.

d. Whether agreements to provide health care and agreements with other health care providers, employees, and third party payors further the Corporation's charitable purposes and do not result in inurement or impermissible private benefit.

# Article VIII

## *Use of outside experts*

In conducting the periodic reviews provided for in Article VII, the Corporation may, but need not, use outside advisors. If outside experts are used their use shall not relieve the board of its responsibility for ensuring that periodic reviews are conducted.

# Appendix B
## Tax-Exempt Organization Reference Chart

**Organization Reference Chart from**
*Tax-Exempt Status for Your Organization*
**Internal Revenue Service Publication 557 (Rev. July 2001)**

| Section of 1986 Code | Description of organization | General nature of activities |
| --- | --- | --- |
| 501(c)(1) | Corporations Organized Under Act of Congress (including Federal Credit Unions) | Instrumentalities of the United States |
| 501(c)(2) | Title Holding Corporation for Exempt Corporation | Holding title to property of an exempt organization |
| 501(c)(3) | Religious, Educational, Charitable, Scientific, Literary, Testing for Public Safety, to Foster National or International Amateur Sports Competition, or Prevention of Cruelty to Children or Animals Organizations | Activities of nature implied by description of class of organization |
| 501(c)(4) | Civic Leagues, Social Welfare Organizations, and Local Associations of Employees | Promotion of community welfare; charitable, educational or recreational |
| 501(c)(5) | Labor, Agricultural, and Horticultural Organizations | Educational or instructive, the purpose being to improve conditions of work, and to improve products and efficiency |

| Section of 1986 Code | Description of organization | General nature of activities |
| --- | --- | --- |
| 501(c)(6) | Business Leagues, Chambers of Commerce, Real Estate Boards, Etc. | Improvement of business conditions of one or more lines of business |
| 501(c)(7) | Social and Recreation Clubs | Pleasure, recreation, social activities |
| 501(c)(8) | Fraternal Beneficiary Societies and Associations | Lodge providing for payment of life, sickness, accident, or other benefits to members |
| 501(c)(9) | Voluntary Employees' Beneficiary Associations | Providing for payment of life, sickness, accident or other benefits to members |
| 501(c)(10) | Domestic Fraternal Societies and Associations | Lodge devoting its net earnings to charitable, fraternal, and other specified purposes. No life, sickness, or accident benefits to members |
| 501(c)(11) | Teachers' Retirement Fund Associations | Teachers' association for payment of retirement benefits |
| 501(c)(12) | Benevolent Life Insurance Associations, Mutual Ditch or Irrigation Companies, Mutual or Cooperative Telephone Companies, Etc. | Activities of a mutually beneficial nature similar to those implied by the description of class or organization |
| 501(c)(13) | Cemetery Companies | Burials and incidental activities |
| 501(c)(14) | State Chartered Credit Unions, Mutual Reserve Funds | Loans to members |
| 501(c)(15) | Mutual Insurance Companies or Associations | Providing insurance to members substantially at cost |
| 501(c)(16) | Cooperative Organizations to Finance Crop Operations | Financing crop operations in conjunction with activities of a marketing or purchasing association |
| 501(c)(17) | Supplemental Unemployment Benefit Trusts | Provides for payment of supplemental unemployment compensation benefits |
| 501(c)(18) | Employee-Funded Pension Trust (created before June 25, 1959) | Payment of benefits under a pension plan funded by employees |

| Section of 1986 Code | Description of organization | General nature of activities |
|---|---|---|
| 501(c)(19) | Post or Organization of Past or Present Members of the Armed Forces | Activities implied by nature of organization |
| 501(c)(21) | Black Lung Benefit Trusts | Funded by coal mine operators to satisfy their liability for disability or death due to black lung diseases |
| 501(c)(22) | Withdrawal Liability Payment Fund | To provide funds to meet the liability of employers withdrawing from a multi-employer pension fund |
| 501(c)(23) | Veterans Organization (created before 1880) | To provide insurance and other benefits to veterans |
| 501(c)(25) | Title Holding Corporations or Trusts with Multiple Parents | Holding title and paying over income from property to 35 or fewer parents or beneficiaries |
| 501(c)(26) | State-Sponsored Organization Providing Health Coverage for High Risk Individuals | Provides health care coverage for high risk individuals |
| 501(c)(27) | State-Sponsored Workers' Compensation Reinsurance Organization | Reimburses members for losses under workers' compensation acts |
| 501(d) | Religious and Apostolic Associations | Regular business activities. Communal religious community |
| 501(e) | Cooperative Hospital Service Organizations | Performs cooperative services for hospitals |
| 501(f) | Cooperative Service Organizations of Operating Educational Organizations | Performs collective investment services for educational organizations |
| 501(k) | Child Care Organization | Provides care for children |
| 501(n) | Charitable Risk Pools | Pools certain insurance risks of § 501(c)(3) organizations |
| 521(a) | Farmers' Cooperative Associations | Cooperative marketing and purchasing for agricultural producers |

| Section of 1986 Code | Description of organization | General nature of activities |
| --- | --- | --- |
| 527 | Political Organizations | A party, committee, fund, association, etc., that directly or indirectly accepts contributions or makes expenditures for political campaigns |

# Appendix C
## Suggested Publications, Periodicals, and Web Sites

The general literature on nonprofit boards and corporations is becoming extensive and this appendix does not purport to cover all titles, particularly in view of the uneven quality of some of the material currently offered on the market. The following, however, merit perhaps more extensive attention:

### Publications

First and foremost is Michael Hone, *Revised Model Nonprofit Corporation Act: Official Text with Official Comments and Statutory Cross-References* (Clifton, New York: Prentice Hall, 1988).

For a general review of the function of the nonprofit board, addressed almost entirely to public benefit boards, see Cyril O. Houle, *Governing Boards* (San Francisco: Jossey-Bass, 1997).

Fisher Howe, *The Board Member's Guide to Fund Raising* (San Francisco: Jossey-Bass, 1991). This is a good general discussion of the subject matter described in the title. Again, it is a work largely dealing with the public benefit corporation.

Daniel L. Kurtz, *Board Liability: Guide for Nonprofit Directors* (Mount Kisco, N.Y., Moyer Bell, 1988) is an excellent analysis of the role of the public benefit corporation director and extends beyond the comparatively narrow issue that the title implies.

Howard Leoner Oleck and Martha E. Stewart, *Nonprofit Corporations, Organizations and Associations*, 6th ed. (Englewood Cliffs, N.J.: Prentice Hall, 1994; 1998/1999 Cumulative Supplement). This is a comprehensive treatise on a wide range of legal and other issues applicable to nonprofit corporations in general, and including discussions of specific kinds of nonprofits.

Thomas Wolf, *Managing a Nonprofit Corporation*, 2nd ed. (New York: Prentice Hall, 1990) is a good general text for public benefit or community organization directors, although it suffers a bit from a frequent use of fictional illustrations of problems.

Last, two specialist publications of high quality are Alan D. Ullberg and Patricia Ullberg, *Museum Trusteeship* (Washington, D.C.: American Association of Museums, 1981), and Barbara Hadley Stanton, *Trustee Handbook,* 6th ed. (Boston: National Association of Independent Schools, 1989).

## Periodicals

Periodicals focusing on the nonprofit sector include the following:

*The Chronicle of Philanthropy*, a newspaper focusing on the nonprofit world (see their Web site at <http://www.philanthropy.com>). The *Chronicle* publishes annually their *Non-Profit Handbook*, with lists of books, periodicals, software, Internet sites and other resources, organized by subject matter (such as "Advocacy," "Boards," and "Fund-Raising").

*Don Kramer's Nonprofit Issues*, a national newsletter reporting on tax and other legal developments affecting nonprofit organizations.

The *Philanthropy News Network* provides a daily on-line news service for nonprofit organizations, at <http://www.pnnonline.org>.

*The NonProfit Counsel: The Law of Tax-Exempt Organizations Monthly*, published by John Wiley & Sons, a monthly newsletter that provides analysis of current developments in tax and related law for nonprofit organizations and their professional advisors.

*The Nonprofit Times*, a business publication directed to nonprofit management, with twelve monthly editions plus bi-monthly special editions on direct marketing and financial management, and an annual nonprofit salary survey (for information and selected articles, see <http://www.nptimes.com>).

## Useful web sites and organizations

A reader interested in pursuing further material in this area may consult the following organizations and their web sites:

BoardSource, 1828 L Street NW, Suite 900, Washington, DC 20036-5104, (202) 452-6262 or (800) 883-6262, <http://www.boardsource.org>, which has an extended bibliography on topics relevant to nonprofit boards.

Jossey-Bass, Inc., 350 Sansome Street, San Francisco, CA 94104, (415) 433-1740, <http://www.josseybass.com>, publishes a wide array of books and other documents on topics of interest to directors and others involved in the nonprofit sector.

The American Society of Corporate Secretaries, 521 Fifth Avenue, New York, NY 10175, (212) 681-2000, <http://www.ascs.org>, publishes a number of materials, mostly intended for the business corporation, but some of which are also relevant or specifically directed to nonprofit corporations. See, for example, "Governance for Nonprofits—A Summary of Organizational Principles and Resources for Directors of Nonprofit Organizations" available on the society's web site or in pamphlet form.

The web site for the Internet Nonprofit Center provides suggested book titles, practical guides, essays, and other resource information about non-profit organizations, as well as Nonprofit FAQ, an "online encyclopedia of information" designed for use by nonprofit organizations. See <http://www.nonprofits.org>.

The National Center for Charitable Statistics (NCCS) is a repository of data on the nonprofit sector in the United States. The NCCS's activities include the development of uniform standards for reporting on the activities of charitable organizations. See NCCS at <http://www.NCCS@ui.urban.org> or contact the NCCS at National Center for Charitable Statistics, 2100 M Street NW, Washington, DC 20037, (202) 261-5801.

The GuideStar web site, <http://www.guidestar.org>, is produced by Philanthropic Research, Inc., and contains a database of information from the Form 990s of over 700,000 U.S. nonprofit organizations.

The Charity Channel web site, <http://www.charitychannel.com>, provides a wide range of discussion forums on nonprofit topics, from "Accountability" to "Volunteer Issues."

The Nonprofit Genie web site, <http://www.genie.org>, is maintained by CompassPoint Nonprofit Services, and contains links to CompassPoint's online newsletter for nonprofit board members (the *Board Café*) and facts on nonprofits and other publications of interest to nonprofit boards, officers, and volunteers.

The Independent Sector provides information on and promotes the range of nonprofit organizations that comprise America's independent sector. See <http://www.independentsector.org>.

The National Council of Nonprofit Associations is a network of state and regional associations of nonprofit organizations, developed to provide nonprofits with services, peer support, and a mechanism for collective advocacy. National Council of Nonprofit Associations, 1900 L Street, NW, Suite 605, Washington, DC 20036-5024, (202) 467-6262, <http://www.ncna.org>.

NonProfit Gateway, <http://www.nonprofit.gov>, provides online links to federal government information and services, and other nonprofit resource information. The NonProfit Gateway was created by a task force composed of the nonprofit liaison officers of federal government departments and independent agencies.